Contents

More
One-Act Plays
Acting for
Students

An anthology
of short one-act
plays for one
to three actors

edited by

Norman A. Bert
and Deb Bert

mp

MERIWETHER PUBLISHING LTD.
Colorado Springs, Colorado

Meriwether Publishing Ltd., Publisher
PO Box 7710
Colorado Springs, CO 80933-7710

Executive Editors: Ted Zapel and Arthur Zapel
Cover design: Janice Melvin

Library of Congress Cataloging-in-Publication Data

More one-act plays for acting students : an anthology of short one-act
plays for one to three actors / edited by Norman A. Bert and Deb Bert.
    p. cm.
Includes bibliographical references
  ISBN 13: 978-1-56608-087-3
  ISBN 10: 1-56608-087-8
1. Acting. 2. One-act plays, American. 3. American drama--20th
century. I. Bert, Norman A. II. Bert, Deb, 1954-
  PN2080.M674 2003
  808.82'41--dc21
                                2003005764

       4   5   6   06   07   08

Part 1
Scripts

Scripts for Two Actors

Labor Day
by Milan Stitt
for Jane Smith Knickerbocker

Milan Stitt is best known for *The Runner Stumbles* which was named Best Broadway Play of 1976 in the annual *Best Plays* book. He is a Company Playwright at Circle Repertory which produced his play, *Back in the Race*. Mr. Stitt is listed in *Notable Names in the American Theatre, Contemporary Authors, Who's Who in the East, ... in the Theatre, ... in Entertainment,* and *... in American Education.*

Labor Day was first performed by New York City's Circle Repertory Company in 1987 for a benefit titled HOLIDAZE. Mr. Stitt directed Stephanie Gordon and Christopher Reeve in this production with set by John Lee Beatty and lights by Dennis Parichy.

Production Suggestions

There is, of course, no need to place the actress in an elevated position relative to the actor; you can hardly position her 17 stories above him in any case. As long as she focuses her telescope downward at the same spot whenever looking at the telephone booth, and as long as the two actors never actually look towards each other, the audience will understand and accept their relative locations in the world of the play.

Although the play could conceivably be performed without any props — the telephones and the telescope could be faked — the telephone rings seem essential to the play. If you have no technicians to operate the phone cues, perhaps the actress can activate them; experiment with a button she operates with her foot.

Thea and Daniel need not be played as near 40 as the script originally specified, but both of them are psychologically and socially mature and sophisticated; play their mental and emotional realities and don't worry about their physical ages.

Address all inquiries concerning performances, readings, or

reprinting of this work *or any portion thereof* to the playwright's agent, William Craver, Writers & Artists Agency, 19 West 44th St., Suite 1000, New York, NY 10036; Fax: 212-398-9877. For details, see "Part II: Securing Rights for Your Production," pages 241 to 250.

1   The action takes place near night fall on Labor Day at a pay phone
2   near a bus stop on the corner of 10th Avenue and 23rd Street in
3   Chelsea, New York City, and on a penthouse terrace in adjacent
4   London Towers, where there is a high-powered telescope.
5   ***CHARACTERS:*** DANIEL — a businessman, dressed in expensive
6   loafers, chinos, and pullover. THEA — a successful businesswoman.
7   ***SETTING:*** A split set: On one side, the telephone stand and bus stop; on
8   the other side, the 17th-story terrace with telescope and telephone.
9
10   *(The pay phone at the corner begins to ring. DANIEL is uncertain*
11   *what to do about the ringing. It's insistent.)*
12   **DANIEL: You've got a wrong number. This is a pay phone.** *(There's*
13   *no response.)* **Hello? Can you hear me?** *(He hangs up, returns to*
14   *bus stop, looks for a bus to arrive. The phone starts ringing again.*
15   *He tries to ignore it ... but can't.)* **Listen, this is a pay phone.** *(He*
16   *listens carefully. Is someone on the line?)* **Is someone there? If**
17   **you're there, you got a wrong number.**
18   **THEA'S VOICE: Maybe not.** *(Lights come up on THEA, a striking*
19   *woman. She's on her 17th-floor terrace, looking down at DANIEL*
20   *through a high-powered telescope.)*
21   **DANIEL: What?**
22   **THEA:** *(Very judgmental)* **You sound OK.** *(Annoyed, DANIEL hangs*
23   *up. THEA pushes the redial button on her portable phone. The*
24   *pay phone rings and rings. Finally, DANIEL can't resist.)*
25   **DANIEL: Look. Whoever you are, I'm not interested.**
26   **THEA: It's going to be a long time before a bus comes. We could**
27   **wait together.**
28   **DANIEL: Yeah? What are you waiting for?**
29   **THEA: The dark. To go to work. Whatever's left.**
30   **DANIEL:** *(About to hang up)* **Forget it. I don't pay for it. And I wish**
31   **you'd stop ringing this —**
32   **THEA: Sex is easy.**
33   **DANIEL: Is it?**
34   **THEA: Anyone can accomplish that.** *(Disappointed)* **I guess I knew**
35   **you'd think that was it.**

1 DANIEL: What am I supposed to think? Is this what you do here
2   in what-do-ya-call-it?
3 THEA: Chelsea. *(A moment)* Understand, we're never going to
4   meet. *(A moment)* So don't worry, OK? *(He looks up the avenue*
5   *for a bus.)* The buses are on holiday schedule.
6 DANIEL: *(Looking up at buildings)* You can see me, can't you?
7 THEA: Does it make you nervous?
8 DANIEL: *(It definitely does!)* No. Where are you?
9 THEA: You'll never know, so you can say whatever you want.
10 DANIEL: I have nothing to say, lady.
11 THEA: *(Disappointed)* Oh, you look like the kind of person who —
12   never mind. Must be the distance. That's what I get for trying
13   something different. *(She hangs up. The more he thinks about it,*
14   *the angrier he gets. He stares at phone, daring it to ring. He looks*
15   *up at buildings ... points to phone ... waits. It rings. He's*
16   *surprised ... hesitates ... then grabs it.)*
17 DANIEL: I do have things to say. But not to you! *(He hangs up,*
18   *looks for bus, but does not return to bus stop. He won't give her*
19   *the satisfaction of looking up at buildings again. The phone rings.*
20   *He picks it up. She hangs up. He yells at the building.)* That's
21   very childish! *(He stalks over to the bus stop. The phone rings.*
22   *He won't answer it. It keeps ringing. Shit. He answers it.)* I can't
23   stand unanswered phones.
24 THEA: That's why I selected you.
25 DANIEL: Selected me?
26 THEA: It's been a long weekend. The usual mix-up ... and galleys —
27   *(Corrects herself, lest he be able to identify her.)* Some work that
28   was supposed to be delivered never arrived.
29 DANIEL: Are you a writer?
30 THEA: Pardon?
31 DANIEL: Galleys. Aren't those what writers correct?
32 THEA: Do you want me to be a writer?
33 DANIEL: I don't care. Whatever.
34 THEA: *(Annoyed)* I'm not indiscriminate, you know? *(A moment)*
35   You're the first one who looked ... worth it.

1   DANIEL: *(A come-on)* You like the way I look? *(A moment)* How
2   long have you been at this?
3   THEA: Not long. *(A moment)* My son's starting at one of those
4   generic universities. Ohio or Indiana. The ones with football.
5   Something or other at Urbana.
6   DANIEL: Illinois.
7   THEA: I should know, shouldn't I? But once you put information
8   in computers and these automatic dialers you forget it. *(A*
9   *moment)* He left Thursday to avoid the traffic. *(A moment)* The
10   Times's as empty as the city on these long weekends ... except
11   for the sales. And I don't have time to go running around for
12   bargains. I did the crossword for once. Why anyone would
13   think it's amusing to know a five-letter word for an Egyptian
14   goddess totally escapes me. The other excitement was running
15   out of half and half. On the way back from Dagostino's, I
16   copied the number of your phone down there.
17   DANIEL: Big cities are a bitch. You're pretty lonely, eh?
18   THEA: No. Realistic, and therefore bored. We're alone from the
19   moment of conception. Except maybe twins ... but they're
20   aberrations. Lonely is only possible if you think something
21   else is possible; it isn't. We live by ourselves, with ourselves
22   until the time runs out.
23   DANIEL: How often do the buses run here?
24   THEA: I don't use buses.
25   DANIEL: Neither do I. But I've seen three cabs all the way up
26   from Center Street. And they were off duty.
27   THEA: You work in Wall Street?
28   DANIEL: *(Echoing her)* Do you want me to? *(No response)* I flew in
29   yesterday. There's a conference tomorrow. I figured I could
30   use the weekend here to catch up on paperwork.
31   THEA: Workaholic?
32   DANIEL: When there's no work, I don't call strangers to avoid an
33   empty life.
34   THEA: But you're talking. *(A moment)* Is your life empty? *(No*
35   *response)* You can say whatever you want. *(No response)* In a

1   civilized world, there would be numbers to call for intelligent
2   conversation on holidays.
3   DANIEL: You can call for sex.
4   THEA: But not for intellect. Do you call those numbers?
5   DANIEL: For sex?
6   THEA: I forgot. You don't have to.
7   DANIEL: Do you?
8   THEA: It's curious how in any conversation men turn so quickly to
9   sex.
10 DANIEL: Faster than women?
11 THEA: Yes.
12 DANIEL: Talk. Let's see how long you can avoid it.
13 THEA: *(After a moment)* My life is not a vacuum. I don't have to fill
14   it with sexual fantasies. *(Sees that he's looking for bus.)* And the
15   only reason I happen to have a telescope to watch you being
16   impatient is that I'm fascinated by celestial phenomena.
17 DANIEL: Voyeurism. Sex.
18 THEA: If it is, it's not particularly gratifying knowing what turns
19   me on actually existed some billions of years ago and is just
20   reaching me now.
21 DANIEL: Lacks immediacy?
22 THEA: Which I think is important to sex. So no, it's not voyeurism.
23 DANIEL: You're still talking about sex.
24 THEA: I'm answering your question ... about sex.
25 DANIEL: *(A moment)* I've never gotten the message of astronomy.
26 THEA: Have you looked?
27 DANIEL: Sure, but if I can't begin to understand it ... and the
28   scientists can't understand it. Black holes, time warps,
29   exploding galaxies, why bother?
30 THEA: But that's the point.
31 DANIEL: Why add to the frustration?
32 THEA: Reality isn't frustration.
33 DANIEL: Must be different in Chelsea than in Stevensville.
34 THEA: Is that on the East Coast?
35 DANIEL: No. It's one of those generic places. Near Chicago.

1 THEA: *(A moment)* Looking at the stars ... it's addictive.
2 DANIEL: Addictions are escapes. Not reality.
3 THEA: No. It's wonderful. The stars ... they keep me in my place.
4   Probably proves God is a man.
5 DANIEL: Does it?
6 THEA: What's left to me in an ever expanding universe is this
7   small place. My small problems. Small responsibilities. I am
8   not the center of the universe. I'm reminded that most of what
9   is I cannot control or change. Nor does anyone expect me to.
10   That's important to know. Essential. Therefore, addictive.
11 DANIEL: I get that when I'm at the lake.
12 THEA: I see. You limit your philosophical inquiries to two weeks a
13   year.
14 DANIEL: *(Enjoying the exchange)* No, anytime I look out a window
15   in my house. The lake never looks quite the same. I limit myself
16   to that which I can touch ... maybe even understand. Outer
17   space to reach inner space seems a convoluted trip to me. If not
18   just an escape. Tranquility is what you do, not what you think.
19   Easy things. Right here. Now. Golf when there's no one but me
20   to leave tracks in the dew. Fishing for hours when you know the
21   fish couldn't possibly be biting. Gathering driftwood that's too
22   interesting to burn. Not talking, not thinking, just being.
23 THEA: *(A moment)* I'm not going to invite you up.
24 DANIEL: Sex, again?
25 THEA: Is that the only way people can wait together?
26 DANIEL: At least, it's waiting closer.
27 THEA: You're very glib, for a man who 'does,' rather than
28   'thinks.' Why is there always such a distance between what we
29   want to be and what we are? I hoped that distance would
30   diminish with time.
31 DANIEL: So did I. *(A moment)* But I'm not coming up. In an over-
32   populated world, non-involvement is a social necessity.
33 THEA: And that suits you? *(Focusing telescope)* You don't have a
34   wedding ring.
35 DANIEL: You want me to say I'll come up. So you can say no.

1   That's the game.
2 THEA: I don't play games. I can't anymore. A belated social
3   retardation has set in. *(Looking at sky)* There are a couple of
4   stars. It's almost dark enough.
5 DANIEL: You're that old? You need candlelight? Scarves over the
6   lamps?
7 THEA: *(After a moment)* I wish it were as simple as you think.
8 DANIEL: Isn't it?
9 THEA: Not anymore. *(She hangs up ... immediately regrets it, redials.*
10   *He watches the phone ring for a moment, then returns to bus stop.*
11   *The phone stops ringing. The light fades on THEA. He looks for a*
12   *bus, returns to phone, looks up ... gestures for her to call. Lights*
13   *come up on THEA who is now looking at the stars through the*
14   *telescope. She can't see his gesture. Lights slowly fade to black.)*
15   *The End*
16
17
18
19
20
21
22
23
24
25
26
27
28
29
30
31
32
33
34
35

I Wanna Be a Cowboy
by Jon Tuttle

Jon Tuttle is Assistant Professor of English at Francis Marion University in Florence, South Carolina. His plays have been produced and broadcast throughout New Mexico and in Los Angeles, New York, Atlanta, and Columbia.

I Wanna Be a Cowboy was a finalist for the Actors Theatre of Louisville's Heidemann award in 1990 and had a staged reading at Los Angeles' FirstStage in 1991. It has also been produced by New York City's Metropolis Players (1990) and Atlanta's Parenthesis Theatre Company (1991 and 1992).

Playwright's Production Suggestions

The temptation will be to make this a play about Dumb Rural People. Resist that. Besides being an extended Texas joke, which is, of course, the least sophisticated type of humor known to man, this play deals with people whose crises are real enough to them. An audience will want to laugh AT them, but then should begin to empathize WITH them. There is an air of tragedy, albeit southern-fried, about them both. Also, listen to the beats: There are peaks and valleys throughout. Explore them.

Address all inquiries concerning performances, readings, or reprinting of this work *or any portion thereof* to Dr. Jon Tuttle, Department of English, Francis Marion University, PO Box 100547, Florence, SC 29501-0547. For details, see "Part II: Securing Rights for Your Production," pages 241 to 250.

1   The action takes place on an early afternoon in August on a bus
2   headed for Dallas, Texas.
3   *CHARACTERS:* WALTON — to us, he is a brutish, malformed Texan.
4   To Nella, he's a chiselled side of Texan manhood, a great
5   Promethean mound of brooding male flesh. He wears a greasy
6   cowboy hat and a Texas A&M T-shirt bleached out under the
7   armpits, jingles quarters in his hand, and looks damned pensive,
8   especially for a Texan. He's slower'n Christmas, but could lift a
9   V-8 engine out of a Ford pick-up. Probably has, too. He will chew
10   on a stick of jerky which is so tough that when he bites it, his head
11   snaps back like it's been shot. NELLA — an 18-year-old, corn-
12   fed squishy squab of a girl, God bless her. Her clothes used to
13   belong to her mother. She's one of those people who could stand
14   in a shopping mall all day and no one would ever see her. Still,
15   her hormones have started whispering to her, and throughout the
16   play will begin screaming. At the beginning, however, she sits
17   stock straight, knees bolted tightly together, and reads a big book.
18   When she speaks, she self-consciously struggles for the right
19   word and correct syntax, and seems to have particular trouble
20   knowing where to put her pronouns.
21   *SETTING:* Two chairs on a stage, side by side: seats on a bus. As the
22   play begins, perhaps the distinct diesel whine of a bus is heard.
23   Otherwise, no other props or effects are necessary.
24
25   *(NELLA and WALTON occupy seats next to each other. She has*
26   *the aisle seat, and would be content to follow her finger through*
27   *her book, except she is so smitten with WALTON, so conscious of*
28   *his presence, that she can't keep herself from stealing quick,*
29   *hopeful glances in his direction. He is oblivious to her. He stares*
30   *wistfully out the window next to his seat, out over the Texan*
31   *tundra, at some faraway notion, and jingles quarters in his beefy*
32   *palm. She is staring at him — or with him, out the window,*
33   *wondering at his deep, blue mood — when the bus suddenly runs*
34   *over something in the road. They jostle in their seats, and she*
35   *emits a tiny, high-pitched squeak that sounds like a sexual tremor.*

1   *He doesn't move or break his stare, but after a moment, he breaks*
2   *the silence:)*
3 WALTON: ... 'Dilla.
4 NELLA: ... Escuse me?
5 WALTON: 'Dilla.
6 NELLA: 'Dilla?
7 WALTON: 'Dilla, Ya hit 'em, they explode. Squirt out both ends
8   like a burrita.
9 NELLA: ... Arma ...dilla?
10 WALTON: *(Still looking out his window)* **Stupidest critters in Texas.**
11   **Sit on the road like a idiot an' watch ya comin'. Then the**
12   **highway department comes along'n paint yella lines right**
13   **over their stupid backs.** *(At the indignity of it)* **Huh. Huh.**
14   *(NELLA contemplates the image, and he yanks off a bite of jerky,*
15   *his head snapping back. Not wanting to lose the conversational*
16   *momentum, she loads up a sentence and misfires.)*
17 NELLA: ... To where are you goin' to?
18 WALTON: ... Dallas.
19 NELLA: ...We are as yet a considerable long distance to go to
20   Dallas ... You cannot see Dallas at this time from where we
21   are ... at.
22 WALTON: *(Turning to her)* **I** *know* **that. Ya think I'm** *stupid?* **Ya**
23   **think I'm some sorta** *idiot?* — **Shee!** *(He yanks off another bite*
24   *and looks back out his window. Pause. Nella resists, but then*
25   *bursts into tears. She sputters, like she's trying to swear at*
26   *herself.)*
27 NELLA: Hep! Kuh! Fut!
28 WALTON: *(Turning again, dumfounded)* ... What?
29 NELLA: Shup! Puft!
30 WALTON: What?
31 NELLA: What am I sayin'? I never know! Kuf!
32 WALTON: Ya got some snot on yer chin.
33 NELLA: *(Quickly wiping it)* I'm sorry! I'm sorry what I implied! I
34   think it all through! I try to be soooo — *(She pants hard, like*
35   *some Lamaze breathing drill, trying to pull herself together. He*

1   *doesn't know what to do.)*
2   **WALTON: ... Want some jerky?**
3   **NELLA:** *(Composing herself)* **No, no thank you. I'm sorry. I'm**
4   **terrible sorry.**
5   **WALTON: 'S OK. Ya got some more on yer cheek.**
6   **NELLA: Thank you. I'm sorry.** *(She wipes her cheek, and he turns*
7   *back to his window. She dries up a bit and tries again, tentatively.)*
8   **What are ... I mean, for what are you looking ... for?**
9   **WALTON: ... I'm scared.**
10   **NELLA: ... Of what are you scared of?** *(But Walton cannot*
11   *articulate it. He just shakes his head, stares, jingles and chews.*
12   *Nella presses on. Indicating his shirt)* **Are you a student at the**
13   **Texas University of A&M?**
14   **WALTON: Pff. Hell no. Not no more.**
15   **NELLA: I am on my way to be a freshman at the Texas Christian**
16   **University. That's in Fort Worth. That's near Dallas.**
17   **WALTON:** *(Sharply)* **I know where Fort Worth is.** *(Her lip quivers,*
18   *but she fights it, and hangs in.)*
19   **NELLA: I am from Clancy, Arkansas. And you?**
20   **WALTON:** *(Out the window: the sum total of all his hopes)* **... I**
21   **wanna be a Cowboy.**
22   **NELLA: A cowboy. How very fascinatin'.**
23   **WALTON:** *(To himself, mostly)* **I'm** *gonna* **be a Cowboy, too. I am.**
24   **NELLA: Like Gene Autry?**
25   **WALTON: Like Walt Garrison.**
26   **NELLA: I do not believe as I with him am familiar. I don't know**
27   **him.**
28   **WALTON:** *(Turning to her now)* **He's my hero. Ever since third**
29   **grade with Miss Slocum. Got his poster up over my bed.**
30   **Greatest Cowboy what ever lived. We got the same name**
31   **almost, too. I'm Walton Dwight Pritchard. He's Walt**
32   **Garrison.** *(He yanks off another bite.)*
33   **NELLA: How very fascinatin'. Does he sing?**
34   **WALTON:** *(Baffled)* **... I dunno.**
35   **NELLA: Do you have your own horse?**

1   WALTON: ... Uh-uh.
2   NELLA: Oh, well, they'll prolly let you borrow one.
3   WALTON: In high school I won a trophy.
4   NELLA: A trophy. How very fascinatin'. My high school, which is
5   in Clancy, they awarded me a scholarship to go to any good
6   Christian school to which I wanted to go to, in so far as much
7   as it was within a reasonable radius and had academic
8   credentials. *(WALTON yanks of a bite.)*
9   WALTON: How come ya talk like that? That the way they talk in
10   Arkansas?
11 NELLA: *(Wells up.)* Hep! I'm sorrow! *(She starts crying again.*
12   *Walton is confused again. He looks at his jerky, contemplates*
13   *offering it again, looks up at her, down at it, back and forth, while*
14   *she tries to regulate her breathing.)* My mamma, she says I got
15   to go to a big school like Texas Christian is, so I can git my
16   social graces on account'a I never know what I'm sayin'.
17   However, I don't wanna go away to college. I just wanna stay
18   at home.
19 WALTON: Yeah, well, college *sucks.*
20 NELLA: When I was a little girl? I wanted to be a cowgirl. On
21   Career Day? At Hazelwood Elementary? I stood up and I said
22   I want to be a cowgirl. But Joey Ray Draper, he said I already
23   was, and then he mooed. By which he meant I was *fat.*
24 WALTON: Grade school sucks too.
25 NELLA: I wanted to wear one a them little cowgirl hats and vests
26   with fringes and all and boots and be like Shirley Jones.
27 WALTON: Who's she?
28 NELLA: She was a cowgirl. You know, from "Oklahoma!"? She
29   had pretty blond hair and she wasn't skinny but she —
30 WALTON: Oh yeah! She was in the poster what they done!
31 NELLA: I don't know 'bout no poster. That was a long time ago.
32 WALTON: That's her! Big ol' blonde right up front. I didn't know
33   she was from Oklahoma, is all. Them cowgirls, my Lord, they
34   sure are a sight, huh?
35 NELLA: I was too fat, though.

1　WALTON:　And you *know* them cowboys, they're gettin' some a
2　　　　that. Be fine by me. That's a laugh, huh! *(He snorts.)* Them
3　　　　cowgirls, that'd be a joke. They woundn't even pay me the
4　　　　time a day. Even if I was a cowboy. Even if I was the greatest
5　　　　cowboy since Walt Garrison.
6　NELLA:　How come?
7　WALTON:　'Cause I'm stupid. *(He yanks off a bite, matter of fact-like.)*
8　NELLA:　Y'are?
9　WALTON:　I'm a idiot. Been that way all my life. Least as far as I
10　　　　can remember. Which ain't very.
11　NELLA:　I was fat once.
12　WALTON:　Ask my daddy. He says I'm stupid to think I'm gonna
13　　　　be a cowboy. He says I should stay in Plano an' be a
14　　　　roughnecker like him on the oil field. He even, look here, he
15　　　　even give me these here quarters so's I can call him when I
16　　　　need a ride back home cause I'm too stupid to be a cowboy.
17　NELLA:　You don't seem stupid to me.
18　WALTON:　I don't?
19　NELLA:　Nope. All the kids at Clancy High School? They were
20　　　　stupid. All the kids at Chester A. Arthur Middle School, they
21　　　　were stupid too, and the kids at Hazelwood Elementary? They
22　　　　were really stupid. You ain't stupid compared to alla them.
23　WALTON:　Eh. I can't open my mouth without stickin' my butt in.
24　NELLA:　Well ... cowboys don't talk much, do they?
25　WALTON:　... That's true, huh.
26　NELLA:　They're famous for their stoic — stois — they don't talk
27　　　　much.
28　WALTON:　All my life, it's all I ever dreamed of. 'Specially Sunday
29　　　　afternoons, when they were on TV.
30　NELLA:　Uh-huh, I watched 'em.
31　WALTON:　Monday nights, too, when they were on. Cowboys were
32　　　　my heroes.
33　NELLA:　Mine too, uh-huh.
34　WALTON:　Really?
35　NELLA:　Cowboys are most people's heroes, I always thought.

1 WALTON: Eh. Nobody ain't got no respect for 'em no more. Not
2   like in the olden days.
3 NELLA: Oh, I think they got a pretty firm place in our … sociology.
4 WALTON: Ya think so?
5 .NELLA: Uh-huh. Look at what all the cowboys stand for. Bravery.
6   Integrity. Hard work.
7 WALTON: America.
8 NELLA: America. Freedom.
9 WALTON: They're against drugs, too.
10 NELLA: And you can't blame them for what happened to the
11   Indians.
12 WALTON: Ya mean the Redskins?
13 NELLA: — Uh-huh. The cowboys, they didn't represent the
14   umperialism inherent in manyfest destiny. Quite the opposite,
15   I'd say. Wouldn't you say?
16 WALTON: Yeah, but I hate the Redskins. What the Cowboys need
17   now is to whomp the hell outa them again, at least one a year,
18   like on Thanksgivin', just like the olden days. Wouldn't you
19   say — what you say your name was?
20 NELLA: Nella. Nella Overholt.
21 WALTON: I mean, lookit where they are. Broncos run right over
22   'em now. How often that usedta happen?
23 NELLA: I didn't know it was that bad.
24 WALTON: It's pitiful. If they ain't careful, they're gonna wind up
25   like …the *Falcons*.
26 NELLA: You mean endangered?
27 WALTON: Exactly. Or Buffalo. Who gives a damn, I mean, who
28   *really* gives a damn 'bout *Buffalo* any more?
29 NELLA: I thought they were extinct.
30 WALTON: They were, fer awhile. Bears, who can say with them.
31   But the Dolphins? Lookit the Dolphins.
32 NELLA: Getting slaughtered by the thousands.
33 WALTON: Exactly!
34 NELLA: Or the California condors.
35 WALTON: … I ain't never heard a them.

1   NELLA: That proves my point.

2   WALTON: Exactly! And that's how the Cowboys are headed! I

3   can't let that happen. No red-blooded, born and bred son a

4   Texas can! I could help 'em get back to where they was, I

5   swear I could! If I could be a Cowboy ... God! Wouldn't

6   people look up to me! Everybody in Plano! Everybody at

7   A&M! Me! Walton Dwight Pritchard! *Cowboy! (The very*

8   *notion has pulled him to his feet. He takes his hat off and places*

9   *it solemnly over his heart. NELLA is getting aroused.)*

10   NELLA: *(Heating up)* Oh, I would! I would!

11   WALTON: Would ya? Would ya really?

12   NELLA: I swear to God I would! Specially when you were on your

13   horse!

14   WALTON: *(Baffled again)* But ... I ain't *got* no horse.

15   NELLA: You gotta believe in yourself, Walter!

16   WALTON: *(Shaking his head sadly)* Eh. It ain't so easy, believin' in

17   yourself, when ... when ...

18   NELLA: When what?

19   WALTON: *(Earnest)* Nellie, yer a smart person, I can tell that. Ya

20   know what yer talkin' 'bout. So I need to ask ya a question

21   here. It's kinda personal though, an' I ain't ever asked it to no

22   girl before. So I need ya to answer straight-forward.

23   NELLA: *(Hoping)* OK.

24   WALTON: *(Experimentally)* Nellie. Do ya think ...

25   NELLA: ...Yes?

26   WALTON: Do ya think ... see, the thing is ...

27   NELLA: Yes? Yes?

28   WALTON: The thing is ... I got a *trophy*, see. An' I'm *strong*. Once,

29   when I was at A&M, I hit a Texas Longhorn. Big sucker, open

30   field, dead run. Broke *two* a his ribs. My Christ, the sound he

31   made when he hit the ground! An' I stood up and waved my

32   fist in the air ... *Yeeeow!* And I spit on him.

33   NELLA: *(Totally turned on; overpowered)* You broke ... the ribs ...

34   of a *longhorn?*

35   WALTON: Uh-huh. How's that? Ya think I could be a Cowboy?

1   NELLA: Sweet Jesus, yes! Yes, I do!
2   WALTON: Yee-hoo! I knew I could! Daddy said I couldn't!
3   Everybody said I couldn't! But I got somethin' in me, see,
4   what says I can. I got *desire*. Ya gotta have desire, Nellie!
5   NELLA: *(She's got it.)* Oh, I *know!* I *know!*
6   WALTON: If ya got desire, Nellie —
7   NELLA: I *know!*
8   WALTON: — Ya can survive bein' stupid. Is what I say. But at
9   A&M, they didn't see it that way. They — eh.
10   NELLA: What? They *what?*!
11   WALTON: Listen to me. You don't want to sit here and listen to me
12   ramblin' on like a idiot.
13   NELLA: Yes, I do! This is the most intelligent conversation I've
14   had since I don't know when!
15   WALTON: Me neither! At A&M, they kicked me out fer bein'
16   stupid. They didn't say exacly that, but I knew it's what they
17   meant. It's what everybody says. My daddy, he says Plano is
18   the place fer a man like me, cause it's only Plano, and
19   everybody's stupid. But I got desire! It burns in me like
20   battery acid! I wanna be a Cowboy! But there's only one
21   thing, one thing what I'm ascared of!
22   NELLA: *(Holding his hand tightly)* What's that, Walter? You can
23   tell me!
24   WALTON: *(The horror, the horror)* … I'm … stupid.
25   NELLA: Oh, Walter!
26   WALTON: A thousand Texans can't be wrong! It burns in me day
27   in and night out! An' the girls? They — pff. Pffff. They never
28   even pay me the time a day. Not like you are here.
29   NELLA: *(Some spite here)* Most girls are *petty* and *mean* and *self-*
30   *centered* and *vain* and *superficial* and *ignorant* and *mean* and
31   they only care about *one thing.*
32   WALTON: *Basketball.*
33   NELLA: Exactly. I hate basketball.
34   WALTON: Basketball *sucks.*
35   NELLA: I hated school altogether.

1   WALTON: Me too. Sucked. If I hear that word *stupid* one more
2   time —
3   NELLA: I was fat. All through high school.
4   WALTON: *(Diplomatically)* ... No.
5   NELLA: I've lost seven pounds over the summer. Of course, there's
6   still room for improvement.
7   WALTON: You ain't too fat.
8   NELLA: Well, no, not no more. Not *as* fat.
9   WALTON: You ain't fat at all.
10   NELLA: Well, I'm —
11   WALTON: No, I've seen fat. Fat's bigger'n what you got there.
12   Fat's all puffy and white an' you can draw yer name in it with
13   yer finger. You ain't fat.
14   NELLA: At my high school reunion I'm going to lose forty-eight
15   pounds. I already lost seven.
16   WALTON: When's that?
17   NELLA: Ten years. I'll be skinny as a post. And when they ask me
18   who I am, I'll say —
19   WALTON: Say, I'm Shelley Jones. Cowgirl!
20   NELLA: Maybe so!
21   WALTON: An when they ask ya to dance, you can laugh in their
22   stupid, ugly faces.
23   NELLA: Well, I don't know if —
24   WALTON: It'll make 'em feel stupid. I know.
25   NELLA: *(Protests too much.)* Well, maybe some of them. Like those
26   idiots who strutted down the hall with their rippling biceps
27   and big shoulders and washboard stomachs and granite
28   thighs and hairy chests and letter jackets and never saw
29   *anybody* but the *cheerleaders.* God, I hated them.
30   WALTON: Cheerleaders are *sluts.*
31   NELLA: I mean the basketball players and baseball players and
32   football players and tennis players and wrestlers and golfers
33   and —
34   WALTON: Ya hated ... football players?
35   NELLA: Are you kidding? They're the worst! I hated them with a

1   *passion.* I hated them with a burning, smoldering *passion!* If I
2   had a nickel for every second I spent *hating* them —
3 WALTON: How come ... ya hated ... football players?
4 NELLA: *(Isn't it obvious?)* ... Because ... football players are
5   stupid! They're idiots. I never met a football player who
6   wasn't as stupid as he could be. Wouldn't you say? *(Pause)*
7 WALTON: ... Yeah. I guess so. *(Pause, WALTON looks out his*
8   *window and begins to jingle his change again. Then he turns back*
9   *to NELLA as if to say something, something hard, but sees her*
10   *there, looking at him expectantly, hopefully. So he puts his hat*
11   *back on and stares out his window. The bus hits something. They*
12   *jostle a bit, and she squeaks again, softly.)*
13 NELLA: *(Happily, confidently)* ... 'Dilla. *(She sits smiling at the back*
14   *of his head.)*
15   *The End*
16
17
18
19
20
21
22
23
24
25
26
27
28
29
30
31
32
33
34
35

Jennifer M. Rowe (seated), DeAnn Albertson (standing) in
Something Happened Here by Madeleine Martin.

Something Happened Here
by Madeleine Martin

Madeleine Martin is the award winning, playwriting alter ego of Deb Bert who is the co-editor of this book. Her plays have been produced in educational settings and off-off Broadway since 1993. Currently she is working on a children's book centered on a dog with silky white hair and placing the finishing touches on a full-length play about life after retiring from the police force.

Production Suggestions

Resist the impulse to play these two young women hysterically. Strong emotion, conflict, and tension can be played effectively with a variety of tempos, volume levels, vocal qualities, and physical gestures. While harder to play than screaming and crying, controlled anger is much more effective in portraying the classic stages of denial and shock that Becky goes through in this play. Experiment with different modes of expression to find the best way of communicating the strong feelings in *Something Happened Here.*

Address all inquiries concerning performances, readings, or reprinting of this work *or any portion thereof* to Deb Bert, PO Box 53521, Lubbock, Texas 79453. For details, see "Part II: Securing Rights for Your Production," pages 241 to 250.

1   The action takes place in the present, late at night in the sparsely
2   furnished living room of an old house.
3   **CHARACTERS:** BECKY — a sixteen-year-old girl. PAM — a
4   sixteen-year-old girl and Becky's best friend.
5   **SETTING:** The room has a couple of over-stuffed chairs, a coffee
6   table, and an end table with an old lamp on it. A mirror hangs by
7   the front door which is located Stage Right. An entry to the Off-
8   stage kitchen and bathroom areas is located Stage Left.
9

10   **BECKY:** *(Entering, followed closely by PAM)* **I am so mad!**
11   **PAM: But you're sure you're OK?**
12   **BECKY: I said I'm OK, OK? I'm just … I dunno … mad.** *(Pause)*
13   **I dunno.**
14   **PAM: Let's see if there's anything ta drink around here. Maybe**
15   **it'd … calm you down … or somethin'.** *(BECKY stares blankly*
16   *at PAM. After a pause, PAM goes into the kitchen. From the*
17   *kitchen)* **Is there any whiskey or vodka in here? Becky? Where**
18   **does Rob keep his booze? Becky?** *(PAM returns to find BECKY*
19   *just standing and staring.)* **Becky!**
20   **BECKY:** *(Jumping)* **Whaaa … Jeez, Pam! Don't sneak up behind**
21   **me like that. What are ya tryin' ta do, anyway …**
22   **PAM: I wasn't sneaking. I was just askin' ya where Rob keeps his**
23   **booze.**
24   **BECKY: Booze? Oh. I dunno. Check the tall cupboard. Beside the**
25   **range. Or mabe the cupboard above the fridge. I dunno.** *(PAM*
26   *disappears into the kitchen again. BECKY sinks into a chair. She*
27   *sighs heavily and drops her head into her hands.)*
28   **PAM:** *(Entering with a six-pack of beer)* **Look what I found …**
29   **Becky? Are you …**
30   **BECKY: Don't. Do not ask me again or I swear I will scream.**
31   *(Seeing the beer)* **Great. Beer. I shoulda known he'd only have**
32   **beer in this place. Whatdaya expect from a grease monkey.**
33   **Cars — and beer.**
34   **PAM: Hey, at least it's somethin'. Here. Have one.**
35   **BECKY:** *(Reluctantly)* **Thanks.**

1 PAM: Whatsa matter? Do ya think he'll mind if we drink it?
2 BECKY: I don't know. I don't really care. And I don't think he'll
3   care either. He ... "loves me," ya know? *(She slumps back and*
4   *winces.)* Oh, ouch!
5 PAM: See? You are hurt! I knew it. Maybe we should call the
6   hospital.
7 BECKY: Right! And tell 'em what?! Tell 'em ... Oh, you bet! *(She*
8   *tries to open her beer.)*
9 PAM: My God, Beck, you're shakin' like a leaf. Gimme that. I'll
10   open it for ya.
11 BECKY: I can open my own damn beer! *(BECKY twists the cap. It*
12   *doesn't respond. She twists harder. Still nothing.)*
13 PAM: Maybe we should call the police.
14 BECKY: And tell em what?! "Come on over an open my beer?"
15   Besides, what are *they* gonna do ... now. I'm just ... "very
16   angry" — as my mom would say ... that's all. *(The beer cap*
17   *suddenly responds and some of the beer foams onto the carpet.)*
18   Oooops! Sorry abut that, Rob. Got some beer on your carpet
19   there! *(She smiles at PAM.)*
20 PAM: *(Sipping her beer)* I was so scared ... when you ... left, ya
21   know? I didn't know what ta do.
22 BECKY: I don't wanna talk about it. It's over.
23 PAM: But it's so awful.
24 BECKY: Yeah, it's awful. But it's over. It was all a big mistake. A
25   big, filthy mistake. *(She looks at her hands.)* And my hands're
26   filthy! *(She puts her beer down and goes into the kitchen to wash*
27   *her hands.)*
28 PAM: I mean, Becky? Don't ya think ya should tell someone? I
29   mean, maybe just call someone ... like, anonymously ... or
30   something?
31 BECKY: *(From the kitchen)* Just shut up, *Pam*. The last thing I need
32   right now is to start makin' anonymous phone calls — from
33   my boyfriend's house. *(She comes back into the room drying her*
34   *hands.)* That would get everybody involved all over the place.
35   My mother. My dad. *Your* mother. Think about it. What're we

1   gonna tell 'em when they start sayin', "Well I thought you
2   were spending the night at Pam's." "No, Pammy said they
3   were spending the night at Becky's."
4 PAM: *(Looking at her beer. Quietly)* I know. It just seemed like a
5   good plan, ya know, with Rob outta town and all. I mean, it's
6   not like he's here or anything. And I thought there'd be a
7   kegger or somethin'. It was all a dumb idea I guess.
8 BECKY: Yeah. Dumb. *(She sits and sips her beer.)* This stuff tastes
9   like horse urine or something. I hate beer. Is it hot in here to
10   you?
11 PAM: Hot?
12 BECKY: Or cold? Maybe it's cold in here. *(Pam stares silently at*
13   *Becky.)* Or anything … maybe … hot? It just doesn't … I
14   dunno … feel right. *(She begins to rock very gently.)* I stink. I
15   should take a shower. And there must be somethin' on this
16   bottle. My hands're sticky. *(She rises to go into the kitchen to*
17   *wash her hands again.)*
18 PAM: There's nothin' on that bottle. Will you listen to me?
19 BECKY: *(Sitting again)* Listen to what?! Listen to you come up
20   with some more good ideas?
21 PAM: I was so scared tonight!
22 BECKY: Yeah? So was I.
23 PAM: *(She nods. Looks at her bottle.)* Where did they take ya?
24 BECKY: They?
25 PAM: They. Him and that other guy?
26 BECKY: They? *(She stares off into space blankly.)* They.
27 PAM: Becky! There were two of them.
28 BECKY: Oh. Yeah. I dunno. He was … his friend … or somethin'.
29   I dunno. I think he was drunk. I tried to wake him up. He was
30   asleep … or something … but he wouldn't wake up.
31 PAM: He didn't *do* something? He didn't try to help you …
32 BECKY: To help? No. No. He dropped him off at … at a house …
33   somewhere. I didn't … I … Well, why didn't *you* do
34   something?!
35 PAM: *Me?* I wasn't even …

1   BECKY: *(Rushing)* Yeah! You! Why didn't you "do something?"
2   You could tell I didn't wanna go with 'em. Ya just stood there.
3   Y'all just stood there! Nobody *did* anything. Y'all just stood
4   there and watched us leave ... *(Suddenly calm)* I don't want to
5   talk about it. *(She swallows a large gulp of beer.)*
6   PAM: *(Softly)* I'm sorry, Becky. I didn't know what ta do. Honest.
7   I didn't.
8   BECKY: I'm sorry. I guess I just wasn't thinkin'. *(Silence)*
9   PAM: Oh, God, how did this happen?
10   BECKY: *Pam?* Please don't tell anybody. Ya gotta promise me
11   that! *Please!*
12   PAM: Alright, alright! Relax! I'm not gonna tell anyone ...
13   BECKY: ... 'cause if you do, they'll find out! Everyone'll find out!
14   My mother! *Your* mother! The police! And then what? Pam,
15   ya gotta promise ...
16   PAM: *(Becoming seriously worried)* Alright, I said, I won't ... ya
17   gotta believe me. Relax, OK? Drink some more of your beer,
18   OK? *(BECKY drinks. They are quiet for several moments.)*
19   BECKY: I was scared too, ya know.
20   PAM: I know.
21   BECKY: But it's not my fault.
22   PAM: Of course it's not your fault. Nobody would blame you for
23   what happened. I don't! It's nobody's fault. It just happened.
24   BECKY: My father would blame me.
25   PAM: Your father?
26   BECKY: He would say, "Told ya not to go down there, didn't I?
27   But ya had to go anyway. Well, it's your own damned fault
28   and you deserve whatever you get!"
29   PAM: *(Quietly — under BECKY's lines)* Oh, Becky ...
30   BECKY: *(Continuing without pausing)* And he's right — I shoulda
31   never gone down there. He's always right ... I shouldn't have
32   ... *(She pulls at her shirt collar.)* It's *hot* in here! *(Pam sees*
33   *bruises that are growing quite red on Becky's neck.)*
34   PAM: Oh my God, Becky ... your neck ... it's ...
35   BECKY: My neck? What ... *(She goes to a mirror hung by the front*

1	*door.)* **Oh no! No way! Wait'll my mom sees that! Oh, she's**
2	**gonna ...**
3	PAM: **See? You** *are* **hurt!** *(Firmly)* **Look, something happened here**
4	**and you gotta tell someone.**
5	BECKY: *(Absorbed in examining her bruises)* **I'm ... not ... hurt ...**
6	**really ...**
7	PAM: **I got an idea.** *(PAM picks up the phone book and scans the*
8	*pages as BECKY continues to examine her bruises.)* **I heard**
9	**about this place ... you can ... call. It's ...**
10	BECKY: *(Still at the mirror)* **It really happened?** *(PAM stands and*
11	*goes to BECKY. She guides BECKY away from the mirror and*
12	*leads BECKY back to her chair.)*
13	PAM: **Look. This is stupid. You gotta tell someone. I heard about**
14	**this place. You can talk to 'em. It's supposed ta be**
15	**confidential.**
16	BECKY: **Confidential?**
17	PAM: *(Smiling)* **Yeah, confidential. It means they won't tell anyone.**
18	**See?** *(She looks closely at BECKY.)* **Never mind. I'll dial, you**
19	**just talk. OK? Please? You're scarin' me!**
20	BECKY: **You dial.**
21	PAM: *(Dials the phone and waits a moment.)* **Here. It's ringing.** *(PAM*
22	*hand the phone to BECKY, who carefully puts the receiver up to*
23	*her ear.)*
24	BECKY: **What?** *(Pause)* **Oh, hello. Yes, I'm callin' to ... uh ... to ...**
25	PAM: **Please, Becky,** *tell* **them.**
26	BECKY: *(Nodding)* **Yeah, um, I'm callin' ... to talk ... to ... huh?**
27	*(Pause)* **Yeah? Well, yeah ... I do. Um, somethin' happened**
28	**here tonight and I guess I was ... raped? Un-huh. Tonight ... I**
29	**dunno ... about an hour ago? ...** *(She looks at PAM*
30	*questioningly. PAM looks at her watch and nods.)* **Yeah, about an**
31	**hour ago. Am I — what? Hurt?** *(Again she looks at PAM, who*
32	*looks expectantly back at BECKY.)* **Yeah, I'm here. No, I don't**
33	**think I am. There's no blood anywhere.** *(Suddenly she becomes*
34	*agitated.)* **No, I** *can't* **call the police! No. I can't ... Hospital?**
35	**No ...** *(She looks at PAM.)* **No, I ... I can't. No, I'm OK ...**

1   **Look, just forget it ... I gotta go now. Bye.** *(She places the*
2   *receiver gently in its cradle.)*
3   PAM: **Well, what did they say?**
4   BECKY: **Well, she asked me if I was hurt, and I told her no, and**
5   **she asked if I'd reported it, and I told her I couldn't, and she**
6   **asked if I'd gone to the hospital, and I told her I couldn't ...**
7   *(She wipes her hands on her jeans.)*
8   PAM: **Yeah? Go on. Wha'd she say ta do?**
9   BECKY: *(Pausing)* **She said that I should prob'ly have some tea**
10   **and that I should prob'ly take a shower to, ya know, calm**
11   **down? An' she said I could call her back later ta talk some**
12   **more if I felt like it. But she said if I wasn't hurt then maybe**
13   **I didn't need ta go ta the hospital ...**
14   PAM: **No! No, way! Even I know better than that! Becky, if you**
15   **wanna go ta the hospital, I'll drive ya there right now.**
16   BECKY: **No! Then everyone'll know and my dad'll kill me! I'm**
17   **not goin'! I'm OK. Everything is OK. Ya gotta believe me.**
18   PAM: **OK. I believe you, OK? Nobody's gonna force ya to do**
19   **anything you don't wanna do, OK?** *(Silence)* **Do you want**
20   **another beer?** *(Silence)* **Look, maybe the lady was right.**
21   **Maybe you should just take a nice hot shower and relax.**
22   **Maybe that would feel good, OK?** *(Silence)* **I know. Look, I'll**
23   **go start a shower for ya. OK? Do ya want me to start a shower**
24   **for you?**
25   BECKY: **Yeah. Start a shower. That'd be good. Yeah.**
26   PAM: **OK. you just sit here real quiet, and I'll be right back ...**
27   **OK?**
28   BECKY: **Yeah. OK.** *(PAM leaves the room to go start BECKY's*
29   *shower. Alone now, BECKY begins to rock again very slowly. She*
30   *sips her beer. She looks at her hands. She takes a very long swig*
31   *of beer and coughs a bit at the taste of it.)* **Yeah. It's OK.**
32   **Everything ... is OK. I'm not hurt.**
33   *The End*
34
35

Ledge

by William Borden

William Borden's plays have won twenty-one national playwriting competitions and have had over two hundred productions. The full version of his play, *The Last Prostitute*, was shown on Lifetime Television and is on video. His novel, *Superstoe*, was republished by Orloff Press. A core Alumnus playwright at the Playwright's Center in Minneapolis, he is playwright with Listen Winds.

Ledge received a staged reading by the Playwrights Center of San Francisco in 1991 and was produced the same year by New York City's Impact Theatre. A film version was produced by San Francisco's Frog Prince Productions in 1992.

Production Suggestions

Since the illusion of being on a narrow ledge at a lethal altitude is essential to this play, you should rehearse it some of the time in a situation that constricts your space and gives you a sense of height. Please do not rehearse at a height that is actually dangerous; a "ledge" three feet above the stage floor should be high enough. Carefully observe your feelings and physical behavior during your first several rehearsals at this height; you will soon become accustomed to the sensation and lose the sense of danger. If you have carefully observed your reaction and play them in each rehearsal and performance, it won't matter if the edge of the "ledge" is nothing but a taped line on the stage floor — you'll still be able to communicate to the audience the illusion that the characters are perched far above a street below.

Although a practical window that actually will fall closed on cue will facilitate a production of this play, you can get along without it. One alternative would be to have an off-stage assistant provide the sound of the closing window; if your production plan doesn't include even a sound effect, it will still work if the actress and actor both "hear" the imaginary slam of the closing window and register their response to the noise.

Address all inquiries concerning performances, readings, or reprinting of this work *or any portion thereof* to William Borden, 7996 S. FM 548, Royse City, TX 75189. For details, See "Part II, Securing Rights for Your Production," pages 241 to 250.

1　　　　The action takes place in the present on a ledge around a building,
2　　　　forty-one stories up.
3　　**CHARACTERS:** TOM — who can be any adult age, but should be
4　　　　about the same age as Mary. MARY — who can be any adult age,
5　　　　but should be about the same age as Tom.
6　　**SETTING:** A narrow ledge around a building, with a window in the
7　　　　building's wall. Faint sounds of traffic from far below.
8
9　　　　*(Lights come up to reveal MARY standing on the ledge of a*
10　　　*building, her back pressed against the building, looking straight*
11　　　*ahead, and inching away from an open window. Far, far below a*
12　　　*horn honks. She looks down, sways, catches her balance, and*
13　　　*stares, petrified, straight ahead. She thinks for a moment. Then*
14　　　*she starts to inch back toward the window — just as TOM climbs*
15　　　*out of the window onto the ledge. He doesn't see her. Determined,*
16　　　*he starts to sidestep along the ledge, toward MARY, until he*
17　　　*bumps into her. They both nearly fall, they regain their precarious*
18　　　*balance, and they stare at each other.)*
19　　**TOM: This is my ledge.**
20　　**MARY: I was here first.**
21　　**TOM: I suppose you made a reservation.**
22　　**MARY: If you're going to jump, jump.**
23　　**TOM: Of course I'm going to jump!** *(Several beats)* **You were here**
24　　　**first.**
25　　**MARY: Go ahead.**
26　　**TOM: You go.**
27　　**MARY: No, you go.**
28　　**TOM: You.**
29　　**MARY: *Jump!***
30　　**TOM: All right.** *(He adjusts his position. He readjusts.)* **You're**
31　　　**crowding me.**
32　　**MARY: I'm sorry!**
33　　**TOM: Could you ...** *(She edges away, giving him room. She slips. He*
34　　　*grabs her.)*
35　　**MARY: Thanks.** *(He readies himself. He stops.)*

1   TOM: How's it going to look?

2   MARY: Messy.

3   TOM: My going first. Who'll pay attention to me, with you still up

4   here, making a spectacle of yourself? They'll just step over me

5   — what's left of me — and they'll be shining spotlights on you

6   and sending reporters out to interview you and I'll be lucky to

7   be a sidebar on the comics page, which is the story of my life.

8   So go on. *(She looks down. Cars honk.)* You climbed out here.

9   *(She gathers her courage.)* You made a decision. *(She readies*

10   *herself.)* You knew there was no reason to put up with it any

11   longer. *(She's ready.)* Stop! *(She stops.)* You jump first, who'll

12   pay any attention to me, up here, a speck on the forty-first

13   floor? You'll get all the attention, as usual.

14   MARY: As usual?

15   TOM: You women. You're always getting the attention. With your

16   legs. Your breasts. Your emotions. Get off.

17   MARY: Off?

18   TOM: Through the window.

19   MARY: You're between me and the window.

20   TOM: There must be another window around the corner.

21   MARY: I might fall.

22   TOM: All right then, jump. I'll wait until they've scraped you up

23   and carried you away in a shoebox, then I'll call attention to

24   myself. Go on, go on, get it over with.

25   MARY: I'll jump when I'm good and ready.

26   TOM: *Jump!*

27   MARY: *No! (Tom pulls out a gun and aims it at her.)* Shoot. *(Tom*

28   *smiles, puts away the gun.)*

29   TOM: You women think you're so clever, so damned clever! Tom

30   Longmyer, murderer? No, no. You can borrow it, if you like.

31   MARY: Why would I want your gun?

32   TOM: You could make sure that way.

33   MARY: Forty-one stories is sure.

34   TOM: I was going to use the revolver, but ...

35   MARY: What?

1   **TOM: I was afraid nobody would notice. A shot, drowned out by**
2   **the bedlam of the city. Shots all the time! Gang warfare, drug**
3   **dealers. Buses make a lot of noise, too. You can't hear yourself**
4   **think.**
5   **MARY: I've never heard myself think. I mean, you think very**
6   **quietly, really. Silently, in fact. Don't you?**
7   **TOM: It's just an expression!**
8   **MARY: But words should mean something. Don't you think?**
9   **TOM:** *(He pulls the gun again.)* **Get off my ledge.**
10   **MARY: You are so insignificant.**
11   **TOM: Don't say that to me.**
12   **MARY: Nothing. An absence.**
13   **TOM: Don't say that to me!**
14   **MARY: Who will miss you?** *(He begins to cry. She watches him coldly*
15   *for a moment.)* **I'm sorry.** *(He bawls.)* **I'm sorry!** *(He wails.)* **I'm**
16   **sorry, Tom!** *(He stops abruptly, smiles.)* **Give me the gun.** *(He*
17   *hands her the gun.)*
18   **TOM: Be careful. The safety's on.**
19   **MARY: How do you turn it off?** *(He switches off the safety.)*
20   **TOM: In the mouth. Blows the brains right out. The temple — the**
21   **bullet can ricochet off the inside of your skull, leave you a**
22   **semiconscious vegetable for the rest of your life.** *(She aims the*
23   *revolver at him.)* **What are you doing?**
24   **MARY: You manipulated me.**
25   **TOM: You shoot me, they'll send you to the chair.**
26   **MARY: I don't care.**
27   **TOM: You wouldn't dare.**
28   **MARY: Wouldn't I?**
29   **TOM: You women —**
30   **MARY: You men.**
31   **TOM: — Always flaunting yourselves —**
32   **MARY: You're all the same!**
33   **TOM: All you want is a love slave!**
34   **MARY: Manipulator!**
35   **TOM: Show-off!** *(She pulls the trigger. The hammer clicks. She pulls*

1   *it several more times.)*
2   TOM: I didn't have the guts.
3   MARY: You're a zero.
4   TOM: I'm not worth your pity.
5   MARY: You're disgusting!
6   TOM: I'm not even that significant.
7   MARY: Get off my ledge!
8   TOM: My ledge!
9   MARY: Mine!
10   TOM: Minemineminemineminemine!
11   MARY: You're so juvenile. *(She tries to edge around him, to get to the*
12   *window.)*
13   TOM: What are you doing?
14   MARY: You've spoiled it.
15   TOM: Be careful. You might fall.
16   MARY: Fat lot you care, Tom Longmyer.
17   TOM: But aren't you going to …?
18   MARY: I don't have to put up with you on the day I'm going to die.
19   I can at least have some privacy. Some quality time to myself
20   as I prepare to … you know. *(She can't get around him.)* You
21   climb around me.
22   TOM: You climb around me.
23   MARY: Come on, I'm getting cold.
24   TOM: I might fall.
25   MARY: Climb around me or I'll push you off. *(He tries, he loses his*
26   *balance, she pulls him back. They're belly to belly, face to face.*
27   *He flings himself back to the building, where he was before,*
28   *between her and the window.)* You're just like my father!
29   Cowardly, weak, ineffectual!
30   TOM: If you're *so* effectual, be my guest. *(He motions her to climb*
31   *around him.)*
32   MARY: It's too windy.
33   TOM: You are so effectual. *(She flings herself before him, grabbing*
34   *at the building. He holds her.)*
35   MARY: Let go. *(He lets go. She starts to fall. He grabs her. They're*

1   *both precarious.)*
2   **TOM: You hold onto the building, I'll hold onto you.** *(They do.*
3   *Several beats)* **I've never been this close to a woman before.**
4   **Without kissing her.**
5   **MARY: Kiss me and I'll jump and take you with me.**
6   **TOM: You had coffee for breakfast.**
7   **MARY: Do I have bad breath? I have mints somewhere ...** *(She*
8   *reaches for her mints, teeters, he hauls her in, their lips brush.)*
9   **TOM: I didn't kiss you! It was an accident! Just a brush ... of lips**
10   **... hardly noticeable ... like me ...**
11   **MARY: You should have shaved. Your death day, the least you**
12   **could have done —**
13   **TOM: Who's going to tell, me smeared on the boulevard like sauce**
14   **on a pizza?**
15   **MARY: If you took a little pride in yourself ...**
16   **TOM: ... I wouldn't be here.** *(Several beats)*
17   **MARY: Tom ...**
18   **TOM: I don't even know your name.**
19   **MARY: Mary. Tom ...**
20   **TOM: Mary what?**
21   **MARY: Mary Freestone. Tom ...** *(He kisses her — a long kiss. She*
22   *kisses him — tenderly, for a long time. They catch their breaths.)*
23   **You're excited.**
24   **TOM: I know.**
25   **MARY: Well stop it.** *(Several beats)*
26   **TOM: I can't.** *(Several beats)* **Mary?**
27   **MARY: What?**
28   **TOM: I don't want to die.**
29   **MARY: You should have planned ahead a little better.**
30   **TOM: Do you?**
31   **MARY: I don't care.**
32   **TOM: Well, then you should move, so if one of us falls, it's you.**
33   **MARY: I mean, I don't care if *you* die. I care if *I* die.**
34   **TOM: I'm losing my erection.**
35   **MARY: That gives us more room.**

1   **TOM: Mary? I want you to live, too.**

2   **MARY: That's nice.** *(She succeeds in getting around him. She inches*

3   *toward the window.)*

4   **TOM: Don't leave me! Mary!**

5   **MARY: Don't be a crybaby.**

6   **TOM:** *(Crying)* **I don't want to die.**

7   **MARY: Why did you come out here if you don't want to die?!**

8   **TOM: I hadn't met you.**

9   **MARY: You're trying to manipulate me.**

10   **TOM: If that's true, I'll kill myself!** *(She waits.)* **You want me to**

11   **jump, just for a tiny manipulation?** *(She waits. He starts to*

12   *jump.)*

13   **MARY: Give me your hand.**

14   **TOM: You don't think I have the integrity to jump?** *(He really*

15   *starts to jump.)*

16   **MARY: Just give me your hand.** *(He clutches her hand. They edge to*

17   *the window. The window, which is barred, falls shut.)*

18   **TOM: What is it?**

19   **MARY: The window fell shut.**

20   **TOM: Open it.**

21   **MARY: It locks automatically.** *(They look at each other.)*

22   **TOM AND MARY: Help!**

23   *The End*

24

25

26

27

28

29

30

31

32

33

34

35

GQ

by Sharon Whitney

Sharon Whitney, who holds the Oregon Playwrights Award and the Pacific Northwest Writers Conference First Prize for Playwriting, is the author of three published books and seven prize-winning plays.

GQ won the LitEruption Competition of the New Rose Theatre in 1991 and had its first production in a showcase of the author's new work by Conant & Conant Booksellers.

Production Suggestions

To make this comedy work right, be sure you realize why both of these yuppie wanna-bes are comic fools: neither is at all self perceptive; they are so much into surface images that they've lost track of any understanding that's more than skin deep. The Quinn actor needs to be aware of the major shift his character makes when Penn leaves — just before Quinn's last speech.

Address all inquiries concerning performances, readings, or reprinting of this work *or any portion thereof* to Sharon Whitney, 2712 SW Patton Rd., Portland, OR 97201.For details, see "Part II: Securing Rights for Your Production," pages 241 to 250.

"Penn," Brent Collier, left, "Quinn," Mark Vincent, right, in GQ *by Sharon Whitney.*

1   The action takes place in the present in a men's shop.

2   ***CHARACTERS:*** PENN — A sensitive fellow. QUINN — His guide

3   and confidant.

4   ***SETTING:*** A rack of clothes and a chair.

5

6   **PENN:** *(Trying on clothes while QUINN lounges in a chair)* **So, OK.**

7   **The red scarf. Do you think she'll like me in red?**

8   **QUINN: Red is, well … red. Maybe it'll get her excited.**

9   **PENN: I thought the line, you know … See how it hangs from my**

10   **neck? The eye kind of travels, huh? Do you think I look**

11   **taller?**

12   **QUINN: I don't know, it's risky.**

13   **PENN: Yeah?**

14   **QUINN: A little bit much … for you.**

15   **PENN: Yeah?**

16   **QUINN: Now don't get hurt feelings. It makes your waist look even**

17   **thicker.**

18   **PENN:** *Thicker.*

19   **QUINN: You asked.**

20   **PENN: Oh, God. The other day I heard her say, "Look at that guy**

21   **— what a pear." Oh, God.**

22   **QUINN: Listen … open up your neckline. That's what I do. A nice**

23   **deep V, with something gold. Show some hair.**

24   **PENN: That's so Mafia … isn't it? What do you think? Could I get**

25   **away with it?**

26   **QUINN: Hey, you want her to look at your gut?**

27   **PENN:** *(Pause)* **She could look at my jacket.** *(He takes a jacket from*

28   *a garment bag.)* **I just bought it. It was in** *GQ.*

29   **QUINN:** *GQ?*

30   **PENN: I spent a week's pay on it.**

31   **QUINN: Huh … You saw it in** *GQ?*

32   **PENN: You don't like it.** *(QUINN is silent.)* **I thought I'd wear it**

33   **with black slacks and a cream-colored shirt.**

34   **QUINN: Cream?**

35   **PENN: I thought the guy in the ad kind of looked like me.** *(QUINN*

39

1	*raises his eyebrows.)* ***Jeeze.***
2	QUINN: *You asked.*
3	PENN: Sorry. *(Quinn sighs.)* I'm just touchy today. For breakfast, I
4	had two chocolate croissants. I inhaled 'em. *(QUINN clucks.)*
5	Nerves.
6	QUINN: Oh, forget it. Why deprive yourself because she's got a
7	thing for Greek gods? *(PENN mews like a lost cat.)* You're a
8	little plump, a little soft around the edges. So what?
9	PENN: *(He whimpers. Long pause)* So. I spend three hundred dollars
10	on a jacket and you say I look like a plate of mashed potatoes.
11	QUINN: You're overreacting.
12	PENN: It's the chocolate.
13	QUINN: *(Rising)* I don't need this.
14	PENN: I'm sorry, I'm sorry. Stay with me, buddy. Please. Tell me.
15	Please. What's wrong with the jacket?
16	QUINN: Well. You need me. OK. The cut is English. It's made for
17	someone who can project a kind of "hounds to the foxes" aura.
18	*(Penn mews.)* And the tweed. On you, it's like an extension of
19	your face. It looks like black and white whiskers.
20	PENN: Hurrah. The Hairy Ape. Three hundred bucks.
21	QUINN: Maybe ... somehow ... you can get around it. Try a blue
22	shirt, or even mauve. If you can kill the effect of the tweed ...
23	get it away from your skin ...
24	PENN: I thought I should show my skin, my hairy chest.
25	QUINN: I was wrong. *(Pause)* Have you ever been draped?
26	PENN: I'm a winter. Black and white.
27	QUINN: Oh.
28	PENN: I'm gong to call her. I'll cancel.
29	QUINN: Oh, no, no, no. Let's work on this. Build you up.
30	PENN: I don't even know what to talk about.
31	QUINN: Ask her about her job. Women like that. It's all they think
32	about, anyway. Their identity depends on it.
33	PENN: I know all about her job. I work in the same office.
34	QUINN: Some common sense, please. Play dumb. Let her run her
35	trip. You don't have to listen, just keep eye contact and

1   remember to say "oh" and "uh huh."

2   PENN: Won't she think I'm slow?

3   QUINN: She'll never notice. Women love to talk about themselves.

4   It makes them think they got the world under control.

5   PENN: I read somewhere I should lean across the table and let her

6   sit back. It's very flattering.

7   QUINN: *(Nodding)* Eat everything on your plate, too. It makes

8   them upset when you order something and tinker with it.

9   PENN: OK.

10   QUINN: Offer to share something, though. That's sexy. Put

11   something small on your fork and offer it with a line like,

12   "This is superb. Will you sample?"

13   PENN: Superb? A fork full of peas?

14   QUINN: Peas?

15   PENN: Roast beef? *(QUINN looks like he's been poisoned.)* No?

16   QUINN: No. For you a sensitive dish. *(PENN is clearly stymied..*

17   *Beat)* Linguine with white clam sauce.

18   PENN: Clams give me hives. How about lasagna?

19   QUINN: Sure. slop it on your tie. *(PENN is lost. Beat)* A green salad

20   with nasturtiums and radicchio. Scallops. Barely warm.

21   PENN: How about lamb chops? Itsy bitsy ones.

22   QUINN: In panties.

23   PENN: Right. Lamb with pants.

24   QUINN: What are you doing after dinner?

25   PENN: I could ask her to see my apartment.

26   QUINN: Oh, I don't know …

27   PENN: I could make her an espresso. I got some little cups and one

28   of those knives that cuts lemon peel. Should I ask her? I know,

29   I'll just trust my intuition.

30   QUINN: That's a myth — about men's intuition.

31   PENN: Yeah?

32   QUINN: Some have it, but most don't. *(PENN groans.)* All right, if

33   you must: get her to take you to her place. If it's a disaster,

34   you can always go home.

35   PENN: What if she puts some moves on me?

1 QUINN: What kind of underwear have you got?

2 PENN: The best. A hundred percent cotton.

3 QUINN: White, right?

4 PENN: You can bleach it.

5 QUINN: Lord ... *(Sighs.)* Calvin Klein has a new silk line. Why

6   don't you go wild and buy a pair of briefs.

7 PENN: She won't get the wrong idea?

8 QUINN: They're for heterosexuals. You can tell. They come in

9   royal blue, banker gray and legal pad yellow.

10 PENN: I'm good in yellow ... at least, I used to be.

11 QUINN: Then you're set. *(PENN gathers his things, prepares to*

12   *leave, then freezes, stricken.)* What? What ...? What ...

13 PENN: I don't know how to walk.

14 QUINN: Let's see. *(Head down, arms bowed, fingers curled under,*

15   *PENN skulks across the stage. QUINN considers him.)* Does

16   "miser's hump" run in your family? *(PENN mews.)* Come on,

17   sport, chest out, chin up ... hup, hup ... not so stiff ...try to

18   look carefree, maybe that would suit you. *(PENN is boggled,*

19   *but he tries walking this way and that.)* By the way, no beer.

20   Stick with white wine in case you spill it. Or maybe a blush,

21   that's classy. But now that I think about it, it's not you. Do ale.

22 PENN: Someone should write a book: "What Every Man Should

23   Know."

24 QUINN: Hmmm. Not a bad idea.

25 PENN: I'm reading "My Father, My Self."

26 QUINN: The son's search for identity?

27 PENN: It really gets me. I cried for half an hour.

28 QUINN: My shrink says it's no good.

29 PENN: Oh. *(Beat)* I'm going to call her. I'll cancel.

30 QUINN: You gonna waste my good advice? *(PENN mews.)* Hang in

31   there.

32 PENN: Will you meet me for breakfast? I'll have to debrief.

33 QUINN: Leave a message on my machine.

34 PENN: I feel so vulnerable.

35 QUINN: Uh-huh.

1   PENN: Thanks for everything.
2   QUINN: Hey buddy. Walk tall. *(PENN exits. QUINN sits a moment,*
3   *then rises, calling Off-stage.)* Clerk ...? Sir ...? Excuse me, sir ...
4   Yes, ha, ha — ha, ha. Oh, no, I wasn't shouting. Sir, could I
5   possibly ... uh, do you suppose ... uh, you know that black
6   and white jacket that was in *GQ?* The tweed? Is there a
7   chance I could try it on? ... Oh, any size — whatever size you
8   got ... I know it's not really me ... but it could be ... Don't
9   you think?

10   *The End*
11
12
13
14
15
16
17
18
19
20
21
22
23
24
25
26
27
28
29
30
31
32
33
34
35

The Shadow
by Conrad Bishop and Elizabeth Fuller

Conrad Bishop and Elizabeth Fuller are directors of the Independent Eye, a national touring ensemble. Their plays have been presented by Actors Theatre of Louisville, Circle Repertory, Denver Center Theatre, and many other theatres nationally, and their radio drama productions have won major awards.

The Shadow was part of the Eye's touring revue repertoire from 1975 to 1980 and is included in their book *Rash Acts*.

Playwrights' Production Suggestions

The Shadow emerged from an extreme variety of personal experiences with the medical profession. This sketch tries to include that range of contradictory feelings — rage at impersonal, sometimes incompetent treatment, the sense of humiliation at the vulnerability of being a patient, and the genuine understanding that these people, whatever their flaws, actually saved the lives of both playwrights. The farcical sequences should be played to the hilt, but the real, deeply felt sequences must be given full value as well — the doctor describing his experience with the woman suffering leukemia is totally real. The style and mood shift faster than flipping through the cable channels.

In the Independent Eye's repertory production, there was no set or special costuming. Two chairs indicated the bed, and the actors sitting in them, legs stretched out in front, were assumed to be in bed. It's also possible to use a third chair as the "foot" of the bed. Whatever the choice, it should allow for the transitions to be instantaneous, like the instant shifts of a dream.

The sketch tries to capture that very vulnerable, unsettled experience of being midway between sleeping and waking, and veering back and forth from one to the other. It's about the fear that Mort and Mara — and all of us — have about being mortal.

Address all inquiries concerning performances, readings, or reprinting of this work *or any portion thereof* to The Independent Eye, 502 Pleasant Hill Road, Sebastopol, CA 95472. for details, see "Part II: Securing Rights for Your Production," pages 241 to 250.

1   The action takes place in MORT and MARA's bedroom.

2   **CHARACTERS:** MORT — the husband. MARA — the wife.

3   **SETTING:** A bed.

4

5   *(MORT and MARA in nightclothes, getting into bed, adjusting*

6   *pillows, bantering but very edgy)*

7   MORT: **Beddy-bye.**

8   MARA: **When do we have to get up?**

9   MORT: **When's your appointment?**

10   MARA: **Nine. Then I'll bring the car back and you go for yours.**

11   MORT: **Why'd you make our checkups on the same day?**

12   MARA: **That way everything's done.**

13   MORT: **Suppose we're both sick?**

14   MARA: **If you're sick you're sick.**

15   MORT: **If I know it I'm sicker.**

16   MARA: **You had too much to drink.**

17   MORT: **Alcohol sterilizes. My germs are clean.**

18   MARA: **They'll look inside you and find pickled gut.**

19   MORT: **Put your sick mind to sleep.**

20   MARA: **I feel strange.**

21   MORT: *(Settling in)* **Get some sleep, honey.**

22   MARA: *(Settling in)* **Don't act like my doctor.** *(Pause. Instant shift of*

23   *worlds: he stands upright, looming over her. She sits, rigid.)*

24   MORT: **Hello, I'm your doctor. How do you feel?**

25   MARA: **All right.**

26   MORT: **Headaches? Hallucinations?**

27   MARA: **No.**

28   MORT: **How old are your parents? Epilepsy? Seizures? Searches?**

29   **When did you have a bath?**

30   MARA: **Never.**

31   MORT: **What did they tell you in school? Do you like the feel of**

32   **cotton sheets? Can you take criticism? Dizzy spells?**

33   **Ringworm? Rats?**

34   MARA: **Nothing.**

35   MORT: **How'd you like to die?**

1   **MARA: Wait!** *(Blurred focus: they are suspended between dream and*
2   *waking.)* **I need sleep.**
3   **MORT: Go to sleep.**
4   **MARA: I feel strange.** *(Again they mesh into the nightmare.)*
5   **MORT: Hello, I'm your doctor. How do you feel?**
6   **MARA: My watch stopped.**
7   **MORT: That's messy. You need a big lead box.**
8   **MARA: I need a nap.**
9   **MORT: Nap. OK. Procedures and risks involved. First we freeze**
10   **you, make a small incision, insert a tube up the aorta, watch**
11   **its progress by fluoroscope. Then we inject the dye. You'll feel**
12   **a burning sensation for fifteen seconds. At this point you**
13   **sometimes have a reaction, but it can't be proven until you**
14   **die. Then we x-ray the remains and before you clog we yank**
15   **out the tubes and try to stop the blood. At this point you often**
16   **think of tall buildings swaying in the wind. We try to keep you**
17   **back from the edge, but there is a slight chance, say half of one**
18   **percent, that you may lose your balance and fall.**
19   **MARA: Am I worried?**
20   **MORT: Twice a day.**
21   **MARA: Risk? Is there any risk?**
22   **MORT: There's always some risk. Less on a passbook account, but**
23   **there you get only five and a half percent. Municipals are still**
24   **a good buy, but if your inner city deteriorates, you're gonna**
25   **have problems with flushing.**
26   **MARA: What about malignancy?**
27   **MORT: It's like inflation. Eats away at what you've got.**
28   **MARA: How long am I in for?**
29   **MORT: Well, you can put it in five-year certificates, but I'd**
30   **recommend a shorter confinement unless you want long-term**
31   **security at the cost of short-term inflammation.**
32   **MARA: Wait! We're not talking about money —**
33   **MORT:** *(Grasping her hand voraciously)* **I am! I'm a doctor! How**
34   **do you feel?**
35   **MARA: Confused!**

1   **MORT:** *(Suddenly solicitous)* **That's natural. And I'd love to help**
2   **you. I'd be more than willing to help you. But I'm a doctor.**
3   **Medicine is not an exact science. Medicine is an art. I'm an**
4   **artist.**
5   **MARA: It's cold.**
6   **MORT: You don't expect all painters to paint rosy pictures. You**
7   **don't expect all writers to write happy endings.**
8   **MARA: Clammy.**
9   **MORT: There's comic medicine and there's serious medicine. My**
10   **medicine makes a statement:** *Nobody lives forever!*
11   **MARA: Ahhhhhhh!** *(He strangles her. She screams. They wake into*
12   *reality, lying side by side in bed.)*
13   **MORT: What's the matter?**
14   **MARA: I was dreaming. You were the doctor.**
15   **MORT: That's a laugh.**
16   **MARA: If you're the doctor you're safe. Nothing to lose.**
17   **MORT: Relax.**
18   **MARA: It's like auto mechanics. You never know.**
19   **MORT: Relax and get to sleep.**
20   **MARA: Beddy-bye.**
21   **MORT: And try not to yell when we start.**
22   **MARA: Start what?**
23   **MORT: Cutting.** *(Nightmare: he grabs her from behind, cuts her*
24   *throat.)*
25   **MARA: Stop it! Stop! I'm the nurse!**
26   **MORT:** *(Releasing her)* **Oh my God. Sorry. Here, let me button you**
27   **up.**
28   **MARA: It's all right, I'm on the pill.**
29   **MORT: Thank God. Read me the appointments, we're behind**
30   **schedule.**
31   **MARA: There's Mr. Pillsbury.**
32   **MORT: Mr. Pillsbury's cancer. I'm sick of his damn cancer.**
33   **Everybody got a cancer. It's his funeral.**
34   **MARA: There's Mrs. Pillsbury, for an abortion.**
35   **MORT: How advanced is the pregnancy?**

1   MARA: He'll be nineteen this fall.
2   MORT: Nurse, people have no respect for human life. They don't
3   deserve to live.
4   MARA: There's Dr. Pillsbury
5   MORT: Dr. Pillsbury? That's not right. I'm Dr. Pillsbury.
6   MARA: You're on the list.
7   MORT: But I'm the doctor.
8   MARA: It's on the list.
9   MORT: You'll be sorry. I'm the doctor. I'll stand up and shake
10   your hand! *(They clasp hands, shake violently.)*
11   BOTH: Hello, I'm your doctor, how do you feel? *(Mort sinks down,*
12   *Mara dominant.)*
13   MORT: Well ... I don't feel any lumps. I really need to get home.
14   My driver's license expires on Friday, I have to study for the
15   test, I have to get my eyes opened. Couldn't I still be the
16   doctor?
17   MARA: I can't find the vein.
18   MORT: The grass needs mowing, it's getting too high to cut.
19   MARA: I can't find the vein.
20   MORT: It's growing too fast. The doctors are amazed.
21   MARA: I'm the doctor, I can't find the vein.
22   MORT: But Friday I'm due to expire!
23   MARA: Gotcha!
24   MORT: Ahhhhhhhhh! *(They wake.)*
25   MARA: Bad dream?
26   MORT: Doctors.
27   MARA: Relax. *(Blurred focus)*
28   MORT: I should have had it out. In school my friends had
29   everything taken out. I should have done it then.
30   MARA: Are you the doctor or the patient?
31   MORT: I forgot.
32   MARA: It's safer to be the doctor.
33   MORT: Can he wear a white hat?
34   MARA: I'll be the doctor, too. Then we're a team.
35   MORT: A medical team.

1   MARA: MDs!
2   MORT: Men in white!
3   MARA: Doctor!
4   MORT: Doc! *(They embrace, then recoil.)*
5   MARA: Oh dear, I contaminated you.
6   MORT: I was sterile. Wait! The operation! *(Focusing on an*
7   *imaginary patient)* But there's nobody here.
8   MARA: That's OK. It's practice. Run scrimmage, get the plays
9   down pat, then we shove the patients under there and let fly.
10   We don't ever check the face.
11 MORT: Unless there's a beard. We don't want a beard in the muck.
12 MARA: What do you think? Rapid Shave? Drano? Easy-Off?
13 MORT: Wait. He's not real. He's imaginary.
14 MARA: Then we better work fast. You take the steak knife, I've got
15   the juicer.
16 MORT: Roger! *(They begin burlesque surgery: broad, gross*
17   *pantomime.)*
18 MARA: Take that out, I saw it move.
19 MORT: Arthritis. Out with his bones.
20 MARA: How about the kidneys?
21 MORT: Feel OK. Oh-oh, bed's wet. Can't have that.
22 MARA: You did a no-no.
23 MORT: Give 'em the heave.
24 MARA: Squeeze that.
25 MORT: Not very fresh.
26 MARA: Mold.
27 MORT: Out.
28 MARA: Let's do a brain test. What are the three justifications for
29   existence? Wrong. Take out the brain.
30 MORT: What about the liver?
31 MARA: We had liver last night.
32 MORT: Well, it's cheap.
33 MARA: Three dollars a pound?
34 MORT: For that we could buy sweetbreads.
35 MARA: He didn't complain of sweetbreads.

1 MORT: Out.
2 MARA: Better wash all this off.
3 MORT: Wait. I got a bite.
4 MARA: All we can do is pray.
5 MORT: Pull out the plug.
6 MARA: Locomotor ataxia.
7 MORT: Dynamite up the kazoo! Take cover! *(Catastrophic*
8   *explosion)*
9 MARA: Got him.
10 MORT: Is he OK?
11 MARA: He's dead.
12 MORT: But he's imaginary.
13 MARA: He is now. *(Blurred focus)*
14 MORT: Hey, what am I doing? I'm not the doctor, I'm supposed to
15   *see* the doctor …
16 MARA: No, come on, you better be the doctor …
17 MORT: I can't speak Latin. I missed the test. Is there a Band-Aid
18   in the house?
19 MARA: We're running out of gas … *(He transforms into a concrete*
20   *character: a fatigued fifty-year-old physician, speaking to us*
21   *directly.)*
22 MORT: I have a patient. Forty years old. Female. White. The most
23   radiant, life-loving woman I know.
24 MARA: She's a patient. She's dying.
25 MORT: She has leukemia. She's dying. I do bone-marrow biopsies.
26   Which are very painful. She's had remission twice. Then it
27   goes on.
28 MARA: She's losing her looks.
29 MORT: She tries to joke.
30 MARA: Symptoms?
31 MORT: Symptoms? I feel a cold sweat. Shaking. I try to laugh.
32 MARA: Prognosis?
33 MORT: Six months.
34 MARA: Side effects?
35 MORT: Side effects?

1   MARA: Any side effects?
2   MORT: You die.
3   MARA: Who dies?
4   MORT: The patient dies.
5   MARA: Who's the patient?
6   MORT: The patient pays the piper.
7   MARA: Then who pays the doctor?
8   MORT: Whoever's dying.
9   MARA: Everyone's dying. *(Pause. Incredulous)*
10   MORT: No ... *(Stark awake, they kneel clumsily side by side on the*
11   *bed, hands in prayer.)* **I'm the patient now.**
12   MARA: I'm the patient too. *(They mumble in shambling unison.)*
13   BOTH: Yea though I walk through the valley of the shadow of —
14   Yea though I walk through the valley of —
15   Yea though —
16   Valley of —
17   Sha —
18   Va —
19   I fear no evil!
20   No evil.
21   Yea though I fear no —
22   Yea though I fear no —
23   Yea though I walk through the valley of
24   The Shadow of —
25   *(Their lips form a word, soundlessly. Fade.)*
26   *The End*
27
28
29
30
31
32
33
34
35

The Lemonade Stand
by Bryan P. Harnetiaux

Bryan Harnetiaux is playwright-in-residence at Spokane Civic Theatre in Spokane, Washington. He has written over twenty plays, eight of which have been published.

The original version of *The Lemonade Stand* was first performed in 1987 at Spokane's Gonzaga University in a production sponsored primarily by the Spokane Christian Coalition. A revised version was a finalist in the Actors Theatre of Louisville's 1991 Ten-Minute-Play contest. A twenty-five minute version of the script is available from The Dramatic Publishing Company of Woodstock, IL.

Playwright's Production Suggestions

Take care in fashioning the lemonade stand: It needs to be durable enough to withstand the business of the play, but fragile enough to collapse when the man kicks it "for emphasis." His first kick should be no more than a gesture, yet it must cause the stand to fall. If the actor has to work too hard to achieve the effect, the Man will wrongly appear to have *intended* to up end the stand. The prop also has symbolic value: Its presence evokes a shared memory of our first, benign experience with capitalism.

Since the play is, in part, about power, you should ask yourselves who has the power at any particular moment; also decide whose house is being foreclosed.

The Woman should not spit violently; this would undermine the dignity of her act. It should be a slow, well-aimed stream of spittle that drops by force of gravity. Also, she should not take any of the money as she exits.

Play the Woman as desperate but dignified, the Man as likeable and well-intentioned.

Address all inquiries concerning performances, readings, or reprinting of this work *or any portion thereof* to the play's licensing agent, The Dramatic Publishing Company, 311 Washington St., Woodstock, IL; 1-800-448-7469. For details, see "Part II: Securing Rights for Your Production," pages 241 to 250.

1　　　The action takes place in the present on a hot summer day at a
2　　　lemonade stand in a poverty-stricken sector of a city.
3　*CHARACTERS:* A WOMAN — her clothes are worn, but neat. Her
4　　　eyes are unsettling. A MAN — enviably fresh and well-
5　　　nourished, he wears a sport coat and tie.
6　*SETTING:* The area is littered with fast-food wrappers and other trash.
7　　　In the center, the lemonade stand is like one a child would make
8　　　out of scraps of batting and butcher paper. On its shelf stands a
9　　　plastic pitcher along with some paper cups and a jar with pennies
10　　　in it. A sign reads "Lemonade." The scene speaks of hot Saturday
11　　　afternoons in childhood, of tender exchanges and important sales
12　　　to dig up movie money.
13
14　MAN: *(He enters preoccupied with a piece of paper and then*
15　　　*discovers the lemonade stand.)* **Hello.** *(The WOMAN, sitting*
16　　　*behind the stand, smiles.)* **Hot today, a scorcher.**
17　WOMAN: **Yes. It is.**
18　MAN: **Unseasonably hot.** *(Explaining)* **Unusual for this time of year.**
19　WOMAN: **You're right, there. It'll go, sooner or later.**
20　MAN: **Yeah. Say, would you know where Oliveras Street is?** *(Handing*
21　　　*her piece of paper)* **What, twenty one hundred block ... There's**
22　　　**a house for sale tomorrow; and I wanted to take a look at the**
23　　　**property.**
24　WOMAN: **No.**
25　MAN: **It can't be far. Just a general direction would help.**
26　WOMAN: *(Indicates vaguely.)* **Somewhere over that way. I don't**
27　　　**know. Why do you want that property; property like that?**
28　MAN: **What?**
29　WOMAN: **You wanna buy property around here?**
30　MAN: **Yes.**
31　WOMAN: **Why?**
32　MAN: **Why not? Investment. You gotta find it; it rarely finds you.**
33　WOMAN: **Bad investment around here. I wouldn't.**
34　MAN: **You wouldn't?**
35　WOMAN: **Maybe somebody's trying to take you.**

1   MAN: Maybe. I'll keep an eye out.

2   WOMAN: Who's selling? The property. Maybe I know them.

3   MAN: A bank. It's a foreclosure.

4   WOMAN: Oh.

5   MAN: Business. What makes the world go round. Selling

6   lemonade, huh?

7   WOMAN: Yes.

8   MAN: One of those things that just sells itself.

9   WOMAN: Yes, it does.

10   MAN: Boy takes me back. *(Wiping face with handkerchief)* Benny

11   LaRuso and me. Our secret was mobility. Had our stand built

12   right on top of my Red Rider wagon. We'd cover forty blocks

13   on a hot afternoon. Long time ago. Well, is it any good?

14   WOMAN: I think so.

15   MAN: It's the stuff to have when it's thirsty out, that's for sure.

16   This your regular corner?

17   WOMAN: No. I don't have a regular corner.

18   MAN: Some say you need a regular corner to build up clientele,

19   customers. Not necessary. We did just fine. It's the product

20   that counts — and somebody with a need. Gotta have that.

21   You move around, then?

22   WOMAN: Huh?

23   MAN: To different locations. You move around?

24   WOMAN: I did this today. Just today.

25   MAN: Trying to get movie money, huh?

26   WOMAN: Yeah. Movie money.

27   MAN: A little slow today.

28   WOMAN: It's been pretty busy. Slow right now. *(Looking in*

29   *pitcher)* I've only got about one glass left.

30   MAN: That's good. Very good. *(Takes out coin purse.)* Well, why

31   don't I take the last glass? Then you'll have it licked.

32   WOMAN: If you want.

33   MAN: If I want? *(Chuckles.)* It'd be kinda fun. It's been a while

34   since I had any. How much?

35   WOMAN: Seven thousand.

1   MAN: *(Fishing for change)* **Pardon?**
2   WOMAN: **Seven thousand dollars.**
3   MAN: *(Has a good laugh; WOMAN joins in.)* **No. Really ...** *(Succumbs*
4   *to laughter again.)* **That's good. In business, you get the customer**
5   **laughing, you get the business. So, what's it go for these days?**
6   WOMAN: **This goes for seven thousand.**
7   MAN: **That's ridiculous. Nobody in their right mind is going to pay**
8   **seven thousand for a glass of lemonade.**
9   WOMAN: **Maybe. It's my lemonade.**
10 MAN: *(Laughing again, although with a different quality, as he starts*
11   *to leave)* **Seven thousand ...** *(Coming back)* **Are you trying to**
12   **make a fool out of me? Seven thousand!** *(Picks up a jar of*
13   *pennies and shakes it.)* **What are these?!**
14 WOMAN: **They're pennies.**
15 MAN: **I know they're pennies! You got them selling lemonade.**
16 WOMAN: **Those were other glasses and other people. You are you,**
17   **and this is my last glass.**
18 MAN: **Ah, you admit you sold it for pennies.**
19 WOMAN: **That's all they had.**
20 MAN: **So that's it. You see me as some mark who'd pay seven**
21   **thousand dollars for a lousy glass of lemonade.**
22 WOMAN: **It's not lousy. It's exceptional lemonade. This is all**
23   **that's left. If you want it, buy it.**
24 MAN: **For seven thousand dollars. I could buy a house in this**
25   **neighborhood for that. A carload of lemons wouldn't cost that**
26   **much. What am I doing here? You're not serious; you can't be**
27   **serious ...** *(He laughs.)* **Alright, I'll give you a buck for it — for**
28   **entertainment value.** *(Hands her a dollar. She does not take it.*
29   *Instead she tears a blank sheet of paper out of an old notebook — or*
30   *perhaps some excess butcher paper off the corner of the stand —*
31   *and hands it to the man.)* **What's this?**
32 WOMAN: **An application.**
33 MAN: **What application? It's a blank piece of paper.**
34 WOMAN: **Just put all you own on the left side and all you owe on**
35   **the right. Add it up and turn it in here.**

1   MAN: You want a net worth statement?

2   WOMAN: If you don't wanna pay my price, you have ta fill it out.

3   MAN: Why?

4   WOMAN: To see if you qualify — for the lower price.

5   MAN: Which is?

6   WOMAN: Three cents.

7   MAN: I offered you a dollar.

8   WOMAN: My price isn't a dollar. It's seven thousand, unless you
9   qualify.

10   MAN: I have no intention of qualifying, and I am not paying seven
11   thousand.

12   WOMAN: Good-bye.

13   MAN: *(Starts to say something, but stops.)* **Good-bye.** *(Starts to leave.)*

14   WOMAN: Could I have my form back?

15   MAN: *(Returning)* Yes, you can have your form back! *(Shoves it at*
16   *her.)* What is so special about this lemonade?!

17   WOMAN: It's my last glass.

18   MAN: You can make more.

19   WOMAN: Not like this. There's no more like this.

20   MAN: You said that. That doesn't tell me anything. What it tastes
21   like, what it's made of, why you wanna charge me seven
22   thousand dollars for it? You want me to spend that kind of
23   money, I don't even know what it tastes like. *(WOMAN ladles*
24   *out a small amount of lemonade and hands MAN the stirring*
25   *spoon.)* What's this cost?

26   WOMAN: Nothing. *(MAN drinks the sample.)*

27   MAN: My God. That's good. That's quite good. Where'd you get
28   this stuff?

29   WOMAN: I made it myself, from scratch. I told you it was
30   exceptional.

31   MAN: Real lemons, right? Big as footballs. Benny and I got ours from
32   the corner market. Big as footballs. He was fun, but couldn't sell
33   anything to save his life. He pulled the wagon, I sold the lemonade.
34   Nice guy, kid. There's something else in this. What is it?

35   WOMAN: You wanna buy it or not?

1   MAN: Not at your price. Hey, I'm trying to be fair. I don't have to
2   be here at all.
3   WOMAN: You were lost and thirsty as I remember. It had nothing
4   to do with bein' fair.
5   MAN: Where do you get off talking to a customer that way. I'm not
6   robbing you. *(Going to his wallet, he sets ten dollars on the*
7   *counter.)* I'll give you ten dollars, that's it. *(WOMAN shakes her*
8   *head.)* You need it and you know it.
9   WOMAN: I close in a couple of minutes.
10   MAN: *I want that lemonade!*
11   WOMAN: That's my price.
12   MAN: Such principles. You can't eat principles. You can't sleep
13   under principles. You can't keep warm with principles. *(Once*
14   *again to his wallet, peels off cash and sets it on the counter.)* One
15   hundred dollars. I don't know why I'm doing it, but there it
16   is. Go ahead. When's the last time you saw a hundred dollars
17   for a glass of lemonade? When's the last time you saw a
18   hundred dollars? Go on, pick it up. *(WOMAN stares at the bills.*
19   *Slowly, a drool of spit drops from her lips onto the money.)* Why
20   you ... worthless piece of ... garbage. I tried to help you.
21   WOMAN: On your terms. At your convenience. For your
22   entertainment. You tried nothing. Nothing.
23   MAN: Seven-thousand-dollar lemonade. I'm talking to a nut. What
24   looney farm did you escape from? The world doesn't work this
25   way! *(During the following, MAN kicks at one of the corners of the*
26   *lemonade stand for emphasis and it collapses. Seeing this, he is at*
27   *first startled but then continues to lay it to ruins. During this,*
28   *WOMAN grabs the pitcher and clutches it.)* You don't set up some
29   flimsy stand and ask for the sky. Nobody owes nobody the sky.
30   And you haven't the decency to go crazy somewhere else, away
31   from those of us who are trying like hell to be reasonable! *(He*
32   *stops; the stand is in shambles.)* Didn't mean to ...
33   WOMAN: Yes, I know ...
34   MAN: Take this. For the stand. *(He goes to hand her the money. She*
35   *does not take it, so he sets it down and starts to go.)* I'm sorry.

1   *(Pause)* **You ask too much.**
2   **WOMAN: You give too little.**
3   **MAN: What was in the lemonade?**
4   **WOMAN: Tears.** *(MAN exits as he came. WOMAN then exits in*
5   *direction of Oliveras Street.)*
6   *The End*
7
8
9
10
11
12
13
14
15
16
17
18
19
20
21
22
23
24
25
26
27
28
29
30
31
32
33
34
35

Breakfast

by Norman A. Bert

Norman Bert, co-editor of this book, pastored a church in Indiana and taught school in Zambia before beginning his career as a university theatre professor. He has led college theatre programs in Pennsylvania, Montana, and Texas. He believes that theatre is more than entertainment and that good plays give their audiences new insights and change the way they live.

Breakfast was first produced by Eastern Montana College's Katoya Players in 1988 and was given a staged reading at the New Play Development Workshop of the Playwright's Program of the Association for Theatre in Higher Education at ATHE's national convention in Chicago in 1990.

Production Suggestions

The action of this play is exceedingly simple — almost minimalist: two people participate in making a decision. But the plethora of options they must deal with is bizarre. It will play most effectively if you refrain from accenting its flatness on the one hand or its absurdity on the other hand. Play it realistically, listen carefully to each other, and react sincerely, and the comedy will take care of itself.

The play has been staged effectively with two women in the roles; since the roles are not gender-specific, it would probably work just as well as a play for two men.

Address all inquiries concerning performances, readings, or reprinting of this work *or any portion thereof* to Norman A. Bert, 5704 Nashville Avenue, Lubbock, Texas 79413-4601. For details, see "Part II: Securing Rights for Your Production," pages 241 to 250.

Ken Quinley and Lisa Kudrna
in Breakfast *by Norman A. Bert.*

1	The action takes place in a coffee shop during breakfast hours.
2	*CHARACTERS:* A FEMALE CUSTOMER — she wears a skirt and
3	blouse and heels, and she carries a handbag. Not tacky; not
4	flamboyant; no statement to make with her clothing. No one
5	would give her a second look. A MALE WAITER — he wears
6	black pants, a white shirt open at the collar, and a black vest.
7	*SETTING:* A table for two. Period. No other coffee-shop set dressings.
8	If possible, the scene should be isolated without suggestion of any
9	surroundings. A vase on the table with a carnation, however,
10	would be a nice touch.
11	
12	*(A CUSTOMER enters the coffee shop. She pauses only long*
13	*enough to see the table before going to sit at it. The WAITER*
14	*approaches.)*
15	**WAITER: Good morning.**
16	**CUSTOMER: Hi.**
17	**WAITER: Would you like to see a menu?**
18	**CUSTOMER: No, that won't be necessary; I know exactly what I**
19	**want.**
20	**WAITER:** *(Taking his order pad and pencil from a hip pocket)* **Fine.**
21	**Coffee — or tea?**
22	**CUSTOMER: Coffee, please.**
23	**WAITER: Regular of decaf?**
24	**CUSTOMER: Regular.**
25	**WAITER: White or black?**
26	**CUSTOMER: White, please.**
27	**WAITER: Milk, cream, or non-dairy whitener?**
28	**CUSTOMER: Milk.**
29	**WAITER: Whole, skim, or two-per?**
30	**CUSTOMER: Two-per.**
31	**WAITER: Sugar?**
32	**CUSTOMER: Artificial sweetener, please.**
33	**WAITER: Liquid or powder?**
34	**CUSTOMER: Oh, you have liquid sweetener? Yes, liquid, please.**
35	**WAITER:** *(Writing it down)* **Fine. And now, something to eat?**

1   CUSTOMER: Yes. Cold cereal, please.

2   WAITER: *(Writing it down)* Cold cereal. What kind, ma'am?

3   CUSTOMER: Oh, it doesn't matter. Just bring anything.

4   WAITER: I'm sorry, but I can't do that. My job is to serve you;

5   your job is to make the decisions. I don't get paid enough to

6   make customers' decisions.

7   CUSTOMER: OK. No problem. What have you got?

8   WAITER: Well, we're not a supermarket. We have a limited

9   selection of the most popular brands. Just tell me what you

10   want; chances are, we got it.

11   CUSTOMER: No, no, no. *Tempt* me. Come on, give me the list.

12   WAITER: *(Sighing)* OK. We got granola and milled. Natural,

13   regular, and strictly artificial. Oat, wheat, rice, corn, barley,

14   and combinations. With fruit and without. Sugared and not

15   sugared. With saccharin and/or Nutrasweet. Kellogg's, Post,

16   Quaker, General Mills, Checker-Board-Square, Nabisco,

17   Malt-O-Meal, and generic.

18   CUSTOMER: That's a *limited* selection?

19   WAITER: This ain't New York, lady. What can I tell ya? If it's not

20   enough choices, an new shipment comes in on Tuesday.

21   CUSTOMER: Well, I can't cope with all that. Just bring me some

22   bran cereal.

23   WAITER: Bran.

24   CUSTOMER: Yeah. You have bran?

25   WAITER: Yeah, we got bran. Flakes or "all-bran" variety?

26   CUSTOMER: What?

27   WAITER: Do ya want the kinda bran that's in flakes, or do ya want

28   the kinda wormy looking stuff. Sorry. Not a nice choice of

29   words, but that's always what it looks like to me.

30   CUSTOMER: Oh, the cat-food-looking stuff.

31   WAITER: Yeah, that's it. Cat food. Gotta remember that. Sounds

32   better than "wormy looking."

33   CUSTOMER: Yes. That's fine. I'll take that kind. I mean, that's

34   the real thing, isn't it? I mean, if you're going to eat healthy,

35   you might as well go all the way, huh?

1   WAITER: Yeah, well, that's up to you. Me, I eat to live. Live and
2   enjoy. Far as I can see, if you eat what you like, you'll
3   eventually get it all, you know?
4   CUSTOMER: Maybe. I'm not so sure. Anyhow, I'll have the
5   wormy kind of bran.
6   WAITER: Good. That narrows it down. Now we got your Real
7   Bran, your Extra Bran, and your Total Bran.
8   CUSTOMER: Oh my God. What's the difference? Just bring me
9   one of them!
10   WAITER: Like I said, lady. They don't pay me to make decisions.
11   It can only get me in trouble.
12   CUSTOMER: OK. So what are they again?
13   WAITER: Real Bran, Extra Bran, and Total Bran.
14   CUSTOMER: I don't know. What's the difference?
15   WAITER: Well, for one thing, they differ in the amount of dietary
16   fiber which is the bulk stuff why people eat bran in the first
17   place.
18   CUSTOMER: Yeah?
19   WAITER: Yeah. Now your Total Bran has twelve grams of fiber
20   per serving while your Extra Bran only has ten and your Real
21   Bran's got only nine.
22   CUSTOMER: Well, that solves it then, doesn't it? I'll take the ...
23   WAITER: Hold it, hold it. Don't you want to know about the
24   sugar? I mean, if you're gonna be healthy, you ought to
25   consider the sugar, too, right?
26   CUSTOMER: Yeah, OK. So tell me about the sugar.
27   WAITER: Well, they all got it in one form or another. Extra Bran's
28   got six grams per serving; Real Bran's got five grams, and
29   Total Bran's only got two grams.
30   CUSTOMER: Well, that settles it then for sure.
31   WAITER: Maybe.
32   CUSTOMER: Maybe?
33   WAITER: Take it from me, the Total Bran needs more sugar. I
34   watch the customers, see, and most of the Total Bran eaters,
35   after one or two bites, they put on a little sugar. They're pretty

1   sneaky about it, but I don't miss much. You put a half
2   teaspoon of sugar on, and you're right up there with the Real
3   Bran and Extra.
4 CUSTOMER: Oh, wow. Well, let me see. I ...
5 WAITER: Yeah, and while you're working on that, you might also
6   consider that your Real Bran's got two hundred sixty
7   milligrams of sodium while your Extra and Total have a
8   hundred and ninety milligrams and two hundred thirty,
9   respectively. Not counting the milk, that is. 'Course I don't
10   know if you're concerned about that or not.
11 CUSTOMER: No, I'm not.
12 WAITER: Fine. They're *your* arteries. Anyhow, like I always say,
13   how can soft food make hard arteries, right?
14 CUSTOMER: So, you mean to choose my cereal, I have to strike
15   some kind of a balance between my bowels, my heart, and my
16   arteries?
17 WAITER: Yeah, that's it. Least that's one way to look at it. Or you
18   can think of it this way — choosing between going fast with a
19   coronary, being paralyzed then zapped again for good with a
20   stroke, or sort of lengthening it out with cancer, you know?
21 CUSTOMER: This is getting harder and harder. Say you know
22   what you ought to do? You ought to make up a chart with the
23   various kinds of cereal and all the variables so people could
24   see it all at a glance and make up their minds that way.
25 WAITER: Do you know how much space that would take up, lady?
26   It'd be a book. I mean we haven't even started on the various
27   vitamin contents and all. And then, if we got into the fruities
28   and sweeties and spookies and other novelty cereals, well, it
29   would just be *impossible.*
30 CUSTOMER: Maybe you could computerize it. I mean, you could
31   get *rich.* Put *all* the cereals in this program and sell it to
32   restaurants.
33 WAITER: I dunno. You know what kind of turn-over there is in the
34   cereal market? Every month there are a few new ones and a
35   couple of the old ones bite the dust.

1   CUSTOMER: So much the better. For an annual fee, you agree to
2   up-date everyone's program monthly. Just think of the
3   possibilities. You could get out of this joint and be on your
4   own.
5   WAITER: What's the matter with this joint? I sort of like it here.
6   Besides, how many restaurants got computers anyway?
7   CUSTOMER: You might be surprised. And if they haven't got
8   them now, they'll get them soon.
9   WAITER: Dunno much about computers, but I can tell you one
10   reason it wouldn't work: taste. When everything's said and
11   done, most people choose a cereal 'cause they just like it.
12   That's individual. You can't computerize taste.
13   CUSTOMER: I think you could quantify it. You just ask the
14   customer, "On a scale of one to ten, how crunchy do you like
15   your cereal, with one being over-cooked oatmeal, and ten
16   being dry granola?" And then you punch the answer in and
17   say, "OK, and on a scale of one to ten with ten being pure
18   sugar and one being like water, how sweet do you like your
19   cereal?" Then you punch *that* in and …
20   WAITER: OK, I get the point. Maybe it's possible.
21   CUSTOMER: It's just a choice. If it's a choice, you can quantify it.
22   Choices come from a balancing of variables. Computers can
23   handle variables.
24   WAITER: Dunno. I still think the *customer* should be able to
25   decide.
26   CUSTOMER: And speaking of choices, I'd design it for the IBM
27   PC.
28   WAITER: IBM PC?
29   CUSTOMER: Yeah, the computer, you know?
30   WAITER: Oh, the IBM PC's a computer.
31   CUSTOMER: Yeah. Although you might want to consider Apple.
32   There are millions of Macs out there. They're more user-
33   friendly.
34   WAITER: User-friendly. Well, that should probably go into
35   making the choice.

1   **CUSTOMER:** Oh yeah, for sure. 'Course if you want cheap,
2   there's Dell. Or Compaq. And then there's Gateway and
3   Toshiba and Cybertron and Alienware and Packard-Bell and
4   H-P and N-E-C and A-B-S and ...
5   **WAITER:** Hold it, hold it, hold it. I can't get into this! I gottanuff
6   problems. Forget the computers.
7   **CUSTOMER:** You mean you choose to ignore the whole wave of
8   the future?
9   **WAITER:** Yeah. Should I feel guilty or something?
10   **CUSTOMER:** No. That's cool. It's your choice.
11   **WAITER:** Fine. Now can we get back to your cereal?
12   **CUSTOMER:** Look I can't deal with this cereal thing. Just bring
13   me an egg and toast.
14   **WAITER:** *(Scratching off "cereal" on his order pad and writing "egg*
15   *w/T")* OK. You want that egg over, up, scrambled, poached, or
16   boiled?
17   **CUSTOMER:** Uh. Up, I think. No — over. Yes, definitely over.
18   **WAITER:** Hard or runny?
19   **CUSTOMER:** Just so the white won't and the yolk will, if you
20   know what I mean.
21   **WAITER:** No problem. White, wheat, or rye toast, bran muffin,
22   English muffin, or bagel?
23   **CUSTOMER:** Wheat toast.
24   **WAITER:** Anything else?
25   **CUSTOMER:** No, that should be just fine.
26   **WAITER:** Fine. Be back with your coffee in a minute.
27   **CUSTOMER:** Thanks. *(The WAITER exits. The CUSTOMER pulls a*
28   *newspaper out of her bag and starts to read. The lights fade out.)*
29   *The End*
30
31
32
33
34
35

Rattle/Rattle

by Wendy MacLaughlin

Wendy MacLaughlin is a program host and theatre critic for public radio and television in Kansas City. Her plays have won awards and been produced around the world.

Rattle/Rattle was a finalist for the Actors Theatre of Louisville's Heidemen Award and was first produced at New York's Nat Horn Theatre as part of the Love Creek Annual One-Act Play Festival.

Production Suggestions

The actors in *Rattle/Rattle* will be wise to do some research into the psychological backgrounds which underlie this play. What are Sally's psychological problems, what is Dr. Waverly's treatment methodology, and what is "transference?" Psychology teachers may be willing to discuss the play with you or at least point you toward helpful reading materials. Also, in order to convincingly play the characters' interaction with the mirror, you should actually rehearse with a mirror occasionally, learning to draw your face without looking at the paper.

Address all inquiries concerning performances, readings or reprinting of this work *or any portion thereof* to Wendy MacLaughlin, 1103-B West 47th St., Kansas City, MO 64112. For details, see "Part II: Securing Rights for Your Production," pages 241 to 250.

1   The action takes place in a room in a psychiatric hospital the day
2   after something happened.
3   *CHARACTERS:* DR. WAVERLY — a nice-looking man. SALLY — a
4   young girl from the farm.
5   *SETTING:* The white room is furnished with a bed, a chair, and a
6   chest. When the actors draw, they look into a two-way mirror in
7   the "fourth wall" facing the audience.
8
9   *(DR. WAVERLY enters SALLY's room. She is propped up in bed*
10   *with a drawing pad in front of her. She draws staring intently into*
11   *the mirror. He observes her for a moment.)*
12   **DOCTOR: How're we doing today?**
13   **SALLY: Don't know about you but I'm disjointed.**
14   **DOCTOR:** *(Writing)* **Disjointed?**
15   **SALLY: Like everything's turned inside out.**
16   **DOCTOR:** *(Writes.)* **Ummm. Inside out.**
17   **SALLY: Why do you repeat what I say?**
18   **DOCTOR: I'm trying to understand how you feel.**
19   **SALLY: Rattled. Rattled.** *(Angry)* **Rattled!**
20   **DOCTOR: You're in a hospital, Sally.**
21   **SALLY: Liar.**
22   **DOCTOR: I never lie, Sally. You may not like what I say but I**
23   **promise you, I don't lie. Lying is abhorrent to me.**
24   **SALLY: Who are you?**
25   **DOCTOR: I'm your doctor. Dr. Waverly.**
26   **SALLY: You a real doctor?**
27   **DOCTOR: I'm your psychiatrist.**
28   **SALLY: I'd rather have a real doctor. What's that thing hanging**
29   **round your neck?**
30   **DOCTOR: This is a stethoscope. To listen to your heart. See?**
31   *(Shows it to her.)*
32   **SALLY: Know what I see?**
33   **DOCTOR: I'd like you to tell me.**
34   **SALLY: I see a psychiatrist trying to act like a real doctor.** *(Stares*
35   *into the mirror and draws.)*

1 DOCTOR: And what do you see in that mirror, Sally?
2 SALLY: My face, stupid.
3 DOCTOR: It's a very nice face.
4 SALLY: Ugly. All of me is … ugly.
5 DOCTOR: Do you remember what happened yesterday?
6 SALLY: I wet my pants.
7 DOCTOR: No.
8 SALLY: In first grade I did. Now why'd I do that? I knew better.
9 DOCTOR: Do you remember the scissors?
10 SALLY: What was I doing with scissors?
11 DOCTOR: Chasing your father.
12 SALLY: There was this girl. Six years old. She'd hide behind the
13   crack in the door, get her mother's eye, go like this, *(Beckons*
14   *with her finger)* then peek around the corner, roll her eyes,
15   smack her lips and say … guess what?
16 DOCTOR: What?
17 SALLY: You know.
18 DOCTOR: No I don't.
19 SALLY: *(Sing song)* Time to eat.
20 DOCTOR: *(Probing)* She was six years old?
21 SALLY: Long as you nursed you weren't supposed to get PG.
22 DOCTOR: PG?
23 SALLY: *(Loud) Pregnant!* Mother didn't want to get pregnant
24   again now did she? You're about the dumbest doctor I ever
25   met. How many children do you have?
26 DOCTOR: One. A boy. A very good boy. Makes straight A's. Going
27   to be a lawyer.
28 SALLY: Do you love him?
29 DOCTOR: More than anything in the world.
30 SALLY: Does he love you?
31 DOCTOR: He lives with his mother. Yes, I think he does love me.
32   However, I'm aware that his mother would tell you a different
33   story.
34 SALLY: My mother was in labor twenty-nine hours and she was
35   sick from the first month I was in her tummy. He told me

1   often enough.

2   DOCTOR: How'd that make you feel?

3   SALLY: He didn't say she didn't love me. He just said she didn't

4   want me. You can only do so much what with the farm, five

5   children and one on the way. But she was glad to have me after

6   I got here, I'm sure of that.

7   DOCTOR: You were sure she was glad.

8   SALLY: *(Strong)* Very sure. I got sick a lot. Asthma, scarlet fever.

9   Mommie let me stay with her on the sleeping porch. Daddy

10   slept ... somewhere else. All I could eat was chicken soup.

11   Mother made so much chicken soup it came out her ears. I

12   don't like chicken soup much. Do you? They probably wanted

13   to throw me out with the whole batch. What'd they want with

14   another baby anyway? Especially a *(Exaggerates)* girl. They

15   feed girls to alligators in China.

16   DOCTOR: That's hard for a girl to understand, isn't it? I'm sorry.

17   SALLY: If it makes you feel bad I won't tell you any more.

18   DOCTOR: I guess I'm just a little surprised you aren't sad about

19   what you're saying.

20   SALLY: Why should I be sad? It's already happened.

21   DOCTOR: Does anything make you sad?

22   SALLY: There was this retarded boy in school. He never smiled.

23   The boys were supposed to wear red beanies, the girls green

24   beanies. One day he came to school wearing a green beanie.

25   Everyone laughed. He was so happy. That's about the saddest

26   thing I can think of.

27   DOCTOR: Does it make you want to cry?

28   SALLY: I never cry. Even when someone dies. What's there to cry

29   about? They're going home. Every day you pick up the paper

30   and read something about mothers abandoning their babies.

31   Now that's something to cry about. Well, I wasn't abandoned,

32   now was I?

33   DOCTOR: No, Sally, you weren't abandoned.

34   SALLY: Mother nursed me so you know she wanted me. I know

35   she wanted the best for me and she knew the best for me was

1   not to be born right then. If I hadn't been born right then, I'd
2   have had a chance to go to someone who really wanted me.
3   See, I'm sure she knew I'd understand. Why would I be
4   nursing my doll if I didn't understand.
5 DOCTOR: Do you still nurse your doll?
6 SALLY: Do you still play doctor?
7 DOCTOR: Tell me about your doll.
8 SALLY: Wendy had long curls and sky blue eyes. We did all my
9   chores together. We loved to gather eggs, reach under their
10   soft white breasts, feel the warm, smooth, oval shells. I took
11   her everywhere, even to the rabbit hutch that time I tried to
12   kill myself.
13 DOCTOR: Do you want to talk about that?
14 SALLY: *(Holds out wrists.)* See this? I cut myself with a razor. Not
15   very deep. Then I rubbed rabbit dung into the cut places.
16   Thought I'd get lockjaw and die.
17 DOCTOR: I'm glad you didn't.
18 SALLY: Then another time we went out in the snow, took off our
19   clothes, lay down and made snow angels. We were supposed to
20   get pneumonia and die but the only one to die was Wendy. Her
21   funeral was so beautiful. I put daisies over her eyes, a
22   butterfly landed on her nose and all the birds sang ... Wendy.
23   She got her name from Peter Pan. She was Peter Pan's
24   mother. *(Draws.)*
25 DOCTOR: What're you drawing?
26 SALLY: My face. I look in the mirror real hard, try to see what I'm
27   thinking. I draw every freckle, every eyelash ... *(Shows him
28   the drawing.)* Does it look like me?
29 DOCTOR: Yes it does. You're quite an artist. Looks like you're
30   flying.
31 SALLY: Flying in space. Like Peter Pan. Flying free forever ...
32   forever ... and forever. Sometimes I draw when I get mad.
33   Scared.
34 DOCTOR: What kind of things make you mad? Scared?
35 SALLY: Oh you know ... dark nights, shadows on the wall,

1   doorknobs rattling … men playing cards, beer stink, Mommie
2   crying … he shouting, "Why'd that kid have to come into our
3   life." I put the pillow over my head. After it got quiet I sneaked
4   downstairs, got my crayons and drew till the sun came in
5   through the window.
6 DOCTOR: Would you show me those pictures?
7 SALLY: Too ugly. Burned 'em. *(Challenging)* You wanna draw?
8 DOCTOR: I can't draw a straight line.
9 SALLY: Better if you don't. All you do is look in that mirror there.
10   The mirror where you and the others watch me.
11 DOCTOR: You're a very smart girl, Sally.
12 SALLY: Girls have to be twice as smart as boys.
13 DOCTOR: That doesn't seem fair, does it?
14 SALLY: Lucky it isn't hard. *(Pats chair.)* Sit down. Right here.
15   *(Hands him paper and pencil.)* First thing you gotta do is look
16   in the mirror and get a feeling.
17 DOCTOR: *(Looks into mirror.)* Don't spend a lot of time looking at
18   myself in the mirror.
19 SALLY: This isn't about looks. About feelings. Think about
20   something that makes you sad. That isn't much of a feeling.
21   Try getting mad. Come on, Doctor, let your blood boil. Come
22   on, you can do better than that. Yell. Scream. I hate you. I hate
23   you. *(Screams.)* I hate you. *(Works herself into a frenzy and starts
24   hitting him.)* I hate you … I hate you … I *hate you!*
25 DOCTOR: *(Protects himself with a pillow.)* Go on. Go on.
26 SALLY: *(Pounding pillow)* Disgusting … stinking … drunken …
27   pig. Stay away … get out … gooooooooo …
28 DOCTOR: Good girl. Hit me harder.
29 SALLY: *(Piercing scream)* Baaaaaastaaaard! *(Slumps down exhausted.)*
30 DOCTOR: *(After a pause, a gentle touch)* Sally.
31 SALLY: *(Jumps like a rabbit.)* Don't you touch me.
32 DOCTOR: *(Calming)* OK, Sally. It's OK.
33 SALLY: Stupid. You're a stupid doctor. You haven't drawn one
34   line. Sit there. Take your pencil, put it down on the paper. Now
35   look at yourself and get mad. *Draw!*

1   DOCTOR: *(Looks into mirror, draws and carefully explains.)* **In the**
2   **art of psychiatry we speak of transference ...**
3   SALLY: **Grit your teeth, wrinkle your forehead. Good.**
4   DOCTOR: **People take their feelings ...**
5   SALLY: **Stare.**
6   DOCTOR: **... emotional reactions and patterns ...**
7   SALLY: **Don't look at the paper.**
8   DOCTOR: **... they live out with their mother, father ...**
9   SALLY: **You're thinking too much.**
10 DOCTOR: **... and project them onto the doctor.**
11 SALLY: **Don't blink your eyes.**
12 DOCTOR: **Sometimes even the doctor begins to feel ...**
13 SALLY: **What you see is going down your arm ...**
14 DOCTOR: **... respond like the very people the patient has created.**
15 SALLY: **... right onto the paper.**
16 DOCTOR: **We begin to become ...**
17 SALLY: **Your feeling will start to come out ...**
18 DOCTOR: **... what the patient thinks ...**
19 SALLY: **... all over the paper.**
20 DOCTOR: **... rather than what we really are.**
21 SALLY: **Let it flow.**
22 DOCTOR: **So ...**
23 SALLY: **Slow and easy.**
24 DOCTOR: **Perhaps ...**
25 SALLY: *(Low)* **Good.**
26 DOCTOR: **I've ah ...**
27 SALLY: *(Whispers.)* **Magic.**
28 DOCTOR: **I ... can't believe it.**
29 SALLY: **What?**
30 DOCTOR: **I ... look like my father.**
31 SALLY: **He looks sad.**
32 DOCTOR: **He was sad.**
33 SALLY: **Why?**
34 DOCTOR: **He wanted me to be perfect.**
35 SALLY: **That can do it.**

1   DOCTOR: When I wasn't he made up stories to make everyone
2   think he was.
3   SALLY: Did he love you?
4   DOCTOR: He wanted me to be a surgeon. He thought all
5   psychiatrists were crazy. "No one has the ability to look into
6   another mind. Nor the right."
7   SALLY: Do you love him?
8   DOCTOR: One day after I got a C in science he sat me down and
9   whispered very precisely, "I don't know how to tell you this
10   and your mother will deny it but I am not your real father."
11   SALLY: *(Fascinated)* Was it true?
12   DOCTOR: Another story but I swore to kill myself before I'd end
13   up like him.
14   SALLY: You ever try?
15   DOCTOR: Almost everyone has thought of trying.
16   SALLY: But did you do it?
17   DOCTOR: Well ... I ... ah ...
18   SALLY: Did you? Did you? *(Pause)* You gonna tell stories like your
19   father?
20   DOCTOR: Once. Once I tried to kill myself.
21   SALLY: Do you want to talk about that?
22   DOCTOR: One rainy night I drove my car into a wall. Expected
23   the engine to come back and smash my chest. It didn't.
24   SALLY: Isn't that always the way. *(Resumes drawing.)* Funny.
25   DOCTOR: What's funny is how often we become what we hate.
26   SALLY: *(Long pause)* I didn't kill him did I?
27   DOCTOR: No.
28   SALLY: I misremember some.
29   DOCTOR: Do you remember what happened yesterday?
30   SALLY: They were laughing.
31   DOCTOR: Who was laughing?
32   SALLY: He and those men.
33   DOCTOR: What were they laughing at?
34   SALLY: He was showing them my pictures. Then he called me
35   Mommie's name. Told them I was his new wife. It made me

1   sick. I was so mad I ran to my room, got my scissors, crawled
2   under the bed and held my breath. Then later the door knob
3   rattled. Rattled. Then he ... he ... I forget.
4   DOCTOR: Do you hate your father, Sally?
5   SALLY: Hate is strong.
6   DOCTOR: Yes.
7   SALLY: Mommie says ... he's lonely.
8   DOCTOR: Are you lonely?
9   SALLY: Not when I draw. When I draw I go inside to a secret
10   place. A place connected to pretty things.
11   DOCTOR: What pretty things?
12   SALLY: Oh you know ... birds ... flowers ... Wendy and the
13   farthest star.
14   DOCTOR: Is that a good place to be?
15   SALLY: I'm happy there.
16   DOCTOR: I'm glad, Sally. Very glad. *(Checks watch.)* Well, I have
17   to go. I'll see you tomorrow.
18   SALLY: Why?
19   DOCTOR: Well ... because ... because I'd like another drawing
20   lesson.
21   SALLY: OK.
22   DOCTOR: *(Starts to leave.)* Good-bye, Sally.
23   SALLY: Doctor Waverly?
24   DOCTOR: Yes.
25   SALLY: Your son look like you?
26   DOCTOR: People say.
27   SALLY: Next time you draw in the mirror, think about him. Forget
28   all that stuff about your father.
29   DOCTOR: In psychiatry we try to remember.
30   SALLY: Better to forget. *(He looks at his drawing, then draws a cross*
31   *over the face. They smile at each other. The lights get bright, then*
32   *fade to black.)*
33   *The End*
34
35

Mother for Hire
by Linda Lee Bower

Linda Lee Bower is an actress, singer, and writer living in the Washington, D.C. area.

Mother for Hire received a staged reading at the First Stage's Playwright's Express in Los Angeles in 1991.

Production Suggestions

Both of these characters have their endearing qualities, and both of them have their hang-ups and shortcomings. To play them well, make the play work, and realize its full comic potential, be sure to discover both their strong points and their less admirable characteristics.

1   The action takes place in the living room of the apartment of
2   SALLY and ANDY — early evening, any day now.
3   *CHARACTERS:* ANDY BROOKS — a graduate student in his late
4   20s working on a Ph.D. in English. He is of medium height or
5   shorter, and from years of hunching over a desk studying, his
6   posture is somewhat slouched. He wears ragged blue jeans, and
7   his hair is shaggy. SALLY PETERSON — a secretary at a
8   brokerage firm in her mid-20s. Tall and well stacked, she wears a
9   smart business suit.
10 *SETTING:* The room is furnished with a sofa, dinette table and chairs,
11   bookshelves with lots of books, a desk, a typewriter on a stand,
12   etc. It has an entry door and a doorway to the bedroom.
13
14   *(ANDY is sitting at the desk, writing, munching potato chips and*
15   *drinking cheap wine. SALLY breezes in, carrying a large pizza box.)*
16 **ANDY:** *(Without looking up)* **Well, it's about time. I had about given**
17   **you up for lost.**
18 **SALLY:** **I had to work late, and then —**
19 **ANDY:** **I hope Pratt and Wiggins didn't work your poor fingers to**
20   **the bone. This paper is due tomorrow, so I'll need you to type**
21   **it for me tonight.**
22 **SALLY:** **What's this one on? The hidden symbolism of the witches**
23   **in the ninety-ninth verse of the Canterbury Tales?**
24 **ANDY:** **Do I detect a touch of scorn for my scholarly pursuits?** *(He*
25   *now catches the smell of the pizza and looks up.)* **At least you**
26   **brought something to eat. I'm starving.** *(He gets up, grabs the*
27   *box, takes it to the table, and opens it.)* **Wow! That is some pizza.**
28 **SALLY:** **All twelve toppings — double.**
29 **ANDY:** **You must have robbed a bank on the way home.**
30 **SALLY:** **It's a celebration!**
31 **ANDY:** **Did you get a raise?**
32 **SALLY:** **Better than that.**
33 **ANDY:** **What could be better than a raise? I have to buy lots of**
34   **books this semester.**
35 **SALLY:** **I'm going to be a mother.**

1   ANDY: What?
2   SALLY: I'm going to have a baby.
3   ANDY: Sally, that is not cause for celebration.
4   SALLY: It is for me.
5   ANDY: Honey, we have been over that before. It's just not the right
6   time.
7   SALLY: Will it ever be the right time for you? First you wanted to
8   finish your B.A. degree. Then your M.A. degree. and now you
9   are on your Ph.D. degree. What will come next? The Zh.D.
10   degree in Esoteric and Unintelligible Poetry? Are you ever
11   going to actually enter the working world? You are prepared
12   for nothing except life in medieval England.
13   ANDY: Aw, come on. I do work.
14   SALLY: When?
15   ANDY: I teach two classes.
16   SALLY: In what?
17   ANDY: Medieval English Literature.
18   SALLY: Exactly.
19   ANDY: I suppose you want me to be a Wall Street tycoon.
20   SALLY: Not necessarily.
21   ANDY: Listen, you have gotten to be pretty uppity since you went
22   to work for that brokerage firm.
23   SALLY: What's wrong with being successful?
24   ANDY: I'm not going to sell my soul for money. I suppose you want
25   me to wear a three-piece suit, too.
26   SALLY: You don't even want to get married.
27   ANDY: We just can't afford to have a baby now.
28   SALLY: You don't have to worry about a thing. You won't have to
29   pay for it, because it isn't your baby.
30   ANDY: You're going to have a baby and it isn't mine?
31   SALLY: Yes and no.
32   ANDY: Which is it?
33   SALLY: Yes I'm going to have a baby, and no, it isn't yours.
34   ANDY: Whose is it?
35   SALLY: Mr. Wiggins.

1 ANDY: Mr. Wiggins? Your boss?

2 SALLY Yes.

3 ANDY: I'll kill you.

4 SALLY: Don't be silly. I'm not even pregnant yet.

5 ANDY: I must be missing something. I thought I understood
6   English pretty well.

7 SALLY: All you have is book learning. You don't have any
8   common sense.

9 ANDY: Well, will you kindly elucidate.

10 SALLY: I'm going to be a surrogate mother.

11 ANDY: A surrogate mother?

12 SALLY: Yes. Mr. and Mrs. Wiggins have decided to have a baby.
13   But Mrs. Wiggins isn't tall enough.

14 ANDY: Tall enough for what?

15 SALLY: Don't be vulgar.

16 ANDY: Well, do they do it standing up?

17 SALLY: They want a tall baby.

18 ANDY: So he'll have to duck his head when he enters the world?

19 SALLY: I mean, they want him to grow up to be tall. Psychologists
20   say that tall men get more respect in the business world than
21   short men.

22 ANDY: *(Looking down at himself and surveying his unimpressive*
23   *stature)* Oh?

24 SALLY: And besides, Mrs. Wiggins doesn't have time.

25 ANDY: Time for what?

26 SALLY: Don't be vulgar.

27 ANDY: I'm not being vulgar. I'm all agog to learn the new
28   technology.

29 SALLY: Well, if you'll just let me tell you how it happened.

30 ANDY: I'm all ears.

31 SALLY: Mrs. Wiggins had an appointment to come to the office
32   this afternoon.

33 ANDY: They do it by appointment?

34 SALLY: Andy!

35 ANDY: It looks like Mr. Wiggins is the one who doesn't have time,

81

1   if his wife had to make an appointment to see him.

2   SALLY: She has a high-powered career herself, and they have to

3   coordinate their schedules. Anyway, she came to the office this

4   afternoon, and that's why I'm a little late.

5   ANDY: Why? Did you have to power up the Xerox machine?

6   SALLY and ANDY: Don't be vulgar.

7   SALLY: She wanted to interview me. She likes me, and I fit the

8   characteristics they want.

9   ANDY: Your typing speed?

10   SALLY: My height. And also my athletic abilities, particularly my

11   great tennis game.

12   ANDY: They want a tall baby who plays tennis.

13   SALLY: Mr. Wiggins says that a good tennis game is a big

14   advantage for a stockbroker. You know, to play with clients,

15   and get to meet people — potential clients — at the tennis

16   club.

17   ANDY: And how much more income per year does the tall baby get

18   for his tennis game?

19   SALLY: More than your entire annual salary, I'm sure.

20   ANDY: And I suppose this tall baby has already been registered at

21   the Harvard Business School.

22   SALLY: Mr. Wiggins is an alumnus.

23   ANDY: And what if this tall baby doesn't want to go to Harvard,

24   or be a stockbroker, or play tennis either?

25   SALLY: Well, he will have all the advantages, and Mr.Wiggins will

26   groom him, so why wouldn't he?

27   ANDY: What if he wants to be — heaven forbid — an impractical

28   English Ph.D. candidate?

29   SALLY: Horrors.

30   ANDY: I'll kill you.

31   SALLY: Don't be silly. Anyway, that is too far away for me to deal

32   with. I'm excited about today. I'm going to have a baby!

33   ANDY: All this came about today?

34   SALLY: Oh, no. Mr Wiggins asked me about it a month ago.

35   ANDY: I always knew Wiggins was a pervert.

1 SALLY: And if everything works out OK — and there is no reason
2   why it wouldn't — I can do it again.
3 ANDY: I don't even want you to do it once.
4 SALLY: Well, that's just too bad. You think your Ph.D. is so all-
5   important that you can't get married and have a baby. I'm
6   going to have one anyway, so there.
7 ANDY: Why didn't you tell me you wanted a baby so much? And
8   that you wanted to get married?
9 SALLY: I have told you many times.
10 ANDY: When?
11 SALLY: All I ever got was "We can't afford it," or "It just isn't the
12   right time."
13 ANDY: But —
14 SALLY: If I put it in the language of Chaucer would you
15   understand? "Whan that Aprill with hise shoutes soote/ The
16   droghte of March hath perced to the roote."
17 ANDY: But what good will it do you to be a surrogate mother? As
18   soon as you have the baby, you will give it to somebody else.
19 SALLY: I'm doing it for the money.
20 ANDY: How much are they paying you?
21 SALLY: They will pay all my medical expenses, plus twenty
22   thousand dollars.
23 ANDY: Twenty thousand dollars?
24 SALLY: All I need to do is have several babies for other women,
25   and then I will have lots of money and I can afford to have my
26   own baby.
27 ANDY: Several?
28 SALLY: Sure.
29 ANDY: Like how many?
30 SALLY: I'm young. I can have babies for ten years, at least. At the
31   rate you're going it will be ten years before you are ready to
32   get married and have a baby. I can get in plenty of practice.
33 ANDY: Listen, Sally, can't we think about this a little?
34 SALLY: I have already thought about it.
35 ANDY: Just like that?

1 SALLY: Yes.

2 ANDY: How can you just do it with a strange man?

3 SALLY: Mr. Wiggins isn't a stranger.

4 ANDY: You've done it with him before? I'll kill you.

5 SALLY: For heaven's sake, Andy. We don't actually do it.

6 ANDY: Oh. How does it work, then?

7 SALLY: It's done with artificial insemination.

8 ANDY: I don't care. It's —

9 SALLY: They want to start it as soon as possible. So I have to keep

10   a temperature chart to determine when I ovulate so I can go

11   to the fertility clinic on the right day. And, I'm sorry to tell

12   you, we can't have relations for a while, so there won't be any,

13   um, interference.

14 ANDY: For ten years? How can you do this to me?

15 SALLY: What do you care? You're always worried — "Did you

16   put it in?" So afraid I might get pregnant. Well, I am going to

17   get pregnant, but you don't have to worry about it.

18 ANDY: Are you really going to get twenty thousand dollars?

19 SALLY: Yes, isn't it wonderful!

20 ANDY: Ah … well, then, in that case, perhaps —

21 SALLY: But you aren't going to get any of it. I'm going to save it

22   for my future baby.

23 ANDY: And whose baby will that be?

24 SALLY: Well, it depends If it still "isn't the right time" for you,

25   then maybe I will go to a sperm bank.

26 ANDY: And where does that leave me?

27 SALLY: Where you have always been. Up in your ivory tower.

28 ANDY: Does this mean you won't type my papers anymore?

29 SALLY: I'm so excited. Mmmm. Let's eat the pizza before it gets

30   cold. *(She separates a wedge and begins to eat.)*

31 ANDY: I'm not hungry anymore. *(Blackout)*

                              The End

32

33

34

35

First Day of Winter
by Sam Smiley

Sam Smiley, a freelance writer, led the Dramatic Writing program at the University of Arizona–Tucson. His book, *Playwriting: The Structure of Action* is the standard work in its field. He has written two other theatre books, numerous plays, and a TV series. He recently finished a screenplay about Spain, *Commando Barcelona*.

First Day of Winter received its first production from the Playwright's Project at the University of Arizona, and Actors Theatre of Louisville selected the piece as a finalist in its national play competition. Producer-director Michael Kane also filmed the play as a festival project in cooperation with California State University–Fullerton.

Production Suggestions

The playwright has laced this play with a plethora of details about these two characters and their relationship; don't overlook a single background item while creating your characters. Avoid dragging the tempo; keep the cues tight and focus throughout on the characters' concentrated reaction to each other.

Address all inquiries concerning performances, readings, or reprinting of this work *or any portion thereof* to Sam Smiley, 5799 Via Amable, Tucson, AZ 85715. for details, see "Part II: Securing Rights for Your Production," pages 241 to 250.

1   The action takes place at dawn in an open field.

2   **CHARACTERS:** LEAH — she is dressed against the cold in jeans, a

3   navy pea coat, wool mittens, and a long maroon scarf. ANDREW —

4   dressed for fashion, not warmth, he wears a suit and tie, dress shoes,

5   and a Burberry trench coat. He has no hat or gloves, and his coat

6   flops open.

7   **SETTING:** A cold wind blows over the dead weeds of the open field

8   toward a distant line of trees silhouetted against the silver sky.

9

10   *(LEAH walks into the field carrying a spade and an antique*

11   *wooden box. She gently sets the wooden box on the earth, shoves*

12   *the spade into the ground, and lifts out dirt. Then with head bowed*

13   *she kneels, picks up the box, and presses it against her chest.*

14   *ANDREW hurries into view and stops momentarily at the edge of*

15   *the field.)*

16   ANDREW: Leah. *(No reply)* Leah, what are you doing out here?

17   *(She shakes her head.)* What? I can't hear you in the wind.

18   LEAH: I didn't say anything.

19   ANDREW: It's winter. *(Looks around.)* You'll freeze to death out

20   here in the open.

21   LEAH: No, I won't.

22   ANDREW: It's five o'clock in the morning! What's going on? I

23   mean, what are you doing out here with a shovel?

24   LEAH: It's a spade.

25   ANDREW: All right, a spade. And what're you holding?

26   LEAH: A box.

27   ANDREW: I can see that. What's inside?

28   LEAH: Andy, you know how I hate questions. That's all I get these

29   days, questions … from everyone — parents, friends, teachers,

30   and especially from —

31   ANDREW: Especially from me. Right? *(Sarcastic)* Well, I'm sorry.

32   LEAH: It would help a lot if you would just please go away. *(Puts*

33   *her forehead against the box.)*

34   ANDREW: C'mon, Leah. Don't do that. Don't cry. Darlin', get up

35   off that cold ground and talk to me. *(She collects herself.)*

86

1   LEAH: I have nothing more to say.

2   ANDREW: We should get out of this wind. I'm freezing.

3   LEAH: Button your coat.

4   ANDREW: Yeah. See? Without you, I'm practically helpless. *(He*

5   *buttons his coat.)*

6   LEAH: Helpless as a shark.

7   ANDREW: That's not very nice.

8   LEAH: I'm tired of being nice. Tired of school, tired of this town,

9   and I am deathly tired of —

10   ANDREW: Me?

11   LEAH: No, of hiding. I want to get on with my life.

12   ANDREW: Then let's go somewhere warm and talk it out.

13   LEAH: I said everything last night.

14   ANDREW: And you think I believed any of it?

15   LEAH: Andrew, don't make it so difficult, for both of us.

16   ANDREW: I won't … if you explain where you've been all night.

17   *(She bows over the wooden box.)* You know, I've always thought

18   that maroon scarf looks like blood running down your neck.

19   Where were you?

20   LEAH: I spent the night helping a friend.

21   ANDREW: Leah, I checked with all your friends — Bonnie, Gina,

22   Max, Darlene — everyone. I went to all your favorite places. I

23   even called Jonathan.

24   LEAH: You didn't! *(She rises.)* You called Jonathan? I haven't

25   spoken to him for a year and a half.

26   ANDREW: He told me that. And I also talked to Professor Carlson.

27   LEAH: Andy!

28   ANDREW: I thought you might have some kind of rehearsal.

29   LEAH: You know perfectly well my final performance was last

30   weekend. I'm done. No more rehearsals or performances.

31   None! I told you that. My degree is finished.

32   ANDREW: Yeah, Carlson reminded me. Said he hadn't seen you

33   since last Saturday night.

34   LEAH: Sometimes I could kill you.

35   ANDREW: Thanks. You know, I don't think Carlson likes me.

1   Every time I'm around him, he watches you like a vulture. I
2   think he's jealous. Has he ever come on to you?
3 LEAH: *(Indignant)* Professor Carlson?
4 ANDREW: OK, look, I'm just tired and upset ... and I'm freezing
5   my tail off. Let's get out of this wind.
6 LEAH: Go away, Andy. I have something important to do.
7 ANDREW: Leah, I have been searching for you all night, the whole
8   lousy night! I didn't even go home. See, I'm still wearing the
9   same clothes. *(LEAH picks up the spade.)* What are you doing?
10   Listen to me a minute, OK? Listen! *(She faces him again.)* Ever
11   since you walked out of that restaurant ... I mean I sat there
12   for all of a minute, finished my Coke, and went after you. But
13   by the time I got outside, you were gone. Poof! Into the night.
14   I looked everywhere — nothing! I called your place about fifty
15   times, checked with your friends, and ... darlin', you better
16   get off that ground before you catch your death.
17 LEAH: Don't worry about me.
18 ANDREW: I am worried out of my mind about you. Leah, I
19   cannot — I know it sounds melodramatic — I cannot live
20   without you. When we're apart, I get this weird sensation.
21   *(Touches his chest.)* Like there's a steel band clamped around
22   my chest, squeezing the breath out of me. I can't let you go.
23   Now, tell me where you were!
24 LEAH: Andrew, I spent last night with my cat Samantha.
25 ANDREW: Oh, yeah sure! Man, my hands are cold.
26 LEAH: Here, take my mittens. *(She starts to remove them, but he*
27   *prevents her by grabbing her hands.)*
28 ANDREW: No, Leah! I want you to have the mittens, all the clothes
29   you want, career, house, money, fame, fortune, travel ...
30   everything your heart desires, because, Leah, I love you. *(He*
31   *draws her close.)*
32 LEAH: You've never said that before, Andy.
33 ANDREW: Haven't I?
34 LEAH: In all the time we've spent together, not once.
35 ANDREW: Well, I do. Very much. *(Kisses her.)* And you love me,

1   too, don't you? *(He lifts her off the ground.)*

2   LEAH: I haven't been able to help myself.

3   ANDREW: That's my girl. *(Sets her down.)*

4   LEAH: I'm touched that you spent the night looking for me.

5   ANDREW: Yeah, well I did.

6   LEAH: It shows you honestly care.

7   ANDREW: I was out of my mind. For all I knew, some skinheads

8   grabbed you in the parking lot and shoved you in a van or

9   something.

10   LEAH: Not knowing is always worse than reality. *(He takes her face*

11   *in his hands.)*

12   ANDREW: Leah, you are so beautiful. *(Lightly kisses her.)* But your

13   lips are ice. Let's get out of this wind.

14   LEAH: No, I have to finish. *(She gestures at the hole.)*

15   ANDREW: What are you doing?

16   LEAH: Digging.

17   ANDREW: Oh, yeah — for gold? *(Laughs a little.)*

18   LEAH: No.

19   ANDREW: Well, it's the wrong time of year for a garden.

20   LEAH: It's a grave. *(That stops him.)*

21   ANDREW: You got to be kidding. *(Again LEAH kneels beside the*

22   *box.)* Leah, what the hell have you got in there? *(She shakes her*

23   *head.)* I don't believe it! You've got to be kidding. Don't tell me

24   you ... *(He gets down on one knee and puts an arm around her*

25   *shoulders.)* Look at me, Leah. Darlin', look at me! *(He turns her*

26   *face toward him.)* You never said anything. You never told me.

27   LEAH: I know. *(She pulls away.)*

28   ANDREW: You should have.

29   LEAH: It doesn't matter now.

30   ANDREW: Of course it matters! *(Loud)* It matters!

31   LEAH: Don't yell at me, Andy.

32   ANDREW: I'm not. I am simply saying you should have told me.

33   *(Beat)* So anyway it's all over now, right?

34   LEAH: Yes, it is past.

35   ANDREW: *(Sudden thought)* Leah, you didn't do it yourself! You

1   should've gone to a hospital, right?
2   LEAH: I did.
3   ANDREW: Oh. In a hospital — and you're all right?
4   LEAH: I'm fine.
5   ANDREW: Now, wait a minute. When did all this happen? Not last
6   night! Is that where you were, in a hospital?
7   LEAH: No. It happened long before last night. Three weeks ago to
8   be exact. Remember when I told you I had a stomach virus?
9   ANDREW: *(Nods.)* But I still don't understand. *(Softly)* What've
10   you got in the box?
11   LEAH: Please, Andrew.
12   ANDREW: Now wait, I want to know. What's in the box?
13   LEAH: I'll tell you. But first, you explain how you found me.
14   ANDREW: What do you mean?
15   LEAH: How did you know to come out here?
16   ANDREW: Simple. I went up the steps over there in back of the
17   house. *(Points.)* I knocked on your apartment door, and no one
18   answered. So I turned on the landing and looked around.
19   From that angle up there I could see a dark figure walking
20   into this field. I mean, you're a dancer, and I'd know you
21   anywhere just from the way you move.
22   LEAH: What phone did you use last night to call my friends?
23   ANDREW: The one in my office.
24   LEAH: You drove clear down to your office?
25   ANDREW: Sure. Better than spending a fortune in quarters.
26   LEAH: Why didn't you bother to drive out here last night?
27   ANDREW: I called your apartment, and no one answered.
28   LEAH: Have you ever been at home but avoided the phone?
29   ANDREW: You were there?
30   LEAH: Andy, it is very odd that you searched for me eight and a
31   half hours without ever coming by to look in my apartment. I
32   think you're lying ... again.
33   ANDREW: Darlin', I swear —
34   LEAH: You're awfully good at it. You didn't search for me all
35   night, did you? You went home to her. Just like always.

1   *(ANDREW presses his lips together and gazes into the distance.*
2   *Pause)* **It's over, Andy. Today's the first day of winter. It's a**
3   **natural time to let it die.** *(LEAH picks up the spade and digs out*
4   *more dirt.)*
5   **ANDREW: Let it die? No, Leah, you want to kill it and bury it.**
6   **Right?** *(She continues digging.)* **I want to know what's in the**
7   **box.** *(She goes on.)* **Come on! Show me!** *(He grabs the spade*
8   *away from her. LEAH picks up the wooden box, sets it on the pile*
9   *of dirt from the grave, and kneels beside it.)*
10   **LEAH: I tacked down the lid. Do you have a pocket knife?**
11   **ANDREW: Me? No.**
12   **LEAH: I can't get it off.**
13   **ANDREW: Here, try one of my keys. My fingers are frozen stiff.**
14   *(He pulls a ring of keys from his pocket and hands them to her.)*
15   **LEAH: Andrew, I don't want to show you this.**
16   **ANDREW: Show me, Leah! You better show me, or ...**
17   *(Momentarily, his frustrations come to focus, and he lifts the*
18   *spade as though he might hit her in back of the head. But of*
19   *course he cannot. He lowers the spade and lets it slide out of his*
20   *hands.)* **Never mind. I don't want to see anything.**
21   **LEAH: No, I want you to.** *(She pries off the lid, lifts the box toward*
22   *him with both hands like an offering. He looks inside.)*
23   **ANDREW: I don't believe it.** *(Tries to laugh.)* **It's a kitten.**
24   **LEAH: What did you expect? Look again.**
25   **ANDREW: One little black ... no, two black kittens.**
26   **LEAH: Look closer.**
27   **ANDREW: One black kitten ... with two heads.** *(Repulsed, he looks*
28   *away.)* **Oh, man, I am freezing to death.**
29   **LEAH: Andrew, last night I helped my cat Samantha give birth to**
30   **a litter. This little one amazed us both. A totally black,**
31   **stillborn kitten with two perfect heads.**
32   **ANDREW: It's just a freak. Call a newspaper or the museum.**
33   *(LEAH replaces the lid on the box.)*
34   **LEAH: I thought of that, but I decided it was better to bring it out**
35   **here, into the open, and return it to the earth ... maybe with a**

1   prayer.

2   ANDREW: Then hurry up and do it so we can go to your

3   apartment and wrap ourselves around each other and get

4   warm.

5   LEAH: Can't you understand? Whatever joy we shared, it's ...

6   ANDREW: ... only temporary, right? Leah, think of all the great

7   times we've had — the hiking, the skiing, the cabin in the

8   woods. You want to end it? I have promised and promised you

9   that one of these days we'll go away together!

10   LEAH: You don't believe that and neither do I and anyway it's too

11   late. It was too late when I went to the hospital.

12   ANDREW: Well, I'll tell you one thing — I can't stay out here

13   another minute. I am freezing to death. *(Beat)* Maybe you're

14   right. Maybe it's time for me to just walk away.

15   LEAH: Good-bye, Andrew.

16   ANDREW: Why in the name of ... why bury a freak kitten?

17   LEAH: Because it was real, because life is so inventive, because I

18   wonder what other strange seeds lie hidden in some secret

19   womb. I only want to cover it peacefully with dark soil ... and

20   a blanket of dried weeds. *(ANDREW nods and walks away.*

21   *LEAH sets the little box into its grave.)*

22   *The End*

23

24

25

26

27

28

29

30

31

32

33

34

35

Hangman

by William Borden

William Borden's plays have won twenty-one national playwriting competitions and have had over over two hundred productions. The film version of his play, *The Last Prostitute*, was shown on Lifetime Television and is on video. His novel, *Superstoe*, was republished by Orloff Press. A Core Alumnus playwright at The Playwright's Center in Minneapolis, he is a playwright with Listening Winds.

Hangman received a staged reading by the Playwrights Center of San Francisco in 1991 and was produced the same year by New York City's Impact Theatre and in the Love Creek One-act Play Festival at New York's Nat Horne Theatre.

Production Suggestions

Both of these men are articulate intellectuals. Be sure to look up the meaning and pronunciation of all words and proper names in your role which are not a part of your normal, everyday conversation. Roger realizes he has made a fool of himself mispronouncing "Proust." Take a lesson from him so *you* don't make a fool of *yourself* on stage mispronouncing words. Start using the rope early in your rehearsals so that it doesn't get in your way in performance. And be very careful; Theodore dies, but we don't want the *actor* to get so much as a rope burn.

Address all inquiries concerning performances, readings, or reprinting of this work *or any portion thereof* to William Borden, 7996 S. FM 548, Royse City, TX 75189. For details, see "Part II: Securing Rights for Your Production," pages 241 to 250.

1   The action takes place in a prison in the present.

2   ***CHARACTERS:*** ROGER — he wears nondescript clothes — trousers,

3   shirt open at the neck — that haven't been changed for days. He

4   also wears a cap of some kind, not very official looking, and a

5   pistol slung around his waist. THEODORE — his shirt and pants

6   are also nondescript and unlaundered.

7   ***SETTING:*** A room with a pipe batten or beam and a stool.

8

9   *(THEODORE, watched by ROGER, stands on a stool, tying a*

10   *rope to a pipe or beam. He finishes and steps off the stool. They*

11   *both appraise it for a moment, then ROGER tugs at the rope. The*

12   *rope comes off. ROGER throws the rope to THEODORE.)*

13   **ROGER: You think I haven't seen everything? Every trick and ruse**

14   **you scum could possibly think of? You think I'm not smart?**

15   **THEODORE: You're very smart.**

16   **ROGER: I am.**

17   **THEODORE: I imagine you have a Ph.D.**

18   **ROGER: Don't get smart with me.** *(THEODORE ties the rope again.)*

19   **THEODORE: This will be a foolproof knot. Guaranteed to kill**

20   **instantly.**

21   **ROGER: Not instantly. We want you to ponder your ways, reflect**

22   **on your errors, as you dangle, swaying slowly in the breeze.**

23   **Then we allow you to expire.**

24   **THEODORE: Expire.**

25   **ROGER: Yes.**

26   **THEODORE: You have an enormous vocabulary.**

27   **ROGER: Thank you.**

28   **THEODORE: A veritable prodigious lexicon in your cerebrum.**

29   **ROGER: I read vociferously. No television, no card games — I**

30   **have the complete collection of The Great Books.**

31   **THEODORE: The Great Books? Who wrote them?**

32   **ROGER: You know those guys, from Homer and the Bible to**

33   **Melville and Prowst.**

34   **THEODORE: Prowst?**

35   **ROGER: You're not too well read yourself, are you?**

1   THEODORE: No, I'm not.
2   ROGER: Prowst was a French guy, wrote in a cork-lined room,
3   suffered from asthma. He pursued the nuances of the past.
4   Cherchez the past. And he was a fag. *(ROGER tests the beam.)*
5   That's better.
6   THEODORE: Might be too sturdy.
7   ROGER: Naw.
8   THEODORE: I might not dangle long enough. I have a lot of sins
9   to reflect upon as I die.
10 ROGER: They go fast. Whole life in a flash. That's the rumor.
11 THEODORE: As I dangle.
12 ROGER: As you dangle.
13 THEODORE: In the breeze.
14 ROGER: In the breeze.
15 THEODORE: What breeze? We're indoors. Miles from daylight.
16   So you've told me.
17 ROGER: Well, just the momentum, as you plunge through the
18   opening, and the rope, you know, jerks you up, as you're
19   plunging down — gives your body what they call a torque, an
20   angular momentum, so your body, as it's expiring, will swing,
21   from its own potential energy.
22 THEODORE: Torque.
23 ROGER: You'll sway in quite graceful circles, or possibly ellipses,
24   around and around.
25 THEODORE: Like a pendulum.
26 ROGER: *Exactement.*
27 THEODORE: I could become a clock.
28 ROGER: If I left you there.
29 THEODORE: Then you were lying about the breeze.
30 ROGER: It was a bit of poetry.
31 THEODORE: Do you write?
32 ROGER: Reports?
33 THEODORE: Poetry.
34 ROGER: Me?
35 THEODORE: Let me hear something.

1   **ROGER:** Naw ...
2   **THEODORE:** Please! *(ROGER pulls out a fat sheaf of scraps of*
3   *paper. Then he looks at THEODORE.)*
4   **ROGER:** You'll laugh. *(THEODORE doesn't answer. ROGER*
5   *hesitates, then starts to read.)*
6   "The rope sings like a nightingale
7   as it snaps across the breeze" —
8   Maybe breeze isn't right there. *(ROGER takes out a pencil.)*
9   "The rope sings like a nightingale
10   as it snaps ... into the ... abyss ... of death."
11   **THEODORE:** "Death" 's trite.
12   **ROGER:** You're right. "Abyss of ... "
13   **THEODORE:** "Like a raven." "Raven" 's better than "nightingale."
14   "Raven" connotes the harshness of the moment.
15   **ROGER:** It's a beautiful moment. Lyrical. And for those who
16   disagree, there's the irony, the poignant reversal of
17   expectation. "Abyss of ... "
18   **THEODORE:** "Horror."
19   **ROGER:** "Abyss of ... "
20   **THEODORE:** "Meaninglessness." "Nothingness." "Darkness."
21   **ROGER:** "Into the abyss of ... "
22   **THEODORE:** "... into the sweet memory of roses." *(ROGER looks*
23   *at him a moment, then writes it down, shoves packet into his*
24   *pocket.)*
25   **ROGER:** *(Reluctantly)* Thanks. *(ROGER tests the knot. It holds.)*
26   Good work.
27   **THEODORE:** Thanks.
28   **ROGER:** Of course it's not a professional job.
29   **THEODORE:** I'm going to hang!
30   **ROGER:** I'd think that would be a particular reason for taking
31   pride in your work. Here. *(ROGER hands THEODORE the*
32   *other end of the rope.)*
33   **THEODORE:** Now what?
34   **ROGER:** The noose. Make the noose.
35   **THEODORE:** *(Throwing down the rope)* No. I won't participate any

1   further in my own murder.
2 ROGER: Execution, my friend. Words are important.
3 THEODORE: Shoot me then! That will make it murder!
4 ROGER: However I do it, it's an execution.
5 THEODORE: No —
6 ROGER: I'm the executioner. It's a matter of definition. The man
7   who writes the dictionary rules the nation. I can execute you
8   now — *(He pulls out the pistol.)* Or you can have another
9   minute or two to enjoy God's bounty on earth, while you tie
10   the rope, while I test it, while we engage in scintillating dialect.
11   Which do you prefer?
12 THEODORE: Shoot me. We might as well get it over with.
13 ROGER: That seems mighty shortsighted, my friend. Who knows
14   what might occur in the next ninety seconds? An earthquake
15   might kill me and free you. The rebels might stage an attack
16   and divert my attention, allowing you to escape. There might
17   be a coup from above. A foreign invasion. The Commander
18   might commit suicide. You might receive a pardon. Don't
19   forget — what's his name? You know, the Russian —
20 THEODORE: Dostoevsky?
21 ROGER: That's the guy. Life is ruled by chance, old boy. Ninety
22   seconds can seem like an eternity.
23 THEODORE: Everything is fated.
24 ROGER: An Augustinian!
25 THEODORE: There is a destiny —
26 ROGER: God's? Or the inevitability of historical materialism?
27   *(THEODORE doesn't answer.)*
28 THEODORE: I think for me ninety seconds will pass quickly.
29 ROGER: Time is relative.
30 THEODORE: Time marches forward inexorably.
31 ROGER: Inexorably.
32 THEODORE: Inexorably. I relish intellectual debate. Don't you? I
33   haven't had a good discussion for a hell of a long time.
34 ROGER: *(ROGER hands the rope again to THEODORE.)* The noose.
35 THEODORE: I don't know how.

1   ROGER: I don't believe it.
2   THEODORE: It's not something you need to know in the normal
3   course of a lifetime. *(Disgusted, ROGER begins to make the noose.)*
4   ROGER: The other executioners, you know, all they want to do is
5   play cards, read girlie magazines. I'm out of my element.
6   THEODORE: I can see that. *(He watches ROGER deftly make the*
7   *noose.)* You're very good.
8   ROGER: Funny thing is, you guys usually have something to talk
9   about. You seem to think more. It must be thinking that makes
10   you dissatisfied with things.
11   THEODORE: It's not only thinking.
12   ROGER: I suppose not.
13   THEODORE: It's feeling, too. You know, intuitively, things aren't
14   right.
15   ROGER: Well, it depends which side you're on, doesn't it? Like for
16   me, things are right. *(He completes the noose. He admires his*
17   *work.)*
18   THEODORE: But they're not.
19   ROGER: Of course they're right. Right as rain.
20   THEODORE: You're not happy.
21   ROGER: *(Angrily)* I'm happy!
22   THEODORE: You're a fish out of water. No intellectual
23   companionship. No one to share ideas with.
24   ROGER: *(Slipping the noose over THEODORE's head)* Now there's
25   where you're wrong, old sport. I have you to converse with.
26   You and your compatriots. All day, every day, one after
27   another, a veritable parade of intellect.
28   THEODORE: Perhaps you'd like to join us.
29   ROGER: Get myself executed?
30   THEODORE: Fight for a cause.
31   ROGER: Die before my time?
32   THEODORE: Live a meaningful life.
33   ROGER: Die like a dog? There's a flaw in your syllogism. *(ROGER*
34   *motions THEODORE onto the stool.)*
35   THEODORE: Don't you feel some dishonesty? Killing people you

1   have so much in common with?

2   ROGER: I don't find it dishonest, no. Poignant, perhaps. Ironic.

3   Tragic, even. It's like playing a part in a great drama. It

4   fulfills me. Whereas you become nameless, faceless, one of

5   many who die futilely.

6   THEODORE: Who knows what's futile?

7   ROGER: It's plain as the noose around your neck.

8   THEODORE: But don't we have some effect? Make some difference?

9   ROGER: Oh, yeah. I learn a lot. I sharpen my wits. You make a big

10   difference to me.

11   THEODORE: Do I?

12   ROGER: Definitely. *(THEODORE climbs onto the stool.)*

13   THEODORE: I mean, do *I?* Do I, Theodore, make a difference to

14   you?

15   ROGER: What do you mean?

16   THEODORE: Or am I just one of many who pass through your life?

17   ROGER: *(Beat)* You're different.

18   THEODORE: How?

19   ROGER: I don't know.

20   THEODORE: What's your name?

21   ROGER: My name?

22   THEODORE: Yes.

23   ROGER: I have no name. So far as you're concerned.

24   THEODORE: Have you no conscience?

25   ROGER: Do you? Wouldn't you kill me if you could? Even after

26   our thrilling conversation? You would. Because I'm on the

27   other side. It would be my fate to die.

28   THEODORE: It would be a chance you would take.

29   ROGER: So you see, I have no choice.

30   THEODORE: You always have a choice.

31   ROGER: Do you? *(ROGER gets ready to kick away the stool.)*

32   THEODORE: One question — *(ROGER pauses.)* Does everyone

33   participate in his own ... death?

34   ROGER: Oh, yes. We think it makes a point. It teaches a lesson.

35   THEODORE: But what good will it do now?

1   ROGER: That's the irony of it, isn't it? Any further last words?
2   *(Several beats. ROGER gets ready to kick away the stool.)*
3   THEODORE: Proost.
4   ROGER: What?
5   THEODORE: Proost! It's pronounced Proost, not Prowst!
6   ROGER: You kidding me?
7   THEODORE: No.
8   ROGER: You're sure?
9   THEODORE: I'm positive.
10   ROGER: You know French?
11   THEODORE: *Tres bien.*
12   ROGER: Proost.
13   THEODORE: Proost.
14   ROGER: I could've gone on for years making a fool of myself.
15   THEODORE: I know. *(Several beats)*
16   ROGER: Well.
17   THEODORE: Right.
18   ROGER: We can't wait forever.
19   THEODORE: No. *(Several beats)*
20   ROGER: Roger.
21   THEODORE: Pardon?
22   ROGER: My name's Roger.
23   THEODORE: Ah. *(Beat)* Theodore.
24   ROGER: Right. *(ROGER starts to kick away the stool, the stage goes*
25   *to black, and there's a strange musical note, as of a string being*
26   *plucked, the overtone lasting for several seconds.)*
27   The rope sings
28   like a nightingale
29   as it snaps
30   into the sweet
31   memory of roses.
32   It's a beautiful moment. Lyrical.
33   *The End*
34
35

Wheelchair Blues

by James I. Schempp

James I. Schempp has been a faculty member at Syracuse University and Murray State University. He has worked at theatres in Pennsylvania, New York, Massachusetts, Ohio, Kentucky, Colorado, and North Dakota.

Wheelchair Blues was selected as a finalist in the Actors Theatre of Louisville Ten Minute Play Contest in 1991 and 1992 and was included in the New Play Development Workshop of the Playwrights Program of the Association for Theatre in Higher Education at ATHE's national convention at Seattle the same year. The Actors Institute of New York presented it off-off-Broadway in 1992.

Production Suggestions

Both of these characters are basically good people, and both of them have their blind spots; in your preparation, come to terms with both the good points and weaknesses of your characters.

If you don't have technical support to supply the sound cues at the beginning and end of the script, the play will still work. At the beginning, the male actor simply needs to set the scene with his entrance business; at the end of the play, if you both freeze and hold for several seconds after the final line, the audience will understand that you are still there when the doors open.

Address all inquiries concerning performances, readings, or reprinting of this work *or any portion thereof* to James I. Schempp, 723 Milligan Lane, West Islip, NY 11795. For details, see "Part II: Securing Rights for Your Production," pages 241 to 250.

1   The action takes place in an open space in front of an auditorium.
2   ***CHARACTERS:*** CHARLOTTE WHEELER — a student in a
3   wheelchair. BARNEY LUFTER — a student who works for the
4   auditorium. He wears a security guard uniform.
5   ***SETTING:*** An open space backed by the doors to the auditorium.
6
7   *(CHARLOTTE WHEELER enters in a wheelchair, which she stops*
8   *at Center Stage. She positions herself carefully, then takes a wrench*
9   *of some type out of a book bag, leans over the side of the chair and*
10   *does some manipulation. There is a crunching sound and*
11   *CHARLOTTE drops the wrench. She tries to move the chair with no*
12   *effect. She gives it her strongest push but it will not move. With a*
13   *determined but resigned smile, she settles back, takes a book from*
14   *her book bag and begins reading. After a beat, BARNEY LUFTER*
15   *enters. He opens the doors of the auditorium to make sure they are*
16   *functioning properly; the sound of the concert washes over the*
17   *stage. He closes the doors and approaches CHARLOTTE.)*
18   **BARNEY:** Uh, you're not planning to sit here much longer are you?
19   **CHARLOTTE:** How was the concert?
20   **BARNEY:** Because that probably won't be a very good place to be
21   in about … *(Checks his watch)* ten minutes.
22   **CHARLOTTE:** I didn't go to the concert because there is a flight
23   of fourteen steps just inside those doors.
24   **BARNEY:** The concert will end then and this place is going to be
25   virtually flooded with thousands of wild-eyed teenagers
26   headed for their cars.
27   **CHARLOTTE:** They are very pretty stairs. Made out of New
28   Hampshire granite. Did you know that?
29   **BARNEY:** *(Nodding his head toward the side of the stage)* You want
30   to come over there with me, we can watch it together. From a
31   safe place.
32   **CHARLOTTE:** Fourteen granite steps. *(Pause)* You sure of the
33   ending time?
34   **BARNEY:** Hm?
35   **CHARLOTTE:** You know for sure when it's gonna end?

1   BARNEY: To the minute. This whole concert is planned to the
2   split-second. Gotta be. You ever seen the lighting effects they
3   use? They gotta know exactly where someone's gonna be
4   every second. Now let's get you out of here.
5   CHARLOTTE: I haven't seen the special effects. I'm not allowed
6   to see them.
7   BARNEY: That's too bad. Really neat stuff. The concert started
8   three minutes late, so the final encore will end in exactly ...
9   *(Consults his watch again)* nine minutes and thirty-five seconds.
10   CHARLOTTE: That long?
11   BARNEY: *(Moving behind chair to push it)* It's a big finish, too. The
12   kids get real hyped up and come crashing out of there like a
13   herd of buffalo. So like I said, you better come out of the way
14   or they'll run right over you. *(The chair doesn't move.)* You got
15   the brakes on or what?
16   CHARLOTTE: It's broken.
17   BARNEY: 'Cause this thing ain't moving.
18   CHARLOTTE: I said, it's broken. I broke it.
19   BARNEY: Yeah? Where's it broken? Maybe I can put it back
20   together.
21   CHARLOTTE: I don't think so. It's in the axle itself.
22   BARNEY: Bad news. *(Trying to make it a joke)* Now why'd you go
23   and break your chair in a dangerous place like this? You
24   trying to get yourself killed?
25   CHARLOTTE: *(Quietly)* Yes.
26   BARNEY: *(Nervous)* Yes? What d'ya mean, yes? You didn't break
27   the chair intentionally, did you?
28   CHARLOTTE: Yes. I did.
29   BARNEY: Why the hell did you do a thing like that?
30   CHARLOTTE: *(Her anger welling out of her)* Because I want
31   someone to say, "Gee, I wonder what she was doing there,
32   *because you know she couldn't get into the concert because there*
33   *is no way to get a wheelchair into that damned auditorium!"*
34   BARNEY: *(Examining the chair)* Maybe I can fix this.
35   CHARLOTTE: *(Recovering slightly)* Did you hear what I said?

1   BARNEY: Huh? Sure. How'd this get broken?
2   CHARLOTTE: It's easy. You just take a wrench and grab that little
3   tab, then turn it with all your might and the axle gets jammed
4   and there's no way to fix it and there's no way to move it.
5   BARNEY: Jeez, lady! This is serious!
6   CHARLOTTE: *(Slowly and with emphasis)* I intentionally disabled
7   my wheelchair. *(Lighter, to herself)* Hey! How about that! Now
8   it's my wheelchair that's handicapped!
9   BARNEY: I gotta get some help to take care of this. *(The noise of the*
10   *concert is heard again as BARNEY reaches for his walkie-talkie.*
11   *CHARLOTTE makes a lunge for it and gets it out of his hand. The*
12   *effort of this pulls her from her chair and she ends up on the*
13   *ground. She sits and places the walkie-talkie beneath her.)*
14   CHARLOTTE: I don't want it taken care of, damn you!
15   BARNEY: *(Lunging)* Hey, give me that radio!
16   CHARLOTTE: *(Pulling a can of Mace from her book bag)* **Don't**
17   **touch me!**
18   BARNEY: OK! OK ...
19   CHARLOTTE: This stuff smells terrible and it hurts worse.
20   BARNEY: I said, OK!
21   CHARLOTTE: I'll use it if I have to!
22   BARNEY: I'm not going to touch you, OK?
23   CHARLOTTE: Stand over there!
24   BARNEY: Just take it easy. The last thing we need right now is for
25   me to be blind!
26   CHARLOTTE: Yeah. One handicap is enough, right?
27   BARNEY: Huh?
28   CHARLOTTE: Skip it. Will you *please* go away!
29   BARNEY: *(At the end of his patience)* Look, lady! I don't know what
30   your problem is, but you are sitting in the path of several
31   thousand people who are going to start coming through those
32   doors in six minutes and fifteen seconds, and they aren't going
33   to see you sitting there, and even if they did, I very much
34   doubt that they will give a care and you could get hurt real
35   bad. Now will you just calm down and let me take you to a

1   more convenient place.
2 CHARLOTTE: I don't *want* to be taken to a more convenient
3   place! That's the point! *Please go away!*
4 BARNEY: No, I will not go away. I have a job to do.
5 CHARLOTTE: Then do it!
6 BARNEY: That's what I'm trying to do. What are you, some kind
7   of protesting nut?
8 CHARLOTTE: I am not a protestor. I am not a nut. I am not a
9   "handicapped person." I am Charlotte Wheeler. And I want
10   to be seen. And I want to be recognized as an individual. And
11   if I can't be seen, then I want to do something to make people
12   aware of me, even if I have to trip them up to do it.
13 BARNEY: OK! OK. *I see you!* Now let's move it. I have other
14   things to do, other doors to check.
15 CHARLOTTE: No you don't.
16 BARNEY: I don't what?
17 CHARLOTTE: You don't see me.
18 BARNEY: Lady, believe me, I see you.
19 CHARLOTTE: Can you see me riding a merry-go-round? I'm sick
20   of places I can't go and cars I can't drive and pay phones I can't
21   reach and toilets I can't get into and classes I can't take, for
22   God's sake, because I can't get up the stairs to the classroom!
23 BARNEY: Look, you *have* to get out of the way. In ... *(Looks at his*
24   *watch)* four minutes and thirty seconds, those doors are gonna
25   open and you're gonna get trashed!
26 CHARLOTTE: Nothing new. It happens every day.
27 BARNEY: *(Pause)* So you're upset because you can't ride a merry-
28   go-round?
29 CHARLOTTE: That was just an example.
30 BARNEY: You're really feeling sorry for yourself, aren't you?
31 CHARLOTTE: Damned right. No one else will do it for me, so I
32   gotta do it myself. *(Pause)* Look, I was out at the Crossroads
33   Mall this afternoon, and I ...
34 BARNEY: You what?
35 CHARLOTTE: Nothing. This is stupid. Will you please leave?

1   BARNEY: You want to get trampled by a herd of rock fans?
2   CHARLOTTE: Smart boy! You finally figured that out, did you?
3   BARNEY: Why?
4   CHARLOTTE: Because I can only be overlooked for so long.
5   *(Turning on BARNEY)* Look. *(He averts his eyes.)* No, I mean
6   *look at me!*
7   BARNEY: If you don't ...
8   CHARLOTTE: Do you know what happens when I roll down the
9   street? People get out of my way, sometimes they open doors for
10   me, but they're always looking three feet over my head! That's
11   where my face would be if I were standing up. When they
12   bother to notice me at all, they talk to me like I'm an idiot!
13   The world is full of schmucks and I am an invisible person!
14   You don't see me, no one sees me! Tonight, when these people
15   come out of the concert, they are going to trample me. And
16   maybe I'll be hurt. Real bad hurt. *(Pause)* What's the worst
17   thing that could happen to me?
18   BARNEY: *(Quietly)* You could get killed.
19   CHARLOTTE: That's not necessarily bad.
20   BARNEY: You could get maimed! You could end up ...
21   CHARLOTTE: In a wheelchair? *(BARNEY has nothing to say. He*
22   *looks at his watch.)*
23   BARNEY: Two and a half minutes. *(Pause)* You're going to just sit
24   there?
25   CHARLOTTE: *(Quietly)* Yes. *(Pause)* I can't play hackey-sack! I
26   can't play Frisbee!
27   BARNEY: "I can't, I can't, I can't!" All you do is whine "I can't!"
28   CHARLOTTE: I went by the pet store. At the mall. *(Pause)* There
29   was a real cute little Scotty in the window. *(Pause)* I had a dog.
30   She died.
31   BARNEY: Look ...
32   CHARLOTTE: Pets are great, y'know? I mean, they don't care if
33   you're sitting down or standing up. All they want is love, and
34   all they give is love. *(Pause, then going on with increasing*
35   *intensity)* And all you have to do is take them for a walk and

1   keep them on a leash so they won't run off into the traffic, but
2   if the leash slips and she runs off anyway, there's no way you
3   can stop her if you can't run ... *(She rushes on with the same*
4   *intensity.)* Have you ever seen me before?
5   BARNEY: We don't have time for this ...
6   CHARLOTTE: You're Barney Lufter. You're a junior in college.
7   You are a member of Theta Chi. You work weekends as a
8   security guard and you're studying pre-law. You drive a little
9   red Chevrolet and you park it in the library parking lot.
10   *(BARNEY is taken by surprise, and for the first time, he looks*
11   *directly at CHARLOTTE.)*
12   BARNEY: How'd you know all that?
13   CHARLOTTE: I see you every day. We pass each other all the
14   time between classes. We even had a class together. Intro to
15   Business Law.
16   BARNEY: Was that you? I didn't recognize you.
17   CHARLOTTE: Of course you didn't! Until I sat here I was
18   invisible to you. You ignored me.
19   BARNEY: I wouldn't exactly say I *ignored* you.
20   CHARLOTTE: That's *exactly* what you did! Three weeks ago ...
21   you probably don't even remember, do you?
22   BARNEY: Remember what?
23   CHARLOTTE: Nothing. Nothing! I'm just so ... *(Collects herself.)*
24   I made an extra special effort to get your attention three
25   weeks ago. It was a Thursday afternoon. I usually leave
26   campus on a special bus at one o'clock in the afternoon on
27   Thursdays, but I made arrangements to stay late because you
28   were going to present a report in Dr. Lee's symposium.
29   BARNEY: *(Remembering the event)* That's right ...
30   CHARLOTTE: I went to the seminar room. I waited outside for
31   you. I knew just what I was going to say. I had it all set out,
32   starting from the first word. I wore my best ...
33   When you came up I said "Hi ... " You just kept walking
34   by. You didn't even acknowledge my existence!
35   I gave it my best shot, I put all I had into that one word,

1   "Hi ... " Everything I *am* was attached to that one word! If
2   you had just picked it up. If you had just *responded!* All of me
3   would have come along with it. That was the opening gambit!
4   Of course you don't remember! Of course you didn't hear!
5   I wasn't there! You just walked past me because I didn't exist!
6   You never saw me.
7   That was the first time I ever tried, I mean really *tried*, to
8   get someone to deal with me on a grown-up, real-person basis.
9   I wanted you to look me in the eyes and treat me like I was
10   something other than a poor idiot child!
11   You could have done so much.
12   But I thought, he's probably thinking about his report. I'll
13   wait until afterwards and try again. So I sat at the back of the
14   room. I hung on every word you said. I gave you all my
15   attention. When you finished, I'm the one who started the
16   applause! You came off the podium and everyone was telling
17   you what a great job you did.
18   When you came past me, you looked right *at* me. I *know*
19   you did. I waited until I could see your eyes, and I said it
20   again. "Hi ... "
21   And you ignored me again. you looked right *at* me, but you
22   never saw me!
23   BARNEY: I don't even remember that.
24   CHARLOTTE: That's the point. *(CHARLOTTE stops, bites her lip*
25   *and stiffens. She cries in spite of herself and tries to keep BARNEY*
26   *from seeing it. BARNEY considers, then reaches a decision. He*
27   *sits down beside her.)*
28   BARNEY: Move over.
29   CHARLOTTE: Will you please go away! It's too late now!
30   BARNEY: Nope. You're gonna sit here, I'm gonna sit here.
31   CHARLOTTE: I don't want you here.
32   BARNEY: I don't want *you* here!
33   CHARLOTTE: Why are you trying to take care of me? I don't
34   want you to take care of me. I'm an adult and I can make my
35   own decisions! Now get the hell out of here.

1   BARNEY: Sorry. If they walk on you, they're gonna have to walk
2   on me too.
3   CHARLOTTE: You're screwing everything up!
4   BARNEY: Life is like that sometimes. You get a nice little plan and
5   someone comes along and messes it up. Someone makes you see
6   something or someone refuses to see something or someone gets
7   converted to your point of view. It's a bitch, but it happens.
8   CHARLOTTE: Why are you doing this?
9   BARNEY: I'm sharing the experience with you.
10   CHARLOTTE: Do you know how dumb that sounds?
11   BARNEY: Sorry.
12   CHARLOTTE: You might get hurt.
13   BARNEY: There's a terrific echo around here.
14   CHARLOTTE: *(After a pause)* Look. You can avoid this. You can
15   just get up and walk. Now will you please do it?
16   BARNEY: What's the matter? Can't you take "yes" for an answer?
17   CHARLOTTE: I …
18   BARNEY: You win! I'm noticing you! *(BARNEY sits in silence as*
19   *they consider the situation. CHARLOTTE hands the walkie-talkie*
20   *back to him.)*
21   CHARLOTTE: Here's your radio.
22   BARNEY: Thanks.
23   CHARLOTTE: You want to use it?
24   BARNEY: Too late now.
25   CHARLOTTE: *(Pause)* How much time?
26   BARNEY: Fifteen seconds.
27   CHARLOTTE: Are you sure you want to do this?
28   BARNEY: No. *(There is another slight pause. Then BARNEY turns to*
29   *CHARLOTTE and looks her directly in the eyes as he extends his*
30   *hand.)* Hi. *(CHARLOTTE takes his hand and holds it.)*
31   CHARLOTTE: Hi. *(The sound of a large crowd is heard approaching*
32   *the closed doors of the auditorium. The sound suddenly increases*
33   *as if the doors have been opened like floodgates. The lights fade*
34   *to black with the crowd noise reaching a crescendo.)*
35   *The End*

Twisted Sister

by Lora Lee Cliff, Cynthia Judge, and Janet Wilson

Writing jointly under the name "Sisters in Partnership," the playwrights are all professional actresses working in theatre, film, and television. Ms. Cliff and Ms. Wilson, specialists in the Sanford Meisner technique of acting, have both taught at the Riverside Shakespeare Company in New York City. Ms. Judge received the Joseph Jefferson Award nomination for her stage work in Chicago.

Twisted Sister received its premiere production by Shadowcast Theatre Works in Richmond, Virginia, in 1991.

Production Suggestions

The actor who plays Sr. Cheryl will have great fun switching back and forth between her different roles; how often, for instance, do you get to play a peppermint patty? The actress will want to develop distinctly different voices, movement patterns, and tempos for each of the different characters. Avoid "hamming it up"; trust the piece to play well, and focus on taking the process as seriously as Sr. Cheryl does.

Far from just being the "straight man," Dr. Blank is the one who really makes this play happen. The actor need not turn his character into a stereotypical shrink; instead he should focus on playing Dr. Blank's objective — discovering and exploring Sr. Cheryl's deeper problems.

Address all inquiries concerning performances, readings, or reprinting of this work *or any portion thereof* to Sisters in Partnership, 300 Harper Court, Normal, IL 61761. For details, see "Part II: Securing Rights for Your Production," pages 241 to 250.

1   The action takes place in a therapist's office.

2 **CHARACTERS:** DR. BLANK — more like a little league coach than a
3   psychotherapist, he wears a baseball cap and a whistle around his
4   neck. Throughout the play, he blows the whistle to trigger Sr.
5   Cheryl's changes of character. SR. CHERYL — more like a
6   precocious child than a nun, she is dressed in traditional nun garb
7   and wears a cardigan sweater.

8 **SETTING:** DR. BLANK's office is furnished with a couch and an easy
9   chair.

10

11   *(SR. CHERYL is lying on the couch clutching her purse while DR.*
12   *BLANK is sitting in an easy chair. He blows the whistle.)*

13 **SR. CHERYL:** *(As her thirteen-year-old self)* **I'm thirteen and I just**
14   **got my period. I've been crabby all day and didn't know why**
15   **and — boom — my period started, first time. I thought God**
16   **was punishing me for being crabby ...**

17 **DR. BLANK: Go on, Sr. Cheryl.**

18 **SR. CHERYL:** *(Sitting up and coming out of "character")* **Dr. Blank,**
19   **all I need is a little help sleeping. If you would just write me**
20   **another prescription ...**

21 **DR. BLANK: Go on with your dream.**

22 **SR. CHERYL: All right.** *(Laying back on the sofa. DR. BLANK blows*
23   *whistle. As her thirteen-year-old self)* **I'm walking home from**
24   **school and I just gotta have some candy — it's all I can think**
25   **about.** *(Jumping up and looking in the "candy store window")*
26   **Then I'm at the candy store and I see the butterscotch, and**
27   **the chocolate-covered cherries. And then I see the chocolate**
28   **mints — and the chocolate creams! And I get really upset**
29   **because then I don't know which I want more. And the lady's**
30   **getting mad 'cause I'm taking a long time to decide. Anyway,**
31   **I look up and there's Daddy — and he smiles at me. Then, all**
32   **of a sudden, he gets this weird look on his face and falls down.**
33   *(Running to the "door")* **So I run over to the door and it's**
34   **locked — I don't know how it got locked — and I keep trying**
35   **it and then I** *(Running back to the "window")* **run back over to**

1 the window to see Daddy — and, and, and — he's laying on
2 the ground and *(Running back to the "door")* I run back to the
3 door to try to get out and I'm screaming and kicking at the
4 door *(Coming out of "character")* and that's it.
5 DR. BLANK: It's great! It's a terrific dream because of all the
6 symbolism — crabby and getting your period. I get this image of
7 crabs. What a marvelous metaphor. I would love to work on this.
8 Now, all you have to do is play out the different characters …
9 SR. CHERYL: What?
10 DR. BLANK: See, Sr. Cheryl, each character in your dream is an
11 aspect of your personality — now, through exploring and
12 tying up the fragmented selves …
13 SR. CHERYL: *(Jumping up and heading for the door)* You're not
14 going to tie me up! Why, Mother Superior …
15 DR. BLANK: *(Intercepting her at the door with his hands up)* Oh no,
16 no, no! Metaphorically speaking, metaphorically speaking!
17 Oh hell, Sr. Cheryl, it's fun! Come on — you'll feel better.
18 Why don't we start with your father. Now, you're outside the
19 candy store. What are you doing there? *(Blows whistle.)*
20 SR. CHERYL: I don't know about this.
21 DR. BLANK: Yes you do, Sister. *(Blows whistle again.)*
22 SR. CHERYL: *(As "Daddy," pacing back and forth)* Whew! I gotta
23 have a break. Too much going on — the pressure! I need a
24 drink, but Thelma won't like it. That Thelma — whoa! Guess
25 I'll just have some candy. *(Dropping the "character")* Is that
26 what you mean?
27 DR. BLANK: Yes. Yes. Go on. Who do you see in the candy store?
28 *(Blows whistle.)*
29 SR. CHERYL: *(As "Daddy")* Hi there, Cheryl! Isn't that funny? She
30 looks kind of happy to see me. Come on, I'll buy you a Coke.
31 DR. BLANK: You seem very fond of her.
32 SR. CHERYL: *(As "Daddy")* Yeah. When she was a little girl, I
33 used to hold her, read to her …
34 DR. BLANK: And now?
35 SR. CHERYL: *(As "Daddy")* I'm a very busy man. I don't have

1   time for ... Come on, Cheryl — now! *(Suddenly stricken with*
2   *chest pains)* God, I don't feel well. Must have been that lousy
3   goose liver I had for lunch. Cheryl, come on out here — you
4   gotta call Mother.
5   DR. BLANK: Are you having a heart attack?
6   SR. CHERYL: *(As "Daddy")* I don't know! Would you just call
7   my office?
8   DR. BLANK: I think we should call an ambulance.
9   SR. CHERYL: *(As "Daddy")* No, I'm fine.
10   DR. BLANK: You don't look fine.
11   SR. CHERYL: *(As "Daddy")* I told you to call my office.
12   DR. BLANK: Boy, you're stubborn, aren't you?
13   SR. CHERYL: *(As "Daddy")* I'm not stubborn. Where the hell is
14   Cheryl?
15   DR. BLANK: She can't open the door. She's struggling with it.
16   SR. CHERYL: *(As "Daddy")* What's so hard about a little door?
17   She had to open it to get in.
18   DR. BLANK: Can't you see she's trying?
19   SR. CHERYL: *(As "Daddy")* Just shut up and don't get into my
20   business.
21   DR. BLANK: How dare you talk to me like that! What makes you
22   so angry?
23   SR. CHERYL: *(As "Daddy")* For Christ's sake, what's a little
24   door? These girls — just like their mother — can't do
25   anything without throwing these little fits. Oh — don't start
26   crying like that. Always crying, that one.
27   DR. BLANK: Aha! So it's her crying that pisses you off!
28   SR. CHERYL: *(Coming out of "character")* C'mon, Dr. Blank. You
29   call this fun?
30   DR. BLANK: How insightful! The internalized father is incapable
31   of taking in your feminine self thereby causing a polarization
32   between your masculine and feminine selves.
33   SR. CHERYL: Forget it! Now just give me my prescription ...
34   DR. BLANK: *(Starts whistling "The Candy Man" and starts a "soft*
35   *shoe" dance.)* I want to go back to the candy store — back to

1   the sweetness. Now I want you to play one of the chocolates.
2   *(He is about to blow his whistle but SR. CHERYL stops him.)*
3   SR. CHERYL: No. I'll be a peppermint patty 'cause that's the best.
4   *(DR. BLANK blows whistle. SR. CHERYL as the "patty" jumping*
5   *on the arm of the couch, crossing her legs and imitating Mae West;*
6   *she "strips" off her sweater as she speaks.)* On top of my melt-in-
7   your-little-mouth chocolate, I have a flashy, shimmery, silvery
8   paper wrapping. Shows you what a good taste I'll be. And over
9   that one, there's a little cellophane wrap to make me very
10   secure and never stale, you know, reliable every time.
11   DR. BLANK: Do you think you can do anything for Cheryl?
12   SR. CHERYL: *(As "patty")* Of course, honey — mmmm ... she's
13   gonna love me. *(As "patty" to SR. CHERYL)* Hi there! Oh, you
14   don't feel good, do you? Well, I'll fix that. Listen, I am so
15   good. Now, undo my cellophane — OK, take away my silver
16   lining — see, I'm all chocolate. Take a bite — the first time is
17   great — that's it. See, I'm a little hard on the outside — ooh,
18   surprise — I'm all white inside — that squishy, gooey,
19   marshmallow — real, real moist ...
20   DR. BLANK: Ahhh ... fascinating ... the pieces of the subconscious
21   are falling into place. There's a real paradox here. On the one
22   extreme, there's this helpless child unable to accomplish a
23   simple task, and then there's the adolescent's smoldering
24   sexuality about to explode. I want to talk to your mother now.
25   She's not exactly in the dream, but I want to talk to her anyway.
26   Sit over here. Thelma, how do you feel about Cheryl growing
27   up? *(Blows whistle.)*
28   SR. CHERYL: *(As "Mama" putting her sweater back on and*
29   *buttoning it)* I do not look forward to having another teenage
30   daughter. She's my favorite, but ... I told her when she was
31   six, I said, "You were a lot nicer when you were three." And
32   it's just gone on that way.
33   DR. BLANK: How does this change her relationship with her father?
34   SR. CHERYL: *(As "Mama")* Her father's uncomfortable about
35   things like this — emotional things. I'll be able to handle her.

1   She'll come to me like she always does.
2   DR. BLANK: So she'd rather come to you than to Daddy — I
3   mean to her father?
4   SR. CHERYL: *(As "Mama")* Oh heavens, yes. Her father thinks a
5   period is a punctuation mark. They're not close.
6   DR. BLANK: Does Cheryl miss that?
7   SR. CHERYL: *(As "Mama")* Oh no. I don't think it fazes her.
8   DR. BLANK: Are you sure about that, Thelma?
9   SR. CHERYL: *(As "Mama")* Yes! Cheryl's father works hard. He's
10   a good provider. And I see to it that his time at home is spent
11   with me.
12   DR. BLANK: You are a selfish woman.
13   SR. CHERYL: *(As "Mama")* You can't talk to me like that!
14   DR. BLANK: OK. Change places and be Cheryl. *(He attempts to*
15   *blow the whistle but "Mama" stops him.)*
16   SR. CHERYL: *(As "Mama")* Wait just a minute! I'm not finished yet!
17   DR. BLANK: *(Blows his whistle and points to the sofa; "Mama"*
18   *refuses to budge; DR. BLANK blows several short sharp blows on*
19   *his whistle and SR. CHERYL complies.)* Now Cheryl — is it true
20   what your mother said?
21   SR. CHERYL: No! Mama won't let me know Daddy 'cause she
22   wants me to be her girl.
23   DR. BLANK: *(Pointing to where "Mama" is sitting)* Tell your
24   mother that.
25   SR. CHERYL: No! I'm not telling her anything. *(Standing up and*
26   *holding out her hand for the prescription)* Just give me my
27   prescription and let me go!
28   DR. BLANK: I'm offering you this creative process in order for
29   you to discover who you really are, and all you want is more
30   pills. I'm so disappointed! Come on, Sr. Cheryl. You can play
31   Mama again. *(SR. CHERYL resumes her "Mama" position.)* You
32   seem a little upset. *(Blows whistle.)*
33   SR. CHERYL: *(As "Mama")* What else can a mother do? What
34   can a mother do? The sacrifices I have made for her. Her
35   sisters did not get the dancing lessons. They did not get a lot

1   of the things she did. She can just go off with her father — be
2   his girl and leave me alone.
3   DR. BLANK: What are you feeling right now?
4   SR. CHERYL: *(As "Mama")* Betrayed. The last of my three
5   blessings has betrayed me.
6   DR. BLANK: The missing link — betrayal. The fact that you're
7   wanting to separate from the symbiotic relationship, but *she*
8   just won't let you!
9   SR. CHERYL: *(As "Mama")* What are you talking about?!
10   *(Grabbing her purse and beating DR. BLANK with it)* Just who
11   do you think you are?
12   DR. BLANK: *(Blocking her blows with his arms)* I think we've done
13   enough for one session, Sr. Cheryl.
14   SR. CHERYL: *(As "Mama," still beating him)* You have a lot of
15   nerve sticking your nose in where it doesn't belong!
16   DR. BLANK: *(Still defending himself)* The session is over! *(He blows*
17   *his whistle.)*
18   SR. CHERYL: *(Ignoring the whistle, "Mama" yanks the whistle out of*
19   *his mouth and tries to cram it down his throat.)* All my daughter
20   wants is a few lousy pills so she can sleep at night. *(DR. BLANK*
21   *searches for his prescription pad.)* I that asking too much? But no!
22   You have to go dragging me into this! Why is it always the
23   mother's fault? And I wasn't even in her damn dream ...
24   DR. BLANK: *(Quickly writing her a prescription)* Here it is!
25   *(Fearfully hands it to "Mama.")*
26   SR. CHERYL: *(As "Mama," snaps it out of his hand.)* I'll give this to
27   Cheryl and I'll be back for more!
28   DR. BLANK: Yes, yes, next week. *(As "Mama" exits, DR. BLANK*
29   *throws himself on the couch.)*
30   *The End*
31
32
33
34
35

He/She/It?

by Jan Baross

Jan Baross, a leading Northwest documentary filmmaker for twenty years, now writes for theatre. In addition to readings and productions in Los Angeles and the Northwest, she has had two plays produced off-off-Broadway.

He/She/It? was first performed by LitEruption in 1992 and was a finalist in the Actors Theatre of Louisville Ten Minute Play Contest in 1991.

Production Suggestions

Both of these characters try to keep their feelings tightly in check. As a result, the play will work better if you underplay the emotions; be closely and clearly in touch with your character's feelings, but avoid vocal fireworks — or at least save them for a very few, carefully chosen moments. The brevity of the lines drives this play forward at a lively pace; don't slow it down with lagging cues and melodramatic pauses. Finally stay in touch with the humor in this script; in the opinion of the playwright, who has seen it done both as a comedy and as a drama, the play works better as a comedy.

Address all inquiries concerning performances, readings, or reprinting of this work *or any portion thereof* to Jan Baross Media, Inc., 6426 SW Barnes Rd., Portland, OR 97221. For details, see "Part II: Securing Rights for Your Production," pages 241 to 250.

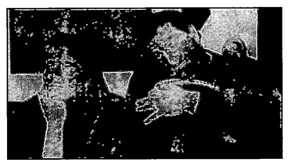

Actors: Karen Voss, Jim Caputo in He/She/It? *Photo by Jan Baross*

1   The action takes place in a living room in the evening in the
2   present.
3   ***CHARACTERS:*** HE — between twenty-five and forty-five years old.
4   SHE — between twenty-five and thirty-five years old.
5   ***SETTING:*** A couple of chairs, end table, sofa — whatever is needed to
6   stage the action.
7
8   *(SHE enters nervously. HE sits reading. Both are intense and*
9   *fighting to keep themselves and each other under control.)*
10   **SHE:** Is she here yet?
11   **HE:** Calm down, will you?
12   **SHE:** This is calm. You know this is calm. You know this is what
13   calm looks like when I do it.
14   **HE:** Do you want a drink?
15   **SHE:** Don't do that.
16   **HE:** What?
17   **SHE:** You didn't hear a word I said.
18   **HE:** Yes, I did. It was clear, like a foghorn.
19   **SHE:** That's her.
20   **HE:** That's a car.
21   **SHE:** So? She doesn't drive?
22   **HE:** She's coming by bus. She'll get off at the corner and ...
23   **SHE:** Walk into our lives and surround us like a big blue mountain
24   range.
25   **HE:** It'll just be a talk. A small talk.
26   **SHE:** A mountain range is coming for tea. How do you talk small
27   to a mountain range?
28   **HE:** You promised to give it a chance.
29   **SHE:** Alright! What do you want? You want ...
30   **HE:** Small talk. Nothing beyond a chat.
31   **SHE:** My stomach is clenched. I can't talk with a clenched stomach.
32   **HE:** Nothing has been decided. Nothing. It's really up to you.
33   **SHE:** Oh, suddenly it's up to me!
34   **HE:** Just say "no," and the whole thing is off.
35   **SHE:** Just say "no."

1   HE: "No." It's simple.
2   SHE: *(Quietly)* No.
3   HE: What?
4   SHE: I said, no!
5   HE: Don't panic!
6   SHE: *No!*
7   HE: What do you mean, when you say "no"?
8   SHE: You said I could say it and it would all be over.
9   HE: Is that what you're really saying?
10 SHE: How many ways are there to say it! No. No. *No!*
11 HE: You can't mean that. You haven't even met her.
12 SHE: It's not *no* to her. It's *no* to you. This is all about you.
13 HE: Is that what you think?
14 SHE: Do you know what happened the last time I said no to you?
15 HE: *(Pause)* Well, what?
16 SHE: I didn't see you for two years.
17 HE: A long weekend. Christ. Your memory.
18 SHE: Longest weekend of my life. I had fourteen affairs, and two
19   abortions.
20 HE: Don't joke about it. I suffered too.
21 SHE: Alright, a long weekend that lasted two years.
22 HE: On and off. You hurt me.
23 SHE: Because I said no.
24 HE: Because I want a child!
25 SHE: I don't.
26 HE: I know.
27 SHE: And if I say no to this new plan, you're gone again. With her.
28 HE: No. I promise to stay.
29 SHE: You'll resent me.
30 HE: I'll get over it.
31 SHE: Over what? What the hell are we talking about?
32 HE: A baby. Mine.
33 SHE: So. Go marry her.
34 HE: She won't marry me.
35 SHE: You asked her to marry you?!

119

1 HE: No. She announced it when we met. She doesn't want to
2   marry, period.
3 SHE: That's how she starts her conversations? Hello, I won't
4   marry you.
5 HE: Pretty close.
6 SHE: She just wants your sperm?
7 HE: My baby.
8 SHE: My husband's baby.
9 HE: Ah baby, you're my wife. I love you.
10 SHE: And her!
11 HE: In a way.
12 SHE: What way?
13 HE: She's motherly. No. Nurturing.
14 SHE: I'm not?
15 HE: You are, in your fashion.
16 SHE: But she'd be a better mother for your child?
17 HE: Our child. All three of us.
18 SHE: We all call her Mom?
19 HE: I won't sleep with her if that's what you're worried about.
20 SHE: Yes! That's what I'm worried about. You mean you haven't?
21 HE: We gave it up when you and I got back together.
22 SHE: And then you both had this fabulous idea that you couldn't
23   wait to share with me.
24 HE: We've talked about artificial insemination.
25 SHE: *We?* Who? Her?
26 HE: And me.
27 SHE: And where was I?
28 HE: On our minds every minute. We don't want to hurt you.
29 SHE: *(Beat)* Hold onto that thought.
30 HE: She has the baby. She lives next door. That's all.
31 SHE: Next door?
32 HE: That's why it's important that you like her.
33 SHE: I don't *want* to like her. I don't even like you at this moment!
34 HE: Do you want me to leave?
35 SHE: Did I say that? I said I don't like you at *this* moment. *This*

1   moment is over. It is now *that* moment. I'll die if you leave me
2   again.
3   HE: I was miserable without you.
4   SHE: It was hell!
5   HE: Worse than hell.
6   SHE: What can we do?
7   HE: We'll visit with her and the baby several times a week. That's
8   all it amounts to.
9   SHE: For God sakes!
10 HE: It won't take anything away from you.
11 SHE: Except you.
12 HE: You've got me. I'm not going anywhere.
13 SHE: Except next door.
14 HE: *(Intensely)* I've got you and I'll never let you go.
15 SHE: You'll never let me go?
16 HE: I love you so much, it makes me tremble.
17 SHE: That's terror.
18 HE: I'm trying to be honest ...
19 SHE: You've always been honest about what *you* want. I know
20   exactly who you are, and it scares the hell out of me.
21 HE: I've got room in my heart for more, that's all.
22 SHE: How much more? Are we going to adopt Czechoslovakia?
23 HE: Sweetheart.
24 SHE: I can't give you everything you want! I don't even want to.
25 HE: I know.
26 SHE: We'd be terrible parents.
27 HE: Absolutely!
28 SHE: We *need* parents.
29 HE: Absolutely.
30 SHE: *(Desperately)* Oh, hell. Yes! Yes! I want to give you a baby! Is
31   that what you want me to say?
32 HE: No. I don't want you to be the baby's mother.
33 SHE: *(Terribly hurt)* I'll be nurturing!
34 HE: Sacrificing won't work. You'd hate the pregnancy, your
35   figure, the demands, time away from your career. And then

1   you'd hate me.
2   SHE: Just like you'll hate me if I say no. What's she like?
3   HE: I told you.
4   SHE: Not like me.
5   HE: She's not as attractive as you are. *(Beat)* She's kind.
6   SHE: Not like me.
7   HE: The world needs career people too.
8   SHE: She can't do what I do.
9   HE: That's right. Your work is very unique.
10   SHE: But you prefer that slutty heifer!
11   HE: Where do you get off insulting a woman because she's nice?!
12   SHE: *(Overlap)* Mooooo!
13   HE: *(Overlap)* You hopeless bitch!
14   SHE: You think you can have it all because your crazy mother
15   handed you the world on a silver Ferrari.
16   HE: Don't you malign kindness because you don't understand it.
17   Not everyone's a paranoid like you!
18   SHE: You want to leave me! Admit it!
19   HE: She was right. She said you'd throw a fit! We knew you'd ...
20   SHE: Oh, excuse me for being paranoid!
21   HE: Stop it, Hon! Stop it! You're doing this crazy stuff to us again.
22   SHE: *What?*
23   HE: What do you really want? Bottom line.
24   SHE: You. All to myself. You. Not wanting a baby. You. Not hating
25   me for saying no. You and me. That's all.
26   HE: That's all I want. You and me.
27   SHE: And baby makes three. And Mamma makes four.
28   HE: *Alright! Alright!* Damn it. Maybe I can't have everything!
29   SHE: My God! Did you really say that?
30   HE: Forget everything I said.
31   SHE: What? You don't really mean it.
32   HE: Maybe it's a passing thing, you know, wanting to be a father.
33   SHE: Now, hey.
34   HE: I lost my passion for sailing.
35   SHE: You got seasick.

1   HE: Maybe I can make myself seasick when I think of babies.
2   SHE: Is she the only solution?
3   HE: She's the only woman I ever met who wants my child and
4   doesn't want to get married.
5   SHE: And you're the only man she knows who wants her to have
6   his child and doesn't want to marry her.
7   HE: Right.
8   SHE: Thank God you found each other.
9   HE: Funny how things work out.
10   SHE: Listen! Is that the bus?
11   HE: Yes.
12   SHE: Well?
13   HE: Will you talk to her?
14   SHE: Did we ever dream we'd be this adult? *(Knocking)*
15   HE: She's knocking.
16   SHE: *(Angrily)* Why doesn't she use the doorbell?
17   HE: Broken.
18   SHE: *(Angrily)* You still haven't fixed it?
19   HE: Priorities.
20   SHE: It's been broken a long time!
21   HE: Yes, a very long time.
22   SHE: You should fix it!
23   HE: *(Beat)* We both should fix it.
24   SHE: *(Beat)* You and me? *(Pause. Softens)* A project for two?
25   HE: Just for two.
26   SHE: *(Smiles.)* We've always fixed it before.
27   HE: *(Laughs.)* We've got so much invested in the thing.
28   SHE: Will you really try?
29   HE: With all my heart.
30   SHE: *(Relief)* Thank God! I love you.
31   HE: I love you. *(Pause. Softly)* Darling.
32   SHE: Yes?
33   HE: Would you mind answering the door?
34   *The End*
35

Absolution
by William Reynolds

William Reynolds earned an M.F.A. from Rutgers University in writing for stage and screen. His play *Something or Nothing* was produced by Rutgers.

Absolution was selected for inclusion in the New Play Development Workshop of the Playwrights Program of the Association for Theatre in Higher Education at ATHE's national convention in Atlanta in 1992.

Production Suggestions

Resist any temptation to turn this into some kind of anti-religious satire. The comedy focuses on the characters' personality quirks, not their religion. Whether you're playing Bobby or the Priest, if you're not Catholic you'll want to do a little research so you understand the religious backgrounds of the play and can believably execute the rituals portrayed.

The character of Bobby may be played as either a boy or a girl. If the latter case is preferred, simply replace all references to "my boy," "my son," and "good boy" with "my girl," "my child," and "good kid," respectively. In programs the name should be spelled "Bobbie" (for Roberta). Also "Melinda's boy" should become "Sam's daughter."

Address all inquiries concerning performances, readings, or reprinting of this work *or any portion thereof* to William Reynolds, 12342 Hunters Chase Drive #2425, Austin, TX 78729. For details, see "Part II: Securing Rights for Your Production," pages 241 to 250.

1   The action takes place in a confessional box in a Catholic church.
2   ***CHARACTERS:*** BOBBY — a very intense young person with an air
3   of desperation. A PRIEST — rather sleepy-eyed, reading a copy
4   of *True Detective.*
5   ***SETTING:*** The confessional box has a partition between the priest's
6   portion and the penitent's portion so that they can't see each other;
7   if possible, the partition should have a small window to speak
8   through. The actors may dispense entirely with the partition as
9   long as their mannerisms make clear that it is present.
10
11   *(The PRIEST yawns and rubs his face in a feeble attempt to wake*
12   *up. But upon hearing sounds of approaching footsteps, he sits up*
13   *and puts the comic book away. BOBBY enters the other side of the*
14   *box and eagerly slides the little window open. He wipes his brow,*
15   *takes a deep breath, and begins to speak.)*
16   **BOBBY: Bless me, Father, for I have sinned. My last confession**
17   **was a week ago.** *(PRIEST nods absently.)* **Father ... Father, are**
18   **you there?**
19   **PRIEST: Hm? What? Uh, yes, my son, go ahead.**
20   **BOBBY: I mean, I've *really* sinned.**
21   **PRIEST: Go on. I'm listening.**
22   **BOBBY: It's too terrible. I'd better warn you.**
23   **PRIEST: Nothing is too terrible for the ears of our Lord. You go**
24   **right on ahead.**
25   **BOBBY: I mean, really terrible.**
26   **PRIEST: Don't be worried, my son. I hear terrible things every**
27   **day. Nature of the priesthood, you know.**
28   **BOBBY: You'll be shocked.**
29   **PRIEST: My dear boy, I will listen with the patience of Job. Only**
30   **please get on with it.** *(He picks up his magazine and glances over*
31   *the cover.)*
32   **BOBBY: I've ... oh, God ... I can't even say it.**
33   **PRIEST: It's all right, my boy. Spit it out.**
34   **BOBBY: I've killed someone.**
35   **PRIEST: I see.** *(Sudden realization)* **Killed someone! ... *Killed* someone?**

1   **BOBBY:** Yes.

2   **PRIEST:** *(Breathless excitement)* **Goodness gracious. That** *is*

3   **something.** *(He rubs his eyes roughly, leans forward.)*

4   **BOBBY:** So you see, Father ... I'm a murderer.

5   **PRIEST:** Well, what do you know about that. How did you do it? I

6   mean, how did it happen?

7   **BOBBY:** It was one of those moments. I just lost control. I can't

8   explain why ...

9   **PRIEST:** Yes, yes, yes. Only what did you *do?*

10   **BOBBY:** I ... It was Ms. Sobel. My teacher. She's had it in for me all

11   semester. Yesterday she kept me after school. She said I

12   plagiarized my term paper. I told her I didn't, I *told* her, but she

13   just laughed. She said she was going to keep me from

14   graduating, and tell my parents ... I was scared to go home, so I

15   just wandered around, I didn't know what I was doing. Anyway,

16   I saw her, out by the rear door, on her way home. And in my

17   head, she was still laughing ... and next thing I knew, I had her

18   by the neck. She tried to yell, but she couldn't, her windpipe was

19   shut off. Then she stopped struggling ... she fell ...

20   **PRIEST:** No blood, then.

21   **BOBBY:** *(Thrown)* **What?**

22   **PRIEST:** Oh, uh, I mean ... *(Picks up his magazine.)* **Strangling.**

23   **Only leaves marks, you know. The only bleeding comes from**

24   **burst blood vessels in the eyes.**

25   **BOBBY:** *(Pause)* **That's gross ... Where was I?**

26   **PRIEST:** We'd just strangled her. So, would you say you're like the

27   **Unavoidable Felon?**

28   **BOBBY:** The what?

29   **PRIEST:** *(Consulting the magazine)* **Oh, you know.** *(Half reading)*

30   "You felt your back was against the wall. It was kill or be

31   killed ... "

32   **BOBBY:** Well, yes, that's what it was. Still, there's no excusing —

33   **PRIEST:** Amazing! Why didn't I catch this on the evening news!

34   Was it on TV?

35   **BOBBY:** No. I mean yes. She was. Last night. But I took it away.

1   The body. Into the river.

2 BOBBY: What river?

3 BOBBY: Who cares what river?!

4 PRIEST: I'm just curious —

5 BOBBY: I'm baring my soul and you ask me what river!

6 PRIEST: Fine, fine, don't get upset.

7 BOBBY: It doesn't matter what river!

8 PRIEST: You're right, I shouldn't be so nosy. Only if you're not

9   willing to discuss the matter, then why exactly are you here?

10 BOBBY: Because I want to confess!

11 PRIEST: Are you going to the police?

12 BOBBY: The police! Who cares about the police? I need to clear

13   my soul! Aren't you shocked by any of this?

14 PRIEST: Oh yes, terrible. *(Confidentially)* Only ... can you tell

15   me ... what did you *feel?* Looking down at that cold body,

16   realizing what you'd done. How does that *feel?*

17 BOBBY: It ... I don't know, it feels awful. Why?

18 PRIEST: Well, I've certainly never murdered anyone. And to

19   actually have a chance to talk to a cold-blooded killer!

20 BOBBY: Father! ...

21 PRIEST: They say it's a thrill, you know. Murderers on talk shows,

22   they all say that. They get this icy feeling all down their spine.

23   Were you thrilled? You know, in an icy sort of way?

24 BOBBY: What in the world are you, some kind of sicko maniac?

25 PRIEST: *(Astonished and puzzled)* But ...

26 BOBBY: I mean, I was thrilled. Yeah, right. I was thrilled.

27 PRIEST: *(After a pause, frowning)* I see. *(Slumping back in his chair)*

28   Was there anything else?

29 BOBBY: Anything *else?* What kind of priest are you? I've

30   committed murder. Murder! I've broken the first

31   commandment. "Thou shalt not kill." I've killed!

32 PRIEST: Mm-hm. Refresh my memory. How did you do it again?

33 BOBBY: Uh ... I waited, around a corner —

34 PRIEST: Which hand was the knife in?

35 BOBBY: What?

1   PRIEST: You don't remember, do you?

2   BOBBY: What ... I do! ... Left.

3   PRIEST: Then you stabbed her after you strangled her?

4   BOBBY: Hang on! You're confusing me!

5   PRIEST: You're confusing yourself. *(Sighs.)* You really should've

6   rehearsed this a little more, you know, before trying it out.

7   Out of respect for my intelligence if nothing else.

8   BOBBY: You have to believe me.

9   PRIEST: Oh, honestly. Any devoted reader of *Detective Magazine*

10   knows that the true murderer doesn't get flustered recalling the

11   details of his crime. *(Sighs.)* Well, I for one am pretty let down.

12   BOBBY: You don't believe me.

13   PRIEST: Not in the least. Now, what is it you want from me?

14   BOBBY: I ... want to be absolved.

15   PRIEST: But, my son, you haven't *done* anything! ...

16   BOBBY: *(Exasperated)* Oh, poop! *(A beat)* Excuse me.

17   PRIEST: That's all right. Now ... why are you here? Really.

18   BOBBY: Father ... do you know who I am?

19   PRIEST: No. You don't have to identify yourself if you don't

20   want to.

21   BOBBY: I do. I'm Robert Mackenzie.

22   PRIEST: Bobby Mackenzie? The kid on the track team who set the

23   record for the —

24   BOBBY: Yeah, yeah.

25   PRIEST: You're Melinda's boy, aren't you? Why, I've never heard

26   anything but compliments about you. Why do you want to go

27   inventing murder stories about yourself? You're a good kid ...

28   BOBBY: Don't say that! I'm sick of that!

29   PRIEST: Ah ...

30   BOBBY: That's all I ever get. Bobby the track star. Bobby the A

31   student ...

32   PRIEST: Bobby the Good Kid.

33   BOBBY: Exactly! I can't do any wrong! Even when I tried to skip

34   school. I got bored sitting at home and wrote my term paper

35   instead. I won a prize and a scholarship.

1 PRIEST: Well, we all have our burdens.

2 BOBBY: OK, OK. Maybe it's selfish of me.

3 PRIEST: Maybe.

4 BOBBY: I'm tired of being the Good Boy. I want to be bad, feel
5 guilty, get yelled at. I want to rob a bank. I want to ... bite a
6 dog.

7 PRIEST: Bite a dog?

8 BOBBY: You see? I can't even think bad! I never do anything
9 shocking. I don't even know how. I'm so perfect. I ... I don't
10 have a life!

11 PRIEST: Ah. Yes. I know how you feel.

12 BOBBY: You do not.

13 PRIEST: Not the perfection bit, of course. We're none of us
14 qualified for that. Only I certainly do know what it's like to be
15 bored with the same old thing. What do you think it's like
16 sitting in this booth listening to other people's lives all day?

17 BOBBY: At least you get to hear what real life is about.

18 PRIEST: Real life. The province of the extremely bored and boring,
19 my son. This is a very dry month for transgressions. I actually got
20 a confession from a chronic jaywalker once. *(Crossing himself)*
21 God rest his soul ... Yesterday I had to listen to a woman
22 describe her sinful thoughts about the doctor who scrapes her
23 feet. And she was the highlight of my week. You're the only
24 interesting confession I've had all year. And you had to make it
25 up. What kind of excitement is that? Thanks for nothing.

26 BOBBY: I'm sorry.

27 PRIEST: Ah, well. You tried ... Listen, it's my turn to make a
28 confession to you.

29 BOBBY: To me?

30 PRIEST: I used to dream about being a secret agent. All that seat-of-
31 the-pants stuff, you know. James Bond, marvelous stuff. I've
32 seen *Dr. No* eight times. That beats Father Johnson's record.

33 BOBBY: Huh. From secret agent to priest.

34 PRIEST: I know, I know. But I ended up doing what was right for
35 me. Not everybody can be James Bond, you know. The world

1   needs ... well, Good Kids.

2 BOBBY: *(A beat)* It's not as much fun.

3 PRIEST: No. But you leave less of a mess behind you.

4 BOBBY: So you're saying I'm better off being me.

5 PRIEST: You make it sound like a curse! A lot of people would
6   love to be Bobby Mackenzie, you know. You actually did it.
7   Congratulate yourself.

8 BOBBY: Thanks. You're OK, too. I mean, you do good work.

9 PRIEST: Thank you.

10 BOBBY: I'm sorry about ... you know, trying to shock you ...

11 PRIEST: Oh, think nothing of it, my son! I was really awake there
12   for a minute. Only who knows, next time it could be the real
13   thing! Now couldn't it! A man can dream.

14 BOBBY: *(Getting up)* I guess I just wanted ... I don't know. I'm so
15   tired of doing everything right.

16 PRIEST: I wish I could help you, really.

17 BOBBY: Oh, never mind. I'm doomed to goodness. Just plain
18   doomed. Thanks for trying ...

19 PRIEST: *(Sudden thought, snapping his fingers)* Just a minute there.
20   I'm not through with you.

21 BOBBY: What?

22 PRIEST: Sit down!

23 BOBBY: But ... you said yourself, I haven't done anything.

24 PRIEST: You call lying to a man of the cloth *nothing?* Do you
25   realize that when you lie to me, you're lying to God?

26 BOBBY: *(Stunned)* I ... I didn't think about it —

27 PRIEST: That's right. You didn't think. Adam and Eve didn't
28   think when they committed original sin, you know. Only that
29   wasn't good enough. God called Adam and Eve to account,
30   and what did they say? "We weren't thinking. It wasn't our
31   fault. We're just having an off day." Whereupon God said,
32   "Right! Out you go!" and stuck them out in the wasteland
33   with barely a fig leaf to call their own. You can go to hell for
34   this sort of thing!

35 BOBBY: I'm sorry, I —

1   **PRIEST:** *(More and more excited)* **I'm talking hellfire, boy! Hellfire**
2   **and bloody damnation! Hell has a special stinking hole for**
3   **liars! The blackest, stinkingest pit in all of the underworld!**
4   **Hot lava and blazing flame rains down upon their writhing**
5   **bodies! And I'm not just talking about a little hopping around**
6   **either! These bodies** *writhe!*
7   **BOBBY:** *(Speechless)* **Gosh! ...**
8   **PRIEST: You'll have to do a great deal better than that. You go**
9   **away and say at least ten Hail Marys and ten Our Fathers and**
10   **don't you set foot in this holy place again until you're**
11   **properly atoned, you little heathen!**
12   **BOBBY: Y-yes, Father.** *(Beaming)* **Wow! ...** *(They are both glowing*
13   *with satisfaction.)*
14   **PRIEST: How was that for some cooking?**
15   **BOBBY: Yeah, that was great. Wow! ...** *(A beat)* **Father? ... Are**
16   **you here at this time every week?**
17   **PRIEST: Where else would I be? I've got no life.** *(BOBBY smiles,*
18   *closes the window, and leaves the box. The PRIEST sighs blankly*
19   *to himself, picks up his "True Detective," and begins to read. He*
20   *then reconsiders, puts the comic book away, and sits up in his*
21   *chair, eagerly awaiting the next confession.)*
22   *The End*
23
24
25
26
27
28
29
30
31
32
33
34
35

The Society
by J. Omar Hansen

Omar Hansen teaches at Brigham Young University – Idaho.

The Society was given a staged reading at the New Play Development Workshop of the Playwrights Program of the Association for Theatre in Higher Education at ATHE's national convention at Seattle in 1991. Later that year it received its premiere production at Salt Lake City's Theatre Works West.

Production Suggestions

Although the playwright conceived of these two characters as male, nothing about this is gender-specific; the play would work equally well with two actresses in the roles or with one male and one female actor. The script permits a variety of styles, tempos, and characterizations; experiment until you find the mode that seems to you to fit best.

Address all inquiries concerning performances, readings, or reprinting of this work *or any portion thereof* to J. Omar Hansen, 4497 S. Cameron Lane, Rexburg, ID 83440. For details, see "Part II: Securing Rights for Your Production," pages 241 to 250.

1   The action takes place in a room.
2   ***CHARACTERS:*** BYRON, KEATS.
3   ***SETTING:*** The room has a table and two chairs. There is one door —
4   closed — and no windows.
5
6   *(Two men are in the room. One is asleep at the table and the other*
7   *sits looking at him. After a beat KEATS bangs on the table and*
8   *BYRON wakes up. They begin.)*
9   **BYRON:** Well.
10   **KEATS:** Yes, well. I agree.
11   **BYRON:** It has been a long time.
12   **KEATS:** It has. A year to be exact.
13   **BYRON:** I am overwhelmed.
14   **KEATS:** We must begin.
15   **BYRON:** Of course, you are right.** *(The two men take their seats at*
16   *the ends of the table. BYRON stands.)* **Let it be known that the**
17   **society of Poets of the World and the Universe comes now to**
18   **a poetic order.**
19   **KEATS:** Nice touch.
20   **BYRON:** Thank you. We shall be favored to hear the minutes read.
21   *(BYRON sits down and KEATS rises with a sheet of line paper.)*
22   **KEATS:** I will now read the minutes of the last meeting. Minutes
23   **read. Opening remarks. Poetry read. Lively discussion. No.**
24   **bloodshed. Dues collected. Closing remarks.** *(KEATS sits.)*
25   **BYRON:** Thank you. We will now have the opening remarks.
26   **Gentlemen, the state of the arts is at an all-time low. The**
27   **theatre is dead. Has been for years. The painterly arts are in**
28   **flux. Music remains melodic and therefore dubious and**
29   **inconsequential. Film never really was an art form. The novel**
30   **is fare for the masses, and the short story gets longer every**
31   **year. It is poetry, and poetry alone, that remains a viable art.**
32   **And why, you will ask? Simply put: we have escaped the foul**
33   **dredge of meaning. The putrid cesspool of reason. We are art**
34   **and art is us. We are poetry and therein a light in and of**
35   **ourselves.** *(KEATS starts to applaud. BYRON stares at KEATS*

1	*with irritation. KEATS stops.)* **We bind ourselves to no outside**
2	**order. Order is chaos. Chaos is order. Here, in this place, and**
3	**this place alone, may the muses reside and flourish.** *(BYRON*
4	*sits down. KEATS applauds loudly.)*
5	**KEATS: Dear me.**
6	**BYRON: Thank you.**
7	**KEATS: That was beautiful.**
8	**BYRON: You are too kind.**
9	**KEATS: I think I must weep.**
10	**BYRON: Don't.**
11	**KEATS: Poetic.**
12	**BYRON: Yes.**
13	**KEATS: The report from the secretary?**
14	**BYRON: Funding has stopped. The government refuses aid.**
15	**KEATS: Death to all tyrants, the presidency to all morons!**
16	**BYRON: Calm yourself.**
17	**KEATS: You are right ... I move we proceed with the reading of**
18	**new works commissioned after last year's conference.**
19	**BYRON: I second. Who shall begin?**
20	**KEATS: May I?**
21	**BYRON: By all means.**
22	**KEATS:** *(KEATS stands. A pause)* **"Trample" ... Horse's hoof ... on**
23	**my ... flat face.** *(He sits. BYRON sits staring in awe.)*
24	**BYRON: What brevity ... I could see it ... The horse ... the hoof ...**
25	**the face. It is a masterpiece. It is utterly meaningless.**
26	**KEATS: You are too kind.**
27	**BYRON: May I?**
28	**KEATS: Oh yes, please. We are off to such a good start.**
29	**BYRON:** *(He stands and puts on reading glasses.)* **"Going to the**
30	**park, and being very cold on a winter's night in Manhattan,**
31	**when I thought I loved, but it was nothing."**
32	**KEATS: That's the title?**
33	**BYRON:** *(Taken aback)* **Yes.**
34	**KEATS: Oh, but I like it. I do. Very poetic.**
35	**BYRON: Oh. Do you think so?**

1   KEATS: Oh, yes. Absolutely.
2   BYRON: ... Ashen black frostbite ... toes ... purple pain ... *(A*
3   *small envelope is pushed under the door. KEATS sees it.)* ... **you,**
4   **black-brown lipped ...**
5   KEATS: Did you see that?
6   BYRON: What?
7   KEATS: There by the door.
8   BYRON: I'm not done.
9   KEATS: Someone pushed an envelope under the door.
10   BYRON: But I'm not done.
11   KEATS: Someone has pushed ...
12   BYRON: It's not fair.
13   KEATS: I ...
14   BYRON: You got to read yours.
15   KEATS: But someone has pushed an envelope under the door.
16   *(This registers to BYRON for the first time. He gasps.)* **Should we**
17   **see what it is?**
18   BYRON: You mean it came from the other side of the door?
19   KEATS: Yes. I don't know what it could mean.
20   BYRON: *(Frightened)* Well, perhaps one of us should see what it is.
21   KEATS: Yes, I agree.
22   BYRON: *(He doesn't want to.)* Do you want me to?
23   KEATS: Well, I'll do it.
24   BYRON: All right. *(KEATS walks over to the door and picks up the*
25   *envelope. He looks at the door with a worried glance and then*
26   *back at BYRON.)*
27   KEATS: Perhaps we should call out to see who put it under the ...
28   BYRON: No! No, don't! It could be the ruin of the society! *(KEATS*
29   *jumps away from the door.)* **What is it?**
30   KEATS: *(He opens the envelope.)* **Why ... it's a poem. It's a poem.**
31   **Do you want me to read it?**
32   BYRON: No, no, it's from the outside. I think we ought to put it
33   back where it ...
34   KEATS: It's rather interesting.
35   BYRON: You didn't read it did you?

1   KEATS: I did. I want to read it to the society.

2   BYRON: I am against it.

3   KEATS: We must be bold.

4   BYRON: Very well. It's on your head. *(BYRON goes to his seat and*

5   *sits. KEATS walks to his seat and stands and then reads.)*

6   KEATS: So much depends ... on what I write ... and what they

7   think ... But never the twain shall meet. *(A long pause)*

8   BYRON: It smacks of meaning!

9   KEATS: What?

10   BYRON: I'll say it again! It smacks of meaning.

11   KEATS: I think you're right. What do we do?

12   BYRON: Put it back.

13   KEATS: Under the door?

14   BYRON: Yes, yes!

15   KEATS: Now?

16   BYRON: The sooner the better. *(KEATS walks over to the door and*

17   *kneels down and almost pushes it under. He stops.)*

18   KEATS: Why do you think they pushed it to us?

19   BYRON: To corrupt us. They want to corrupt us! Push it back!

20   KEATS: But ... the door ... this has never happened before.

21   There's someone out there.

22   BYRON: Corruption.

23   KEATS: Really?

24   BYRON: If you won't push it back at least leave it on the floor and

25   read some more poetry. Come ... read.

26   KEATS: Perhaps you're right.

27   BYRON: Read another of your poems.

28   KEATS: But yours wasn't finished.

29   BYRON: That's all right. Read. *(KEATS looks at the table for a*

30   *minute and then stands with another poem. He looks at the*

31   *envelope by the door.)* Don't look at it! *(KEATS looks away. He*

32   *looks again at his poem.)*

33   KEATS: "The Night" ... Cool blackness ... More of less ... It is a ...

34   BYRON: That rhymed!

35   KEATS: No it didn't.

1   BYRON: Yes it did. You read a rhyme.

2   KEATS: No I didn't!

3   BYRON: I know a read rhyme when it rends my ear. That was a
4   rhyme.

5   KEATS: Well ... perhaps. Sometimes I like rhyme.

6   BYRON: What?

7   KEATS: I like rhymes!

8   BYRON: I don't believe it. The corruption has started. That
9   envelope! It will be the ruin of us all. I must destroy it!
10   *(BYRON lunges towards the envelope but KEATS overtakes him*
11   *and physically keeps him from the envelope.)* Let me destroy it,
12   I tell you!

13 KEATS: Stop it! Stop it! You're being absurd!

14 BYRON: Thank you.

15 KEATS: I didn't mean it as a compliment.

16 BYRON: How else should I take it?

17 KEATS: I'm going out the door.

18 BYRON: *(BYRON gasps in horror.)* No!

19 KEATS: I think I must.

20 BYRON: You don't understand. You are young. There is
21   corruption out there. There is meaning out there!

22 KEATS: How do you know?

23 BYRON: I can't tell you!

24 KEATS: *(He goes to BYRON and confronts him.)* I want to know!

25 BYRON: *(Sobbing, he falls to his knees.)* I can't! Don't make me.
26   Please don't make me!

27 KEATS: *(He grabs BYRON by the lapel.)* *Tell me!*

28 BYRON: *(Slowly)* ... I know ... because I went through the door!
29   But I was lucky. I saw the corruption. I saw meaning and
30   knew it would destroy me. How I found the room again, I
31   don't know. But you mustn't try it. You won't return. Others
32   have gone. The society remains here. But they don't return.
33   Please, listen to me.

34 KEATS: But what did it mean? Never the twain shall meet?

35 BYRON: Don't you see what's happening to you? You asked what

1   it meant. Do you hear what you said?

2   KEATS: Did I say that?

3   BYRON: You did. *(KEATS walks over to the door and picks up the*

4   *envelope.)* **Don't do it! Don't do it! ... Push it back under.**

5   **Come away from the door.** *(For a long pause KEATS stands with*

6   *the envelope in his hand. Finally he pushes it back under the door.*

7   *He walks slowly back to BYRON who embraces him.)* **Dear boy,**

8   **you have won. The battle is won ... I think we should continue**

9   **... But no more poems. After this they might be perceived as**

10   **purposeful. Come, let's return and finish the conference.**

11   **There still is left the collection of dues.** *(They both go back to the*

12   *table. BYRON takes a plate that was sitting on the table, blows off*

13   *the dust and pushes it over to KEATS' side of the table. KEATS*

14   *looks at it with a worried look. He feels in his pocket. He pushes*

15   *the plate over to BYRON's side of the table. BYRON turns and*

16   *sees it. He looks a little embarrassed.)* **... Now for the final**

17   **remarks ... Once again we are reaffirmed. We are the last**

18   **bastion of artistry. We live to be as art.**

19   KEATS: That's very beautiful.

20   BYRON: Thank you. We are adjourned. Come embrace me. It has

21   been a marvelous experience.

22   KEATS: Yes.

23   BYRON: Till next year?

24   KEATS: Next year. *(BYRON smiles and then goes to a corner of the*

25   *room farthest from the door. He lays down and sleeps. KEATS*

26   *watches him and then looks at the door. He walks over to BYRON*

27   *and sees that he is asleep. He looks at the door and then at*

28   *BYRON. He walks to the door. He tries the knob and it opens. He*

29   *looks back at BYRON. He exits out the door. BYRON begins to*

30   *snore quietly as the lights fade to black.)*

31   *The End*

32

33

34

35

To the Airport
by Julianne Bernstein

Julianne Bernstein Theodoropulos received her M.F.A. in playwriting from Rutgers University and serves as guest artist and teacher for Thespian festivals throughout the country, at McCarter Theatre in Princeton, and at George Street Playhouse in New Jersey.

Playwright's Production Suggestions

Do not take for granted how important *talking* and *listening* are to the development of Ted and Marcia's relationship and to the successful presentation of this play. Marcia's problem is that she doesn't listen; Ted gets her to do that. Ted is afraid to express himself; Marcia encourages him to do so. Also, work with the physical reality of your play — Marcia yelling to the sixth floor of an apartment building from the street below as well as from inside the taxicab; the sights and sounds of traffic; and of course, Kennedy Airport — approaching it, arriving, and turning around. It is a simple play that requires close attention to detail and your acting partner.

Address all inquiries concerning performances, readings, or reprinting of this work *or any portion thereof* to Julianne Theodoropulos, 811 Corinthian Avenue, Philadelphia, PA 19130. For details, see "Part II: Securing Rights for Your Production," pages 241 to 250.

1   The action takes place in New York City.

2   ***CHARACTERS:*** MARCIA — in her early thirties. TED — a taxicab

3   driver.

4   ***SETTING:*** The play begins in front of a high-rise apartment building.

5   TED's taxi is represented by the cab's seats — six straight chairs

6   arranged in two rows.

7

8   *(TED sits in his taxicab. He is parked and waiting. He beeps the*

9   *horn, which sounds twice. He pulls out a postcard from his shirt*

10   *pocket, reads it, smiles and puts it back. He beeps the horn again.*

11   *He looks at his clipboard, confirms the address, gets out, goes*

12   *around the cab and looks up. He gets back in the taxicab. He*

13   *switches from "park" to "drive" when the sound of a large heavy*

14   *door slamming and a woman's voice is heard.)*

15   **WOMAN'S VOICE: You bastard! I don't care if you stay and rot!**

16.   **Along with the Chinese take-out you took out last Friday!**

17   **Don't you follow me! I don't want to see your face!** *(It is*

18   *MARCIA. She enters with several large suitcases. She throws*

19   *them down on the ground and speaks Upstage Right, as if she's*

20   *yelling to the sixth floor of a high-rise.)* **Don't follow me! You**

21   **hear me?!** *(TED honks the horn.)*

22   **MARCIA:** *(To TED)* **Yeah, yeah. I'm comin'.**

23   **TED: If this isn't a good time, I could come back later.**

24   **MARCIA: And what am I gonna do with you *later?* Kennedy**

25   **Airport. *Now!***

26   **TED: You sure you wanna get in this cab? In your state of mind?**

27   **MARCIA: If you're here to make my life miserable, you can take a**

28   **number.** *(Pause)* **Bobby?! Hey, Bobby, do you hear me?!**

29   **TED:** *(Pause)* **I can't believe he don't hear ya.**

30   **MARCIA:** *(To TED)* **Shut off that goddamn engine. Shut it off!**

31   **TED: I got the meter goin'.**

32   **MARCIA: For what? You're charging me to stand on the curb? To**

33   **mind my own business? Did you hear me? I said shut if off!** *(He*

34   *does so.)* **I'm tired of it! Five years I'm with you, what do I get?**

35   ***No* ring. *No* promise, even. I'm tellin' you. A dishwasher is no**

1   real sign of love. No, sir. You can't even say it. "Marriage,"
2   Bobby. The word is "marriage." I can see it now. My fortieth
3   birthday. My fiftieth. And still no ring. You'll bring me another
4   sweet, forget-me-not appliance, you will. *(Pause)* A little gold
5   won't kill you, Bobby. A little gold won't break you!
6 TED: Excuse me, but —
7 MARCIA: *(To TED)* What? What?!
8 TED: Two-thirty-five West 41st? Sixth floor? Is that who you're
9   talkin' to? The sixth floor?
10 MARCIA: No, I got a special problem with my neck, and I'm
11   talking to the couple in the basement. Come on. The bags.
12   They're growing mold out here. *(TED gets out; he loads the*
13   *baggage in the trunk. MARCIA looking up)* And don't call. You
14   better not call. I'm changing my name. The long distance
15   operator'll laugh in your face. "Who?" "Marcia who?" they'll
16   ask. "Who the hell you talkin' about?" "There's no ... " Aha!
17   You thought I'd say it ... my name. My new name. Well,
18   forget it! *(TED Is finished loading the suitcases. He walks up to*
19   *her and opens her door.)* What's this? Limo service? I'll open
20   my own door, thank you. *(She gets in and slides to the left.*
21   *TED's about to shut the door.)* I'll shut my own door. Double
22   thank you! *(Leaving the door open, he steps around to the front,*
23   *and gets into the driver's seat. MARCIA slides back to the right to*
24   *shut the door, but instead, gets out again.)* I'm shutting this door,
25   Bobby. I got my hand on the handle and I'm closin' it shut! Do
26   you hear me?! *(Pause)* Do you get what I'm sayin'?!
27 TED: Lady, I got a life, too, you know!
28 MARCIA: *(Quickly moving into the cab, and "threatening him at*
29   *gunpoint")* Go ahead. Start the meter. I dare you. *(Calling out*
30   *the window)* I'm leavin' now, Bobby? Bobby, you hear me?
31   You can start cryin'. Shed those buckets, Bucko! Cry! Cry!
32   Cry! *(She slams the door shut, sits still, and listens. After a beat)*
33   Turn the key. *(Pause)* Turn the key, I said. *(He does. Sound of*
34   *the engine is heard.)* Hear that, Bobby? *(She slides to the middle*
35   *of the seat.)* Go. *(Pause)* Drive. *(He switches gears, checks his*

1   *· mirror and drives.)*ₜ

2   TED: *(He does so.)* **Boy, he sure did a number on you. At least he**

3   **didn't throw you and your Wandering Jew out on the**

4   **pavement!**

5   MARCIA: **What?!**

6   TED: **I had a pick-up in Queens just last night. This nice lookin'**

7   **guy. He had real good skin. Sittin' there with a pillowcase full**

8   **of clothes and his favorite Wandering Jew wandering all over**

9   **the street. He didn't know what to do. The roots were torn to**

10   **pieces — all the leaves were flyin' towards Flatbush.**

11   MARCIA: **So? What do you want? A** *medal* **for pickin' him up? A**

12   *prize* **for doin' your job? All you guys — you want medals,**

13   **trophies for just gettin' up in the mornin'!** *(Pause)* **Just get me**

14   **out of here. I wanna go — go where no** *man* **has gone before.**

15   TED: **Yeah? Where's that? You goin' overseas?**

16   MARCIA: **Yeah. Overseas. Way overseas.**

17   TED: **Yeah? Wow. Can you believe I got no postcards from**

18   **overseas? Plenty of domestics, but not a single card from**

19   **overseas.**

20   MARCIA: **What the hell are you talkin' about?** *(He pulls out his*

21   *card; he hands it to her.)* **What am I supposed to do with this?**

22   TED: **Write me. I'll write you back.**

23   MARCIA: **Excuse me?**

24   TED: **But I gotta have your address. Your zip code.**

25   MARCIA: **That's goddamn ridiculous. That's goddamn illegal.**

26   TED: **Hey, there's no way it'll work without the zip. It'll get lost**

27   **and chewed up by those U.S. Postal pigs. It's gotta have a zip.**

28   **You got mine. Now gimme yours. I'll write you.**

29   MARCIA: **What? Like a letter?**

30   TED: **Or a card if that's your pleasure.**

31   MARCIA: **What the hell for?**

32   TED: **Hey, it sounds like you could use your own personal Abby.**

33   MARCIA: **Who?**

34   TED: **Abby. Dear Abby. Come on. What's your zip? Gimme your**

35   **zip.**

1   MARCIA: You're crazy. I'll give you that. You're a loonie. I'll give
2   you that much. *(Pause)* Now, be quiet. I got so much stuff tyin'
3   up my brain right now. I wish I were dead. Yeah. Pretend I'm
4   dead. Pretend you're driving a hearse. *(Silence. To herself)* He
5   don't understand. He don't listen to me. That's the problem.
6   He don't listen. He don't hear. I don't care about gettin'
7   married. I mean, I'd like it and all. But I love him. I tell him
8   that. But he don't believe me. I just want him to believe me.
9   To hear me. *(Bitingly)* Well?
10   TED: Well, what?
11   MARCIA: You hear me? Are you deaf as well?
12   TED: No. I heard.
13   MARCIA: Yeah, what'd I say? Tell me what I said.
14   TED: You said: He don't understand. That, like, he don't listen to
15   you. That *that's* the problem. That, like, he don't listen. That
16   he don't hear. That you don't care about like gettin' married.
17   You'd like, like it and all, but that you love him. And you tell
18   him that. But like he don't believe you. That you just want
19   him to believe you. To hear you. *(Pause)* Well?
20   MARCIA: *(Pause)* Right. You got it. Word for word. Like you got
21   the back seat bugged.
22   TED: You know the best thing? Gettin' cards from places I dream
23   about. I mean, I had a pick-up on Times Square 'bout a year
24   ago, and guess where he was from? Guess.
25   MARCIA: I don't know. Paris?
26   TED: Kansas. I pick him up in the middle of Times Square, right
27   under the Sony sign. Another real nice guy. Though his skin
28   wasn't as clear. But we got to talkin'. Turns out he came to
29   New York City to be somethin'. I don't know what. He didn't
30   know what. It didn't work out. So we struck up a
31   correspondence, and now I get cards from Kansas. Corn
32   country and all that. I got Kansas all over my kitchen. How
33   about it? All I need is the zip on two-thirty-five West —
34   MARCIA: I'm leavin'. That's not my zip code anymore. I'm
35   leavin'. Get it? I'm leavin'. *(Silence)*

1 TED: How come?
2 MARCIA: I don't know.
3 TED: Me, neither. I mean here and now. I don't know. But via the
4   U.S. mail, I usually got this figured by now. Now, I'm aware of
5   the rising cost of postage these days; I can't help that — but
6   my advice will always be first-rate.
7 MARCIA: You know. That's all I ever wanted from him. Was his
8   first-rate effort. I mean, I know he's gettin' old. Me, too. We're
9   not runnin' naked through the living room to get to the Jiffy
10   Pop popcorn anymore. It's just what happens after so many
11   years. And sex is ... well ... it is what it is.
12 TED: It is?
13 MARCIA: It is.
14 TED: Sounds like you're going through maybe a mid-life thing.
15 MARCIA: Me? Mid-life? What kind of a stupid-ass thing is that to
16   say? That's supposed to *help* me? Give me direction? A
17   confirmation that I'm having a mid-life thing?
18 TED: I told you I'm no good in person, face-to-face. One on one.
19   Ah, but on a postcard or sealed up in a letter? Pure gold.
20   Believe me. Really. This one guy was writin' me all the way
21   from Delaware. You know, the valley? He was having a hell of
22   a time with his teenage daughter. She wanted to run away to
23   Soho with her boyfriend and open up a store selling *his* oil
24   paintings of traffic in Ohio and other suburbs, and *her*
25   bracelets made out of gum wrappers and little wet rocks.
26 MARCIA: Wrappers and rocks? What'd you tell the father?
27 TED: A bunch of stuff. I mean, it was pourin' out of me. Like I was
28   writin' fortune cookies or horoscopes. Like I was talkin' right
29   out of the Ten Commandments.
30 MARCIA: So? What'd you tell him?
31 TED: After six pounds of stationery, I tell him to get off his tucas
32   and go to the grand opening of his kid's store. I say to him,
33   "Your own children will show you the way." That's what I
34   wrote. Their little shop's on Bleeker Street, right next to the
35   Lebanese Deli. It's very popular.

1   MARCIA: But the father. He was against it.
2   TED: Not after he saw what a good business they were doin'. He
3   sent me a picture of his daughter. Oh, what a doll. A lovely
4   shot of her workin' behind the counter. Dressed real
5   responsible and all. A skirt with a blouse and a bow. Quite a
6   lady, you know? *(Silence)*
7   MARCIA: Uh-oh.
8   TED: What?
9   MARCIA: Just follow the road. Terminal A.
10   TED: Yeah. Quick. Gimme your zip code. We'll get a
11   correspondence goin'.
12   MARCIA: It's no good anymore.
13   TED: Come on. Just write me and tell me how you're doin'. I'll
14   interpret what I read, and tell you what I think.
15   MARCIA: No! You're not gettin' my code. It's my code. Mine.
16   TED: *(Pause)* You need me to write you.
17   MARCIA: You don't know what I need.
18   TED: Yeah, I do.
19   MARCIA: Then tell me. Tell me. Tell me everything you know and
20   make me see it in a different way. Make me see him in a
21   different way.
22   TED: Whoa. You just can't order up advice like ... like ... it's
23   a pastrami sandwich or something. I need time to think ...
24   time to ...
25   MARCIA: What? What?
26   TED: Let me have my card.
27   MARCIA: But I thought you —
28   TED: I'll give it back. I'll give it right back. *(TED takes a pen from*
29   *his shirt pocket, and the card which MARCIA hands him. He*
30   *scribbles a note on the back of the card.)*
31   MARCIA: Hey, don't write while you're drivin'.
32   TED: I've been driving for fifteen years. I can put up a house of
33   cards while I'm driving.
34   MARCIA: If we have even a little fender bender — you're dead,
35   buddy.

1   **TED:** Be quiet. This is it. This is what you been waitin' for.

2   **MARCIA:** Just shut up and take the red arrow. No, the blue. Yeah,

3   the blue ...

4   **TED:** Hang on.

5   **MARCIA:** I got a plane to catch. Let's go.

6   **TED:** What airline?

7   **MARCIA:** I'm not sure.

8   **TED:** What's your ticket say? Check your ticket.

9   **MARCIA:** Ticket?

10   **TED:** You don't have a ticket?

11   **MARCIA:** Not yet.

12   **TED:** You're expectin' to fly overseas with a ticket you bought ten

13   minutes before?

14   **MARCIA:** What's wrong with that?

15   **TED:** That's stupid. You know how much you gotta pay?

16   **MARCIA:** I got money.

17   **TED:** You need a lot if you want a ticket right up front. I mean,

18   unless you buy a year in advance, they'll charge you a

19   thousand dollars just to fly to Detroit.

20   **MARCIA:** Nobody's gonna pay that much to go to Detroit.

21   **TED:** Hey, if you're stupid enough to fly to Detroit, you deserve to

22   pay that much! *(MARCIA starts weeping.)* Hey, you're not

23   stupid. I didn't mean it.

24   **MARCIA:** I get so tired of talkin' to him about it.

25   **TED:** You call that *talkin'?* You have to yell like that? He wasn't

26   across the country, he was right there.

27   **MARCIA:** He was in the other room. In the bathroom. The shower.

28   With his Walkman over his ears. How else am I going to talk

29   to him?

30   **TED:** It sounds like he was checkin' out.

31   **MARCIA:** I know what he was doin'.

32   **TED:** *(Looking in the rear-view mirror)* Ah, get out of my face.

33   **MARCIA:** Hey, all I said was —

34   **TED:** Not you. I got these Good Humor trucks tailing me.

35   **MARCIA:** *(Pause)* I hate talkin' in the bathroom. It makes me

1   uncomfortable. *(He hands her the card. She reads.)* **After you**
2   **take a shower with him, go to the kitchen ... and pop up some**
3   **Jiffy Pop.** *(Pause)* **Forget the towel.** *(Silence. Taking a deep*
4   *breath)* **There. Follow that road right there.**
5 TED: **It takes you right out of the airport.**
6 MARCIA: **I know.**
7 TED: **You gonna be OK?**
8 MARCIA: **I'll see.** *(Pause)* **I don't have a card for me.**
9 TED: **Yeah, I know. I know.**
10 MARCIA: **But I got yours. Thanks.** *(Pause)* **20331. That's my zip.**
11   **I don't know how long that'll be it. But that's it. That's my**
12   **zip. 20331. For now, that is.**
13 TED: *(Smiling)* **20331.**
14   *The End*
15
16
17
18
19
20
21
22
23
24
25
26
27
28
29
30
31
32
33
34
35

A No Play
by Sarah Provost

Sarah Provost, playwright, poet, and screenwriter, has won multiple playwriting awards and has had her plays performed off-Broadway and at regional and university theatres. She has also published a prize-winning volume of poetry and has had several screenplays optioned for feature films and a CBS Movie of the Week.

A No Play was first produced in 1990 at the Captain Partridge Theatre of Wesleyan University in Middletown, Connecticut, with Kathleen White directing and Maggie Roberts and Andy McPhee in the roles.

Production Suggestions

During the portions of the play when your character has the one-word responses, guard against tuning out and going on automatic pilot; stay engaged with your character during these sequences, react to your partner appropriately, and make your one-word responses *meaningful*. Be sure you understand — and play — the subtext for all of your character's "no's."

Address all inquiries concerning performances, readings, or reprinting of this work *or any portion thereof* to Sarah Provost, c/o Lee Kappleman, Agency for Performing Arts, 9000 Sunset Boulevard #1200, Los Angeles, CA 90069. For details, see "Part II: Securing Rights for Your Production," pages 241 to 250.

1   The action takes place in the present in the kitchen of a middle-
2   class apartment in a medium-sized city.
3   **CHARACTERS:** ANNIE — she wears a skirt and blouse of a business
4   suit with a happi-coat as an apron. She has changed her pumps for
5   bedroom slippers. AVERY — Annie's husband. He is clad in
6   conservative business clothes.
7   **SETTING:** The play requires a kitchen table with two chairs, a stove,
8   a door, and a counter.
9
10 *(ANNIE is discovered at the stove. She sets the table for two with*
11 *wine glasses and candles and stirs a pot of tomato sauce, singing*
12 *"Yes, We Have No Bananas." AVERY drags himself through the*
13 *door carrying a briefcase, which he sets in the middle of the table.*
14 *He goes to a counter, his back to ANNIE, picks up a pile of junk*
15 *mail and sorts through it.)*
16 ANNIE: **Hi, honey! How you doing? Wasn't it a beautiful day? I do**
17 **hate to see summer end, but the fall sky is just so blue! And the**
18 **first cool weather makes me feel like cooking. So guess what**
19 **we're having tonight? La-a-a-sagna!** *(AVERY continues to sort*
20 *through the mail without looking up.)* **Avery? Didn't you hear**
21 **me?** *(He looks up briefly, a bit quizzical, then shakes his head.)*
22 AVERY: **No.**
23 ANNIE: **We're having lasagna! I hope you're hungry.**
24 AVERY: **No.**
25 ANNIE: **Not hungry for lasagna? Whoa! Are you OK?**
26 AVERY: **No.**
27 ANNIE: **Oh, poor baby! I'm sorry. What's the matter, is your**
28 **stomach upset? Do you want some Tums or something?**
29 AVERY: **No.**
30 ANNIE: **Headache?**
31 AVERY: **No.**
32 ANNIE: **Well, what is it then?** *(He shrugs and exits to the bedroom,*
33 *taking off his tie.)* **Honey? Do you want to lie down for a while?**
34 AVERY: *(Off)* **No.**
35 ANNIE: **Then come keep me company while I finish this up. I'll**

149

1   put it in the fridge and we can nuke it up tomorrow. You'll feel
2   better then, huh? *(He returns minus jacket and tie, wearing a*
3   *similar happi-coat.)*
4 AVERY: No.
5 ANNIE: Oh, I get it. We're just in a lousy mood tonight. Obviously,
6   this man needs a hug! *(He accepts her embrace briefly, then*
7   *fends her off.)* What'sa matter, baby, is Walt on your back
8   about that report? Did Adam win the football pool again?
9 AVERY: No.
10 ANNIE: Then what is it, for God's sake! Aren't you going to tell me
11   what's bothering you? *(AVERY considers for a moment, then*
12   *speaks decisively as he pours himself a hefty scotch on the rocks.)*
13 AVERY: No.
14 ANNIE: Why not? Huh? Avery? If you're not sick, and it's not a
15   problem at work ... Oh. Oh, I know. This is about the gerbil,
16   isn't it? Some busybody happened to be passing by and
17   couldn't wait to tell you about it, huh? Well, you could at least
18   do me the courtesy of hearing my side of it before you get all
19   judgmental! *(He looks up at her, mystified.)*
20   Here's what happened. See, when I went to the mall for my
21   Jazzercize class, this skirt is getting so tight, and I went by the
22   pet store — I know it's out of the way, but I always have to
23   check for kittens in the window. Don't give me that look, I'm
24   not going to bring any home, not after the fit you threw last
25   time. But oh, there was one in the window, a little baby gray
26   with long hair, absolutely gorgeous, but he was asleep, so flat
27   out, he looked like a rug. I just thought it was cute, y'know,
28   and went on to my class. But when I walked past again and it
29   was an hour later and he hadn't moved, well, I thought he
30   might be ... y'know ...
31   So I went in and asked the guy in the store — skinny kid
32   with long greasy hair — to check on the kitten, and he looked
33   at me like I was nuts and said, "He's sleeping, lady." And I
34   could tell that he was just waiting for me to leave. He wasn't
35   going to do anything! And with all that long hair, I couldn't

1   even tell if he was breathing. The cat.

2   So I told the guy I wanted to buy the cat and could I see

3   him. Well, he opened the pen and picked the kitty up, none too

4   carefully, and gave him to me. That cat could make Rip Van

5   Winkle look insomniac! He just draped himself over my arm

6   and went on sleeping, but I put my face right up next to his

7   little pink nose and I could feel that he was breathing, so I

8   gave him back. He was OK. The guy was snippy 'cause I

9   fibbed about buying it, but I felt better that I'd checked.

10   Now see, I don't usually actually go *in* the pet store 'cause

11   once I'm in there I always have to see the puppies too and all

12   the other little critters, I can't even not look at the lizards and

13   tarantulas and all the ugly stuff. So I was way in the back of

14   the store where the gerbils and hamsters and guinea pigs and

15   bunnies are — they had the cutest little miniature lop-eared

16   bunny, I'd've brought it home in a minute if ... *(AVERY shoots*

17   *her a dark look.)*

18   Well, anyway, I was back there in the Rodent Round-up

19   when I saw this little black gerbil peeking out from under the

20   cover on top of his cage! Actually I couldn't tell it was a gerbil

21   at first 'cause all I could see were his little quivery whiskers. But

22   sure enough he was on top of his cage and not in it! At first I just

23   told him he was a mighty clever little rascal, but then I began to

24   get worried. What would happen to him? Maybe he couldn't get

25   back in his cage to eat, or somebody might step on him, or lord,

26   he could even wander into the kitten's cage by mistake. Though

27   I don't suppose that snoozy little guy'd be much of a threat.

28   So anyway, I called the kid and he got all snotty, grabbed the

29   poor little thing and just threw him back in his cage! *Threw*

30   him! I tried to talk sensibly to him about how he shouldn't be

31   working in a pet store if that's the way he felt about animals,

32   but he just got really snotty and, Avery, he as much as accused

33   me of letting the little guy out in the first place! So I ... well, I

34   *did* open the cage and let the gerbils out. And the hamsters and

35   the guinea pigs and the little bunny too. And they were all

1   hopping around, you know, so happy! So while he was trying to
2   catch them I let the birds out and they flew out into the mall,
3   some them, and as I was leaving I let the puppies out and they
4   started to chase the gerbils and mice and stuff, but I knew
5   they'd never catch them. I even opened the kitten's pen, but he
6   was still asleep. Now I know you probably think I over-reacted,
7   but if you had got a taste of that guy's attitude you would have
8   done just the same thing, wouldn't you? Hm?
9 AVERY: *(After a beat; bemused)* No.
10 ANNIE: That *is* what you're upset about, isn't it?
11 AVERY: No.
12 ANNIE: You didn't know about it?
13 AVERY: No.
14 ANNIE: Oh. Well if it wasn't that, then what is it? God, I hate it
15   when you get mad at me and won't tell me what I've done! It's
16   not fair! Is it because I've put on a few pounds?
17 AVERY: No.
18 ANNIE: Because I *am* going back to Jazzercise ... Oh! If this is
19   about the dent in the car, that wasn't my fault! Is that what's
20   making you so crabby?
21 AVERY: *(He hadn't known about that either.)* No. *(ANNIE begins to*
22   *get weepy and mushy, goes to him and clings to his arm as he tries*
23   *to read the paper.)*
24 ANNIE: Avery, honey, don't do this to me! I love you so much, and
25   it makes me crazy when you won't talk to me. Tell me what's
26   bothering you. I'll fix it! What am I doing that's wrong?
27   Avery? I'm not going to go away until you tell me what's
28   upsetting you, and don't say it's *me* because you were in a
29   crappy mood the moment you walked in here tonight, and I'm
30   not going to take it!
31 AVERY: No? *(Insulted and angry at his snotty tone, she begins to*
32   *sniffle.)*
33 ANNIE: You can't treat me like this! This is not the person I want to
34   be. Listen to me! You've got me all whiney and clingy and
35   miserable, and that's not the way I am at all. I'm a very happy

1   person, Avery, very happy, or I was until I got mixed up with
2   you! I'm an optimist, Avery, one of those people who always
3   sees the glass as half full and the skies are partly sunny. You
4   know that. You said it's what you loved about me, remember?
5   How I could just chatter along — like a little bird, you said —
6   and talk you out of a bad mood, cheer you right up. Now you
7   look at me like that guy in the store did. And you know what,
8   Avery? I'm beginning to feel like that damn gerbil! Maybe it's
9   time I stuck my nose out of the cage. Because that's what it feels
10   like these days, Avery, like a gerbil cage! *(She begins to sob.)*
11   And I keep running on my little wheel, trying to make you
12   happy, but Avery, you are not a happy person! I am a happy
13   person! I'm hopeful and cheerful and I always believe that
14   things will work out for the best, and I never give up hope on
15   anything except ... I am now. I'm leaving Avery. *(She starts out*
16   *of the room, all injured dignity.)*
17   **AVERY:** *No!*
18   **ANNIE:** No?
19   **AVERY:** No. *(He goes to her, takes her arm, leads her back to sit at the*
20   *table. He offers her his hanky and waits while she wipes her eyes*
21   *and blows her nose. There is a long pause, then:)* You really
22   don't understand me at all, do you?
23   **ANNIE:** *(Sniffling and sullen)* No.
24   **AVERY:** No matter how many times we go through this, you never
25   learn. It isn't always about you. Sometimes I'm just in a bad
26   mood, OK? I've got a right to be in a bad mood now and then,
27   don't I?
28   **ANNIE:** No.
29   **AVERY:** Well, maybe I carry it a little far sometimes, but Christ!
30   You drive me crazy! You just push at me and push at me until
31   I want to — Rargh! But that doesn't mean I don't care about
32   you. Can't you understand that?
33   **ANNIE:** No.
34   **AVERY:** What the hell is it with women? What do you want from
35   me? You want me to kiss your toes three times a day? Moon

1   around writing love poems? You want diamonds and fur coats
2   and roses, is that it?
3 ANNIE: No!
4 AVERY: I'm sorry if I'm not all lovey-dovey every minute of the
5   day. But sometimes I just get this kind of ... do you know what
6   existential dread is?
7 ANNIE: No.
8 AVERY: Have you ever read Heidegger?
9 ANNIE: No.
10 AVERY: Sartre?
11 ANNIE: No.
12 AVERY: Schopenhauer?
13 ANNIE: *(That name sounds familiar at first, but ...)* Uh ... No.
14 AVERY: Well, you ought to. I mean, he talks about how reality is
15   just made up of this blind impelling force, and everyone has
16   this force, and we call it will, OK? But our wills are all
17   contradictory, so we're destined to be miserable. You see?
18 ANNIE: No.
19 AVERY: Like right now. I want to be left alone and you want to
20   harass me. So we're both miserable. But it's more than that,
21   even. It's not just other people, you got fate to contend with
22   too. I mean, don't you sometimes get the feeling there's a big
23   cloud over your head and everyone can see it but you, and
24   some day when you least expect it a fist is going to come out of
25   that cloud and bash you one?
26 ANNIE: No!
27 AVERY: Open your eyes! You're an optimist, huh? An optimist is
28   just someone who refuses to see what's in front of her. *(ANNIE,*
29   *miffed, starts layering the lasagna into a casserole dish.)*
30   How can you go around prattling about gerbils when the
31   world is full of despair? When we have bombs and diseases
32   and banks going belly-up and we can't even hide under our
33   electric blankets anymore or the radiation'll get us! The sky is
34   falling, for Christ's sake, right through the hole in the ozone!
35   Everybody in the Middle East is ready to nuke everybody else

1	and Africa's going to blow up any minute. To say nothing of
2	Central America! You think it's all Tupperware and Twinkies
3	out there? Every time you turn around there's some maniac
4	holed up in a HoJo with an Uzi. I mean, God, how can you go
5	to work every day and read the paper every night and still
6	keep so damn sunny-side up? *(She turns away, puts the lasagna*
7	*in the refrigerator and continues to stand with her back to him.)*
8	Oh, don't get all teary-eyed on me again. I'm not attacking
9	you personally. I'm just trying to explain why sometimes I
10	don't feel like being Mr. Happy. For all we know, the whole
11	thing could slide into oblivion tomorrow, and I'll end up on
12	the sidewalk selling pencils and drinking Mad Dog. For God's
13	sake, Annie, doesn't the thought of nuclear winter mean
14	anything to you?
15	ANNIE: *(Defiantly)* No!
16	AVERY: What about Social Security going bankrupt and medical
17	insurance getting sky high and neither one of us getting any
18	younger? You have to wear reading glasses and I have to get
19	my gums flapped and osteoporosis and prostate trouble are
20	waiting in the wings. Doesn't that worry you?
21	ANNIE: No.
22	AVERY: Haven't you noticed there's less snow every year? Doesn't
23	global warming bother you at all?
24	ANNIE: No.
25	AVERY: The depletion of the rain forest?
26	ANNIE: No.
27	AVERY: Recombinant DNA? Alluvial flood plains? *What about*
28	*Tibet? (He's worked himself into a towering rage. A beat, then, in*
29	*his face:)*
30	ANNIE: No.
31	AVERY: Dammit, woman, don't you ever think about anything
32	outside yourself?
33	ANNIE: No! *(A beat)* Wait a minute. That's not true. I pulled off
34	the road today to look at that gorgeous sunset. Did you?
35	AVERY: No.

1   ANNIE: Did you notice the autumn crocuses blossoming under the
2   shrubs?
3   AVERY: No.
4   ANNIE: How about the trees on the way home? All russet and
5   amber and —
6   AVERY: No! Dammit, Annie, do you really think that sunsets and
7   rainbows and fuzzy gray kittens can make it all up to the
8   homeless?
9   ANNIE: No. But do you think grumping around the house will
10   alleviate the crisis in Algeria?
11   AVERY: No ... Wait a minute. There isn't any "crisis in Algeria!"
12   ANNIE: No? Well, what about the crisis here? And what about me?
13   Does making me unhappy make anything else any better?
14   AVERY: No! I don't want to make you unhappy. But can't you just
15   ignore me and be happy on your own?
16   ANNIE: No. Because no matter how happy I am, it makes me
17   unhappy to see you all unhappy. Because I love you. And so I
18   want to make you happy but you just want me to get out of
19   your face. I guess that isn't the way to make you happy, huh?
20   AVERY: *(Softly)* No. You weren't really going to leave me, were you?
21   ANNIE: No. Not unless you want me to.
22   AVERY: No. I love you too, Annie. Can't you just put up with me?
23   ANNIE: Maybe. But God, Avery, couldn't you make more of an
24   effort?
25   AVERY: Maybe. *(He goes to her, kisses her.)* We could nuke that
26   lasagna a little later, couldn't we?
27   ANNIE: Yes. *(They kiss again. And again. AVERY starts to move them*
28   *toward the bedroom.)*
29   AVERY: Yes?
30   ANNIE: Yes.
31   *The End*
32
33
34
35

Scripts for Three or Four Actors

A Ringing in My Ears
by Debra Bruch

In addition to teaching and directing theatre at Michigan Technological University, Debra Bruch has also been active in Camp Quality, a camping experience for children with life-threatening diseases. Her surname is pronounced "Brew."

A Ringing in My Ears was selected for inclusion in the New Play Development Workshop of the Playwrights Program of the Association for Theatre in Higher Education at ATHE's national convention at Seattle in 1991.

Production Suggestions

Any of these three characters may be played by actors of either sex.

Keep the tempo of this play lively and rapid. If you don't have technical support for the designated lighting effects, simply discover non-technical substitutes. For instance, actors who are supposed to be in black-out portions of the stage might stand with their backs to the "visible" actor(s). Scene breaks might be pointed up with actor-generated sound cues (gongs?) or with title cards on easels which the actors change; or the action might be played continuously without pointing up the scene breaks at all.

A Ringing in My Ears calls for a relatively large number of props; you will be wise to compile a props list at your second or third rehearsal and divide up responsibility for supplying the various items. Since the effectiveness of the play depends on a seamless handling of props, you will want to have the actual props in your rehearsals at an early point. Rehearse the slapstick business (paddling and ear-pulling) carefully so that no one gets hurt.

And have fun. Your audience is going to love this play.

Address all inquiries concerning performances, readings, or reprinting of this work *or any portion thereof* to Dr. Debra Bruch, Assistant Professor of Theatre, Department of Humanities, College of Science and Arts, Michigan Technological University, 1400 Townsend Dr., Houghton MI 49931-1295. For details, see "Part II: Securing Rights for Your Production," pages 241 to 250.

1   The action takes place in a university.

2   ***CHARACTERS:*** STUDENT. ACTOR 1 — as SECRETARY, s/he

3   wears a beret; as VOICE, s/he wears a black mesh bag over

4   her/his head; as ENGLISH PROFESSOR, s/he wears a battered

5   professor's skullcap. ACTOR 2 — as THEATRE PROFESSOR,

6   s/he wears a professor's skullcap; as VOICE, s/he wears a black

7   mesh bag.

8   ***SETTING:*** The set provides four main areas: Up Center Stage, the

9   Secretary's desk is raised high off the floor on a platform. "The

10   University" is painted on the front of the desk. Steps lead up to the

11   desk. Stage Left is a stool and a paddle. Stage Right is a bicycle

12   set in such a way that a person can pedal without going anywhere.

13   Down Center is bare stage.

14

15   **Scene One**

16

17   *(Lights are on the SECRETARY's desk. The rest of the set is in*

18   *darkness. Presently, a flare of trumpet is heard and the STUDENT*

19   *immediately enters.)*

20 **STUDENT:** *(Loudly and proudly)* **I have come to earn my big brass**

21   **balls!**

22 **ACTOR #1 (Secretary):** *(Shuffles papers, then without looking up)*

23   **Why are you here?**

24 **STUDENT:** *(A flare of trumpet, then louder and prouder)* **I have come**

25   **to earn my big brass balls!**

26 **ACTOR #1 (Secretary):** *(Without looking up, writes.)* **Come-to-earn-**

27   **big** — *(Flare of trumpet)*

28 **STUDENT:** *(Loudest and proudest)* **Yes! I have come to earn my big**

29   **brass balls!**

30 **ACTOR #1 (Secretary):** *(Without looking up)* **Number, please.**

31 **STUDENT:** *(Very small)* **Number? Wouldn't you rather have my**

32   **name?**

33 **ACTOR #1 (Secretary):** *(Looks up.)* **You can choose any name you**

34   **want after you earn your big brass balls.** *(Flare of trumpet.*

35   *Then to ACTOR #2, who is flaring the trumpet)* **Will you knock it**

1	off already? Waves. Waves. Nothing but waves. What's your
2	number?
3	STUDENT: 315046.
4	ACTOR #1 (Secretary): *(Writes.)* 3-1-5-0-4-6. Makes — waves.
5	STUDENT: Can I go have lunch now?
6	ACTOR #1 (Secretary): *(Handing the STUDENT papers)* Fill these
7	out in triplicate: Admission to Program. P-1. What is your
8	emphasis? Why are you here? P-2. You, too, can have a
9	program committee. Perhaps within the next five years you
10	can come up with a program? P-3. Writing a prospectus is
11	easy. The hard part is finding out what a prospectus is. P-4.
12	How comprehensively can you comprehend the questions on
13	the comprehensive exam? P-5. Did you do everything to
14	regulations? How well can you adjust? What quality of clay
15	are you? Better fill out a set for yourself. We tend to lose
16	things around here.
17	STUDENT: Thanks.
18	ACTOR #1 (Secretary): *(While putting make-up on the STUDENT's*
19	*face)* Go find out what you can take, look up the classes and
20	copy off all the little numbers onto this little bitty card, have
21	the card signed by somebody you can pass off as your advisor,
22	go stand in line to pick up course cards, go stand in line to get
23	your card stamped by the Dean's office, go stand in line to get
24	your I.D. And if you make a mistake, don't worry about it.
25	You can always drop and add later.
26	STUDENT: This is it, then? I'm at the beginning of the yellow
27	brick road? Ready to trot down the pathway of learning?
28	ACTOR #1 (Secretary): And after that, you can go stand in line at
29	McDonald's and get something deep-fried to eat.
30	STUDENT: Say, are they solid or hollow?
31	ACTOR #1 (Secretary): What?
32	STUDENT: The balls.
33	ACTOR #1 (Secretary): I wouldn't know. I do know, however, that
34	when they clank together they make a terrible noise. *(Closely)*
35	But I've heard that when you bash them against your head,

1   you'll hear a ringing in your ears.

2

3   **Scene Two**

4

5   *(The STUDENT is standing alone, lighted. Everything else is*
6   *dark. The STUDENT takes a handkerchief and, attempting to take*
7   *off the make-up, manages to smear it over his face.)*
8   STUDENT: That wasn't so bad. But I do wish my heart would stop
9   pounding. Now that I've pulled that off, I've got to learn the
10   game. I'll show them. I'll be top dog around here. Show them
11   I'm my own master! Damn, but I wish my heart would stop
12   pounding!
13   ACTOR #1 (Voice): Who are you? *(The STUDENT is startled.)* Who
14   — are — you?
15   STUDENT: 315046. Does that satisfy you? Do you want more
16   specifics? *(No answer)* I had blond hair once but it turned
17   color on me through no fault of my own. I'm nine foot six-and-
18   a-half inches tall. Intelligent enough to grasp the meaning of
19   Copernicus' change of the order of things, but I can't for the
20   life of me figure out how to get the cap off of a medicine bottle.
21   I'm attempting a metamorphosis, but sometimes I don't know
22   where I've been.
23   ACTOR #1 (Voice): Student 315046. Classification: Basic Twit …
24   I'm going to give you some advice, 315046. Listen well and
25   remember. Your studenthood may depend on it … Il faut
26   pourtant que tu t'acceptes. Tu vas redevenir un homme, avec
27   tout ce que cela comporte de taches, de ratures et aussi de
28   joies. Toute notre vie avec notre belle morale et notre ch ère
29   liberté, cela consiste en fin de compte à nous accepter tels que
30   nous sommes. Accepte-toi.
31   STUDENT: *(Frantically trying to get out a notebook and pencil, trying*
32   *to write)* Oh! Oh! Hold it. Wait a minute. I lost you after
33   "depend on it." Could you repeat that please?
34   ACTOR #1 (Voice): Accepte-toi.
35   STUDENT: *(Tries to write and understand at the same time.)* Ack —

162

1   ack — ack.
2   ACTOR #1 (Voice): Accepte-toi.
3   STUDENT: T — t — t — I — I — I — don't —
4   ACTOR #1 (Voice): Where are you?
5   STUDENT: *(Writes.)* Where-are-you. Huh? Oh! *(Laughs nervously.)*
6   Got me. Umm. Let's see. There's a light in my eyes.
7   Everything else is dark. Black. I must be standing in the
8   middle of my own mind.
9   ACTOR #2 (Theatre Professor): *(Enters.)* No. No. No. You've got it
10   all wrong! Look around you. What is actually going on here?
11   STUDENT: *(Totally intimidated)* Oh, gee. I don't know.
12   ACTOR #2 (Theatre Professor): What are you standing on, twit?
13   STUDENT: A floor?
14   ACTOR #2 (Theatre Professor): What kind of floor?
15   STUDENT: A stage.
16   ACTOR #2 (Theatre Professor): Bingo! Now where's the light
17   coming from?
18   STUDENT: God?
19   ACTOR #2 (Theatre Professor): Close, but no cigar.
20   STUDENT: Rats! And I thought I was being singled out to work some
21   miracle for the good of mankind ... It must come from a lamp.
22   ACTOR #2 (Theatre Professor): What else do you see?
23   STUDENT: I see curtains, all sorts of rods and things ... Good
24   grief! There's people out there! All over the place! Hey! That
25   guy with the blond hair is a friend of mine. I know him well,
26   the little creep!
27   ACTOR #2 (Theatre Professor): Audience, actors, stage, curtains,
28   lights and what have you got?
29   STUDENT: The theatre?
30   ACTOR #2 (Theatre Professor): My heartfelt congratulations,
31   315046. Your existence has been qualified. *(The SECRETARY's*
32   *desk is lighted. The ACTOR #1 [Secretary] is seen reading a Zane*
33   *Grey book. ACTOR #2 [Theatre Professor] takes the STUDENT's*
34   *papers.)* I'll take these. Your studenthood is in my hands now,
35   and very capable hands they are. *(Crosses to the SECRETARY's*

1   *desk.)* Here. File these under "things to look forward to." I

2   must study these at two o'clock today. I'm a theatre professor.

3   It's my job.

4   ACTOR #1 (Secretary): You have a meeting at two o'clock today.

5   ACTOR #2 (Theatre Professor): Then I'll look at them tomorrow

6   and tomorrow and tomorrow and tomorrow. *(Looks at the*

7   *STUDENT.)* There's something wrong here. Something smells

8   a bit fishy.

9   ACTOR #1 (Secretary): I've heard that fishmongering is in fashion.

10 ACTOR #2 (Theatre-Professor): No, no, no. Something else. *(To the*

11   *STUDENT)* You're a bit short. I'm sorry, but you don't

12   measure up to our expectations. You don't seem to fit the

13   image we've been looking for.

14 STUDENT: But I'm trying to fit! Honest!

15 ACTOR #2 (Theatre Professor): All right. *(Goes to the*

16   *SECRETARY's desk and pulls out a large cowboy hat, suspenders,*

17   *and a pipe; crosses back to the STUDENT and dresses him up.)*

18   There's still something wrong. How tall are you?

19 STUDENT: I'm nine-foot six-and-a-half inches tall.

20 ACTOR #2 (Theatre Professor): Are you sure?

21 STUDENT: That's what I see when I look in a mirror.

22 ACTOR #1 (Secretary): That's fine for you, 315046. But your

23   image of yourself may not be the perceptions of other people.

24 ACTOR #2 (Theatre Professor): I think I've got it. Creativity is

25   such a wonderful attribute to one's personality. *(The ACTOR*

26   *#1 [Secretary] hands him a pair of stilts that she pulled from*

27   *behind her desk.)* Just what you need. *(Helps the STUDENT get*

28   *on the stilts and stay there.)* There! Perfect! You are now

29   precisely the image I can accept.

30 ACTOR #1 (Secretary): *(Dryly)* I don't know. It looks a bit stilted

31   to me.

32

33   **Scene Three**

34

35   *(The stool and paddle set is lighted. Everything else is dark. The*

*ACTOR #2 [Theatre Professor] is holding a yellow legal pad that has
writing on it. The STUDENT is bent over the stool and the ACTOR
#1 [English Professor] is holding the paddle, ready to strike.)*

ACTOR #2 (Theatre Professor): History, by its very nature,
implies a past event. In drama, history is given in the form of
antecedent action. Antecedent action, by its very nature, is
action never acted, and as never-existed action, it is but an
image of what could have been. Furthermore, antecedent
action, when used, influences what actually happens on the
stage. Therefore, ac — ac — ack — *(The ACTOR #1 [English
Professor] pounds him once on the back.)* ac — cept!

ACTOR #1 (English Professor): Gesundheit!

ACTOR #2 (Theatre Professor): Thanks. Therefore, action on
stage is based upon an image of an action, or a mirage. An
action in the theatre is an event in itself, but the action itself
admits to being representative of what could have been. The
theatre event is an image that is but is not, viewed by people
who are. Therefore, history in theatre is a mirage that is not
relating to a mirage that is.

ACTOR #1 (English Professor): Do you understand? Must we spell
it out for you?

STUDENT: Uh! Uh! *No!*

ACTOR #1 (English Professor): Then upchuck!

STUDENT: You mean, you mean — although I really exist, as long
as I'm doing what I'm doing here, I'm nothing but a mirage.

ACTOR #2 (Theatre Professor): Bingo! *(The ACTOR #1 [English
Professor] strikes.)*

STUDENT: Ow!

ACTOR #2 (Theatre Professor): Although not directly related,
Edwin Forrest and H. Beerbohm Tree had something in
common. Forrest battled the new American frontier on stage
by acting and acting what he acted. And Tree helped English
actors keep acting the way they act.

ACTOR #1 (English Professor): Do you understand? Must we
spell it out for you?

1   STUDENT: Uh! Uh! *No!*

2   ACTOR #1 (English Professor): Then upchuck!

3   STUDENT: Although Forrest had a bigger tail to wag, they both

4   had a very thick bark.

5   ACTOR #2 (Theatre Professor): Bingo! *(The ACTOR #1 [English*

6   *Professor] strikes.)*

7   STUDENT: Ow! Does it have to be so degrading and painful?

8   ACTOR #2 (Theatre Professor): Absolutely.

9   STUDENT: Well, I've had enough! *(The STUDENT gets up.)*

10   ACTOR #2 (Theatre Professor): What are you doing?!

11   STUDENT: What's it look like?

12   ACTOR #2 (Theatre Professor): This isn't right! Get back!

13   STUDENT: Why?

14   ACTOR #2 (Theatre Professor): You have to! You have to listen to

15   me! To *me!(The ACTOR #2 [Theatre Professor] grabs the*

16   *STUDENT's ear and the ACTOR #1 [English Professor] grabs his*

17   *other ear. They have a tug of war while each professor says*

18   *"Listen to me!" Finally —)*

19   STUDENT: *Bugger off! (They stop.)*

20   ACTOR #1 (English Professor): What did he say?

21   ACTOR #2 (Theatre Professor): I think he said bugger off. *(The two*

22   *PROFESSORS huddle, leaving the STUDENT to collapse on the*

23   *floor.)*

24   ACTOR #1 (English Professor): I think he's nearly spent. What do

25   you say?

26   ACTOR #2 (Theatre Professor): I say let's put him through it.

27   ACTOR #1 (English Professor): Do you think he's ready?

28   ACTOR #2 (Theatre Professor): Who cares if he's ready or not?

29   ACTOR #1 (English Professor): Oh. OK. *(They part.)*

30   ACTOR #2 (Theatre Professor): Had enough basics, twit?

31   STUDENT: Huh?

32   ACTOR #2 (Theatre Professor): I said, had enough basics?

33   STUDENT: I guess so.

34   ACTOR #1 (English Professor): What makes you guess so?

35   STUDENT: I hanker to apply what I've learned.

1   ACTOR #2 (Theatre Professor): Well, then. I do believe you're
2   ready for the big time.
3   STUDENT: You mean — ?
4   ACTOR #1 (English Professor): The Seminar! *(They help the*
5   *STUDENT onto the stilts and begin to cross.)*
6
7   **Scene Four**
8
9   *(The bicycle area is lighted. Everything else is dark. The*
10   *STUDENT, on stilts, the ACTOR #1 [English Professor], and the*
11   *ACTOR #2 [Theatre Professor] enter. The STUDENT gets down*
12   *off the stilts.)*
13   ACTOR #2 (Theatre Professor): Now we come to learning in depth.
14   The process of learning transformed into the process of being.
15   ACTOR #1 (English Professor): Mind and body, emotion, intellect,
16   and soul must work together if you want to go the distance.
17   ACTOR #2 (Theatre Professor): Go the distance and you'll end up
18   at a point of no return.
19   STUDENT: I see. You don't want to suck my blood. You want me
20   to suck it for you and put it in a glass.
21   ACTOR #2 (Theatre Professor): Well, 315046. Are you ready?
22   STUDENT: *(Gets on the bicycle.)* Ready. *(The PROFESSORS huddle.)*
23   ACTOR #1 (English Professor): So what are we gonna do?
24   ACTOR #2 (Theatre Professor): Philosophy should make him
25   squirm.
26   ACTOR #1 (English Professor): Existentialism?
27   ACTOR #2 (Theatre Professor): What else?
28   ACTOR #1 (English Professor): Camus?
29   ACTOR #2 (Theatre Professor): Of course! Sisyphus.
30   ACTOR #1 (English Professor): Ah! Sisyphus! I just love
31   Sisyphus!
32   ACTOR #2 (Theatre Professor): OK, then. Let's do it. *(They break.)*
33   Well, don't just sit there, haul it! *(The STUDENT starts to*
34   *pedal.)* Upon examining Plato's *Ion*, it seems clear that
35   Socrates put down Ion, however gentle or subtle that may be.

1   What is your opinion, 315046? Was the ending an end to the
2   quest, or was Socrates merely trying to pacify someone else?
3   STUDENT: Socrates thought too much of himself to fall off the
4   bike. The ending was legit.
5   ACTOR #2 (Theatre Professor): Do you think Ion left with a red
6   face?
7   STUDENT: Can't tell. There's no indication in the text. An answer
8   would be mere mirage.
9   ACTOR #2 (Theatre Professor): What do you think of Aristotle?
10   STUDENT: He's OK I guess.
11   ACTOR #2 (Theatre Professor): What is catharsis?
12   STUDENT: I … I … I know … I … I … don't know. *(The ENGLISH*
13   *PROFESSOR excitedly draws the THEATRE PROFESSOR aside.)*
14   ACTOR #2 (Theatre Professor): What?!
15   ACTOR #1 (English Professor): Did you hear him?!
16   ACTOR #2 (Theatre Professor): *What?!*
17   ACTOR #1 (English Professor): He said he knows he doesn't know!
18   ACTOR #2 (Theatre Professor): He did?
19   ACTOR #1 (English Professor): He did.
20   ACTOR #2 (Theatre Professor): *(Thinks.)* He did! *(To STUDENT)*
21   Don't stop now! Keep going!
22   ACTOR #1 (English Professor): Such ripe-for-the-picking! Such
23   humility! Such mental maturity! Such … what should I say …
24   ACTOR #2 (Theatre Professor): Insecurity.
25   ACTOR #1 (English Professor): That's it!
26   ACTOR #2 (Theatre Professor): Let's do it! *(To STUDENT)* OK.
27   Off you go.
28   STUDENT: Huh? What?
29   ACTOR #1 (English Professor): *Such vocabulary! (The THEATRE*
30   *PROFESSOR begins to help the STUDENT onto the stilts. Then,*
31   *suddenly —)* How tall are you?
32   STUDENT: Huh?
33   ACTOR #1 (English Professor): How — tall — are — you?
34   STUDENT: I'm — I'm — I'm — *(Gives the stilts to the THEATRE*
35   *PROFESSOR.)* I'm as tall as I need to be.

1   ACTOR #1 (English Professor): *(To the THEATRE PROFESSOR)* It
2   begins?
3   ACTOR #2 (Theatre Professor): It begins to end.
4
5   Scene Five
6
7   *(The STUDENT is alone in the light. The two ACTORS [voices]*
8   *surround him, but they are in the dark.)*
9   STUDENT: What? What now? *Oh!* Comps! The Comprehensive
10   Exam! Oh no!
11   ACTOR #2 (Voice): 315046. Now is the time to think all thoughts
12   and dream all dreams. Are you ready?
13   STUDENT: Ready. I guess I'm ready. I must be ready, huh? *(All*
14   *speak at once, creating a chaos of sound.)*
15   ACTOR #2 (Voice): Outline the history of the regional theatre
16   movement in the U.S. since 1945 —
17   ACTOR #1 (Voice): Identify and discuss the historical precedent
18   for the so-called absurdist movement in drama —
19   STUDENT: Let's see. Regional movement is absurd because if it
20   was regional, it wouldn't move.
21   ACTOR #1 (Voice): Two of the greatest periods of drama the world
22   has ever seen employed three-quarter thrust staging —
23   ACTOR #2 (Voice): Defend the contention that tragi-comedy rather
24   than tragedy is the proper mode for theatre production —
25   STUDENT: The thrust of tragedy —
26   ACTOR #1 (Voice): — similar staging has met with great success
27   recently in this country. Given this premise, what role —
28   ACTOR #2 (Voice): The advent of the Stanislavski system
29   stimulated great controversy about an actor's —
30   STUDENT: — stimulates —
31   ACTOR #1 (Voice): — does three-quarter thrust staging have
32   between audience and performance and how can that
33   relationship —
34   ACTOR #2 (Voice): — method of expression —
35   STUDENT: — the expression of —

1   ACTOR #1 (Voice): — be identified —
2   STUDENT: — self identification. *(Dead silence)* Self identification.
3   Self identification.
4   ACTOR #1 (Voice): Student 315046! 315046! You must now answer
5   the ultimate question: What is reality?
6   STUDENT: What? What?!
7   ACTOR #2 (Voice): Accepte toi. Accepte toi. Accepte toi. Accepte
8   toi.
9   STUDENT: Wait! Wait! I hear this ringing —
10   ACTOR #1 (Voice): Answer me! What is reality?
11   STUDENT: OK! OK! *(ACTORS #1 and #2 take the black bags off of*
12   *their heads and don the skullcaps.)*
13   ACTOR #1 (English Professor): What is reality?
14   ACTOR #2 (Theatre Professor): What is reality?
15   STUDENT: *(Pause)* Reality is the interaction of all of my mind's
16   perceptions.
17   ACTOR #2 (Theatre Professor): And what do you perceive?
18   STUDENT: Nothing. Nothing at all.
19   ACTOR #1 (English Professor): Oh, come now. You must perceive
20   something.
21   STUDENT: *(Takes off the added equipment.)* Then I perceive myself
22   — the working of both heart and head that define who I am.
23   ACTOR #1 (English Professor): And who are you?
24   STUDENT: A human being.
25   ACTOR #1 (English Professor): Is there anything — or anybody
26   — else?
27   STUDENT: What?
28   ACTOR #2 (Theatre Professor): Do you want to be different? Do
29   you want to change?
30   STUDENT: No. I accept myself. I've become a person, with all that
31   it carries of sin, forgetfulness, and happiness. Life, with its fine
32   morality and precious freedom, comes in the end of one thing:
33   that I accept myself as I am.
34   ACTOR #1 (English Professor): The metamorphosis is complete!
35   ACTOR #2 (Theatre Professor): Congratulations, 315046! You

1   **have earned your big brass balls!** *(A flare of trumpets. Lights*
2   *up. The ACTOR #1 [English Professor] hands the ACTOR #2*
3   *[Theatre Professor] a pair of big brass balls. He then hangs them*
4   *around the STUDENT's neck.)*
5   **STUDENT: I have earned my big brass balls!**
6   *The End*
7
8
9
10
11
12
13
14
15
16
17
18
19
20
21
22
23
24
25
26
27
28
29
30
31
32
33
34
35

The Tortilla Curtain
by Patrick Baliani

Patrick Baliani earned an M.F.A. in creative writing/fiction from the University of Arizona. He is a member of Old Pueblo Playwrights in Tucson.

The Tortilla Curtain was given a staged reading at the New Play Development Workshop of the Playwrights Program of the Association for Theatre in Higher Education at ATHE's national convention at Seattle in 1991.

Production Suggestions

If, as suggested by the stage directions, Mike is going to speak English with a Mexican accent, and if you, the actor of this character, are not Hispanic, you will need to work systematically to achieve a credible accent. If you aren't willing or able to do this, you might be wiser to play the character without a Spanish accent: A standard American accent will be better than a badly executed or inconsistent Mexican one. If you want to accept this play as an opportunity to develop a good Mexican accent, you might want to use David Allen Stern's *Acting With an Accent: Spanish* available from Dialect Accent Specialists, Inc., 606 N. Larchmont Blvd., Suite 4C, Los Angeles, CA 90004, or from the publisher of this book.

If you are limited to three actors and do not have the technical support for electronic production of the intercom Voice, you might try having the actress in your group play the Voice. If you do this, the actress should develop a distinctly different voice for the guards' superior so that the audience is not confused into thinking Wily Coyote's sidekick and the guards' boss are the same character.

In the process of working on accents, character voices, etc., remember that these things are just window-dressings for the heart of the matter — creating believable characters and real-izing their interactions.

Address all inquiries concerning performances, readings, or reprinting of this work *or any portion thereof* to Patrick Baliani, 1750 Camino Cielo, Tucson, AZ 85718. For details, see "Part II: Securing Rights for Your Production," pages 241 to 250.

1   The action takes place in a United States Customs office in
2   Nogales, Arizona, in the present.
3 **CHARACTERS:** MIKE SANCHEZ — thirty years old, Mexican
4   American, dressed in uniform: Beige shirt, badge, holster, and
5   brown pants. JOE BENSON — about twenty-five, a blond Anglo,
6   and also dressed in uniform. SUPERVISOR'S VOICE. YOUNG
7   WOMAN — striking in appearance, wearing a miniskirt.
8 **SETTING:** The office is adjacent to the walk-through checkpoint. This
9   room allows agents to double-check, through reflective glass, the
10   flow of people crossing into the U.S.A.; it also serves, when
11   needed, as a place to hold interrogations, strip searches, etc. Two
12   chairs face the audience and the unseen glass partition. A few
13   official portraits (perhaps of Presidents Bill Clinton and Carlos
14   Salinas de Gortari) hang on the walls, as well as the United States
15   and Mexican flags, crisscrossed near the only door. There is a
16   desk to one side of the room, with an intercom, phone, scattered
17   forms and reports, etc.
18
19   *(Late one afternoon toward the end of a slow shift, MIKE*
20   *SANCHEZ sits facing the audience, sipping his coffee, peering*
21   *through an [unseen] one-way mirror at the flow of people going*
22   *through Customs. JOE BENSON enters.)*
23 **MIKE:** *(With a Mexican accent)* **Joe! Good to see you, buddy. I**
24   **thought my shift would never end.** *(MIKE grabs his jacket,*
25   *makes for the door.)*
26 **JOE: Not so fast, speedy.** *(He points to his watch.)* **I don't come on**
27   **till four.**
28 **MIKE:** *(Slumps back down.)* **You *would* get here early.**
29 **JOE:** *(Primping himself)* **I need to get ready.**
30 **MIKE:** *(Has heard it all before.)* **Yeah, yeah.**
31 **JOE: Don't *you* start in on me. Not today.**
32 **MIKE: I know, I know …**
33 **JOE/MIKE:** *(Simultaneously)* **I'm not in the mood.** *(MIKE goes back*
34   *to gazing out the window. JOE pins on his badge, checks his*
35   *holster, and peers out over MIKE's shoulder.)*

1   JOE: Any sign of "Wily Coyote"?

2   MIKE: Not yet. Word has it he's coming through, though. *(The*
3   *intercom crackles to life; an authoritative female VOICE asks:)*

4   VOICE: Mike Sanchez. What's the update on those three *locos* you
5   stopped?

6   MIKE: *(Addresses the intercom.)* I put through an OTM and wrote
7   up two EWI's.

8   VOICE: Did you have them O.R.'d?

9   MIKE: They were BCD'd.

10 VOICE: It's about time. *(The intercom crackles off. MIKE silently*
11   *mouths the words, "It's about time," into the intercom, mimicking*
12   *her voice.)*

13 MIKE: *(To JOE)* A little CMB. *(Pause)* Covering my butt. *(Pause.*
14   *He motions with his hand that she is always talking.)* The woman
15   drives *me* "loco."

16 JOE: In more ways than one.

17 MIKE: Listen, amigo. *(Points to the intercom.)* She would know
18   very well who is the boss — off the job.

19 JOE: *(Sarcastically)* Big man.

20 MIKE: She is probably waiting for me to ask her out.

21 JOE: Ask her out?!

22 MIKE: Why do you think she is in such a hurry to get me through
23   work today?

24 JOE: Dream on!

25 MIKE: She must be hot-cha-cha to trot-trot-trot.

26 JOE: The supervisor?

27 MIKE: Claro. And she knows it, too. *(Pause)* So how was your
28   burrito?

29 JOE: What ... How did you know I had a burrito?

30 MIKE: Hombre, if it is my job to look out this window and see
31   Nogales pass before me, then I can also look out this window
32   and see you coming from the cantina on your way over here.

33 JOE: Makes sense.

34 MIKE: And if I can see that, I can also make out the enchilada
35   sauce still on your chin.

1   JOE: *(Embarrassed, wipes his chin.)* Uh ... yeah.
2   MIKE: But what I don't know — what I can't see — is why your
3   wife doesn't make you lunch to bring here so you don't waste
4   your money in that hole.
5   JOE: Make me lunch? Are you kidding? I'm lucky if she makes me
6   toast in the morning. And don't talk to me about wasting
7   money. *(He pulls a pair of tickets from his shirt pocket.)* I got
8   suckered over there at the cantina into buying these two
9   bullfight tickets. The guy said they were good for next week.
10   Only thing is, I find out after he's gone, there *is* no bullfight
11   next week. It's this afternoon.
12   MIKE: So?
13   JOE: So I gotta work. Or did you want to work my shift for me?
14   MIKE: Not me, hombre.
15   JOE: I didn't think so. *(Pause)* Say, you want them? *(MIKE shakes*
16   *his head.)* I'll give them to you for half price.
17   MIKE: Half price or no price — I got better things to do.
18   JOE: I'll bet. *(JOE settles himself in the chair beside MIKE, who's got*
19   *his eye on something outside.)*
20   MIKE: So ... what's this about your wife not treating you right?
21   You two have another fight?
22   JOE: Another war.
23   MIKE: *(Turns to JOE.)* I don't understand you, man. You always
24   come in here with the long face of a burro that's not been fed
25   in a week. *(Looks out again.)* No wonder you eat at the cantina.
26   JOE: Tell me about it.
27   MIKE: You know what your trouble is?
28   JOE: Uh-uh.
29   MIKE: You married a gringa. You should know better.
30   JOE: Hey, Mary's all right. Mary's good to me in a lot of ways.
31   Mary's —
32   MIKE: All that and more, my friend. But she is still a gringa. She
33   expects — demands — certain things. She is what you Anglos
34   call "lib-er-a-ted." *(He pauses.)* Tell you what. I'm going to
35   teach you something. *(He leans toward JOE, as if divulging a*

176

1   *secret.)* **Women say they want a man to be sensitive. But deep**
2   **down, all women — Latinas, gringas, you name them — they**
3   **want a man to exert authority.**
4 **JOE: Authority?**
5 **MIKE: Control!**
6 **JOE:** *(Skeptically)* **Control, huh?**
7 **MIKE:** *(Makes a fist.)* **Power!**
8 **JOE:** *(Still sarcastic)* **Right.**
9 **MIKE:** *(Adamantly)* **You have to impose your *will* on the situation.**
10   *Master* **it.** *(Pause)* **Think of it as a job that is yours to do. Like**
11   **this one. You don't always enjoy it, but you do it anyway. For**
12   **her sake as well as yours. Now, as soon as your woman gets in**
13   **the way of what you have to do, you have to do it all the more.**
14   **When you are in the bullring, *you* are the matador. You are**
15   **the *jefe*.**
16 **JOE: Easy for you to say.**
17 **MIKE: Easy for me to do.**
18 **JOE: I'll believe it when I see it.**
19 **MIKE: Why do you think women love a good bullfight, anyway?**
20 **JOE: They do?**
21 **MIKE: It's the power — the *control* — of the matador they go to see.**
22 **JOE: Not to mention those little butt-hugging suits.**
23 **MIKE: That too.**
24 **JOE:** *(Points abruptly.)* **Geez! Look at her!**
25 **MIKE:** *(Smiles broadly.)* **It's about time you noticed. I've had my**
26   **eye on her for a while.**
27 **JOE: No!**
28 **MIKE: Sure. The whole time she's been in line.**
29 **JOE: You didn't point her out?!**
30 **MIKE: You got eyes, don't you?** *(MIKE and JOE lean up against the*
31   *window, turning their heads and craning their necks as the woman*
32   *they've spotted — unseen by the audience — passes outside.)*
33 **JOE: Thank God for miniskirts!**
34 **MIKE:** *(Stoops to follow her legs with his eyes.)* **Ay ya yai! Muchas**
35   **curvas y yo no tengo frenos!** *(Translation: Wow! So many curves*

1   *and I've got no brakes!)*

2   **JOE: Ditto! Whatever that means!**

3   **MIKE:** *(Stoops lower and lower until he is almost eye-level with the*

4   *floor, and looking up, shouts:)* **Mucho jamón por dos juevos!**

5   *(Translation: That's a lot of ham for just two eggs!)*

6   **JOE:** *(Slumps back in his seat.)* **Ditto! Ditto!**

7   **MIKE:** *(He stands, regains his cool, then boasting:)* **Stick with me,**

8   **my friend, and you will learn to spot these things a mile away.**

9   **You don't work the *frontera* — the tortilla curtain — for ten**

10   **years, including overtime, without picking up a thing or two.**

11   **JOE:** *(Trying to be macho)* **I'd ... like to pick *her* up.**

12   **MIKE: And if your wife found out, you'd be eating breakfast and**

13   **dinner at the cantina as well.** *(He laughs.)* **I'm out of here, my**

14   **friend.** *(He cranes his neck again, as if to spot the woman in the*

15   *distance, and gestures suggestively with his hips.)* **Want to guess**

16   **where I'm going?** *(The door opens. A striking young woman,*

17   *wearing a miniskirt, walks in and closes the door behind her.)*

18   **JOE/MIKE:** *(Simultaneously)* **— What the —? — Caramba!**

19   **WOMAN:** *(Innocently)* **Excuse me ... I mean ...** *(With an American*

20   *accent)* **Buenas tarde. Do you speak —?**

21   **MIKE: I do! I do! And may I say that your Spanish is ...** *(Takes a*

22   *deep breath.)* **Invigorating.**

23   **WOMAN: You're just saying that.**

24   **MIKE: No, no. Of course not. I would never say something just to**

25   **say it. Definitely not.**

26   **JOE: Say, how did you get in here?**

27   **WOMAN: Actually, I'm not exactly sure I'm in the right place.**

28   **JOE: I'm not sure you are either.**

29   **MIKE: I'll decide that.**

30   **WOMAN: I was asking for directions —**

31   **MIKE: I *do* give directions. Joe! Keep watch on the window, will**

32   **you?**

33   **JOE: Directions?**

34   **WOMAN:** *(Moves toward JOE, wary of MIKE.)* **I went through**

35   **Customs and they sent me here. They said *you* could give me**

1   directions.

2   MIKE: *(Steps between them.)* They meant me, señorita.

3   WOMAN: They said to look for ... *(She blushes)* a handsome man ...

4   MIKE: Allow me to introduce myself.

5   WOMAN: With blond hair.

6   MIKE: *(Ignoring this, stands erect, beaming.)* I am Mike Sanchez. At
7   your service!

8   WOMAN: *(Still edging toward JOE, trying to read his name tag)* And
9   you are ...

10 MIKE: *(Before JOE can speak)* This is Joe Benson, my subordinate.

11 JOE: Subordinate?

12 WOMAN: *(Offers JOE her hand.)* My name is Linda.

13 MIKE: *(Steps between them again.)* Linda! What a perfect name for
14   you. Do you know that *linda*, in Spanish, means "exceedingly
15   beautiful"?

16 JOE: I thought it meant "pretty."

17 WOMAN: *(Unfolds a slip of paper.)* Perhaps you can tell me where
18   I might find ... *(She reads from the paper, in her American
19   accent.)* La plaza de toros?

20 MIKE: The bullring!

21 JOE: You're going to the bullring? *(The WOMAN nods.)*

22 MIKE: Of course!

23 JOE: *(Dismayed)* A woman like you ... ?

24 WOMAN: The trip wasn't my idea. It's just that —

25 MIKE: No need to explain.

26 WOMAN: You see, I've never been to Nogales and —

27 MIKE: Never been to Nogales! Then you must experience it, Miss
28   Linda. I insist.

29 WOMAN: There's ... a lot to do?

30 MIKE: There is a world to do. Exquisite dining. Exotic dancing.

31 WOMAN: I heard the water isn't too safe to —

32 MIKE: And once you have gone to one bullfight, you will return
33   again and again.

34 WOMAN: But you don't understand. *(To JOE, imploring:)* I do
35   have to get to the plaza soon.

1   JOE: Well, I suppose in that case —

2   MIKE: In that case — *(He snatches the tickets from JOE's pocket.)*

3   You should know that I go there all the time.

4   JOE: What?

5   MIKE: Even more often than that.

6   JOE: He's full of it. A minute ago —

7   MIKE: A minute ago I was telling my subordinate about the match

8   today. At four-thirty. We have two tickets. See? But he has just

9   now come on duty, and will be here for the next *six hours. (To*

10   *JOE)* Won't you, amigo?

11   JOE: Yes, but —

12   WOMAN: Six hours! That's a long time. Do you take a break?

13   JOE: I don't need a break!

14   WOMAN: But you must get tired.

15   MIKE: As I was saying, the bullring is thirty minutes away. I could

16   give you directions but it is a little tricky to get there. *(He*

17   *grimaces and gestures confusingly with his hands.)* You must

18   turn here, turn there. Go down these steps, up that street.

19   *(With a look of concern)* Not the best part of town, especially for

20   a señorita ... forgive me ... as beautiful as you.

21   WOMAN: Mr. Benson — *(Fending off MIKE)* I mean, Joe — I

22   don't think your partner understands ...

23   MIKE: I understand you, Señorita Linda!

24   WOMAN: *(Clutching JOE)* Can't you control him?

25   MIKE: Control! The outcome of power! *(He strips off his jacket.)*

26   The matador's strength!

27   WOMAN: Put a leash on him or something?

28   MIKE: *(Henceforth, gestures like a matador in the bullring.)* Though

29   I have been gouged many times, I am more invincible than

30   ever!

31   WOMAN: Get away!

32   JOE: Mike.

33   MIKE: *(Still gesturing)* And I would like to share my secrets of

34   strength with you!

35   WOMAN: But you're uncouth, unkempt, and ...

1   **JOE: Mike!**

2   **WOMAN:** *(Eyeing MIKE's movements)* **Uncoordinated!**

3   **MIKE:** *(Wrapped up in himself, gesturing)* **I am an experience you**
4   **will never forget!**

5   **WOMAN: With the brains of a bean! You men are all alike. You**
6   **haven't understood a thing!**

7   **JOE:** *(Overlapping)* **Not all of us.**

8   **WOMAN: What did you say?**

9   **JOE:** *(Forcing himself to be assertive)* **I said, not all of us.**

10   **WOMAN: You mean you're not like that, Joe? You understand?**

11   **JOE:** *(At attention, his back to the audience)* **I'm not! I mean, I do!**
12   *(Sincerely)* **Understand, that is.**

13   **WOMAN:** *(On tiptoes, peeking over JOE's shoulder, she sighs.)* **I'm**
14   **so glad.** *(Pause)*

15   **MIKE:** *(Arrogantly)* **Do you wish to enjoy this bullfight with me or**
16   **not?**

17   **WOMAN:** *(Indignantly)* **Enjoy it? I don't even want to** *see* **it. I'm**
18   **meeting a friend in the lot there. We're driving to Hermosillo.**

19   **MIKE: A friend? Hermosillo?**

20   **WOMAN: I wouldn't be caught dead at a bullfight!**

21   **JOE: Ha!**

22   **MIKE:** *(Reaches out to her.)* **Forgive me, señorita.**

23   **WOMAN:** *(Pulls away.)* **What could possibly be more disgusting**
24   **than a bullfight?**

25   **MIKE: Well … they are not pretty, that's true.**

26   **WOMAN: They're** *revolting* **is what they are …**

27   **MIKE: Uh, perhaps, in some ways …**

28   **WOMAN: As for directions …** *(Walks to the door, opens it.)* **I guess**
29   **I came to the wrong place.**

30   **MIKE:** *(Steps after her.)* **Well, no. Not really.** *(She slams the door in*
31   *his face.)*

32   **JOE:** *(Slumps into his chair. Pause)* **Way to go, Don Juan.**

33   **MIKE:** *(Mumbles to himself in Spanish, then:)* **Ahh, to hell with it!**
34   **I'm going home.** *(MIKE opens the door. Abruptly, the VOICE on*
35   *the intercom booms out.)*

1   VOICE: Mike Sanchez. What on earth are you doing down there?
2   "Wily Coyote" just walked through customs. The guard gave
3   you the signal. You were supposed to pick him up! Are you
4   blind? Or just asleep? *(MIKE and JOE gape at each other; the*
5   *VOICE continues.)* **Answer me!**
6   MIKE: *(Fumbles with the intercom button.)* **Uh ... you got a**
7   **description?**
8   VOICE: Description my behind! *You* know what he looks like!
9   JOE: *(Butting in)* Was ... "Coyote" alone?
10 VOICE: No. He was seen with a tall blonde in a miniskirt. They got
11   away together!
12 MIKE: Uh ... in that case —
13 JOE: *(Stands over MIKE.)* In that case, I'll get my *superior,*
14   Sanchez, on it right away. *(To MIKE, putting a hand on his*
15   *shoulder, with a sardonic grin.)* Isn't that right, *jefe?*
16   *The End*
17
18
19
20
21
22
23
24
25
26
27
28
29
30
31
32
33
34
35

Birthday Party

by Madeleine Martin and Norman A. Bert

Martin and Bert have collaborated on several plays. In the case of *Birthday Party*, Madeleine conceived the play and drafted the first version. Norman revised the script, and then Madeleine revised it again. They continued this process until they were both satisfied with the script.

Playwrights' Production Suggestions

Although Cloe, the grandmother, is older, she need not be played with an aged voice or posture. The presentational style of the play, which combines typical dialog with direct audience address, makes this kind of realism unnecessary. By no means should she be played as a feeble old woman; keep the focus on her self-centered character and her relationship with Angela.

Address all inquiries concerning performances, readings, or reprinting of this work *or any portion thereof* to Madeleine Martin, PO Box 53521, Lubbock, TX 79453. For details, see "Part II: Securing Rights for Your Production," pages 241 to 250.

1   The action takes place in the present in a hospital and later in
2   Angela's home.
3   **CHARACTERS:** ANGELA— a new mother, 22 years old; the wife of
4   Brad. BRAD—Angela's husband, 19 years old. A new father.
5   CLOE—Angela's 60-year-old grandmother.
6   **SETTING:** A bed and a bedside chair.
7
8   *(ANGELA, giving birth, makes typical mother-in-labor sounds.*
9   *BRAD stands by helplessly.)*
10   **ANGELA: I need drugs! Drugs!**
11   **CLOE:** *(She scurries in and elbows BRAD out of the way.)* **Midwife'll**
12   **give you the same as you had last time ... whatever that was.**
13   **ANGELA: That didn't work. Serious drugs! I need drugs.** *(She grabs*
14   *CLOE's face and screams into it.)* **Get me an epidural.** *Now!*
15   **CLOE:** *(Steps forward and addresses audience.)* **They always scream**
16   **for an epidural about this time. Personally, I'd a given her the**
17   **epidural 'bout an hour ago. But I'm just her gramma; what**
18   **do I know? Then the doc pops in — looks like he's about**
19   **twelve — and gives her the epidural. "There," he says, "You**
20   **should be feeling the effects momentarily."**
21   **ANGELA:** *(Hops out of bed and addresses audience.)* **And I do. I feel**
22   **nothing. No more pain, thank God. No more contractions. I**
23   **mean, I've been doing this labor routine for over twelve hours.**
24   **I deserve a break, don't I? The rest should be a piece of cake.**
25   *(She gets back into bed as BRAD addresses audience.)*
26   **BRAD: I know it's going to be a boy. My son! I already bought him**
27   **a soccer ball.**
28   **ANGELA:** *(In bed)* **It's a girl. I want a girl. For no other reason than**
29   **that she needs her own name. Brad wants to name the baby**
30   **"Bradley." That's his name; every baby deserves its own name!**
31   **CLOE:** *(Completes last phrase with ANGELA.)* **— deserves its own**
32   **name. That's what I told Angela. What's this hair-brained**
33   **idea of "Bradley Brodski Jr." As if that's something to be**
34   **proud of. "Oh Gramma!" she says to me.** *(She indicates*
35   *BRAD.)* **He didn't even graduate high school. He works**

1   stocking shelves at Wal-Mart. *(Pause)* I raised her, you know.
2   As if she was my daughter 'stead of my granddaughter.
3   Dancin' lessons, baton lessons — I gave her those things.
4   Somebody had to. Her mother wouldn't. Couldn't.
5 ANGELA: Oh my God! I think the baby's coming! Doctor! Doctor!
6 CLOE: And Junior Doc's yelling, "Push, Angela! Push!"
7 ANGELA: *(Addressing audience)* I've never seen him before today.
8   I wonder what his name is. 'Least he knows my name. He
9   looks awfully young —
10 CLOE: *(In the doctor's voice.)* Angela, you must push now!
11 ANGELA: *(Addressing audience)* But I can't. The epidural has
12   done its job too well.
13 CLOE: Then he yells, "Nurse — get a VE unit in here, stat!" He
14   actually said "stat," just like on ER. Must be a real doctor.
15 BRAD: Wonder if Bud'll like cars? Gonna call him "Bud." 'Course
16   he will — like cars. Only natural.
17 ANGELA: *(Sits up and addresses the audience.)* I don't know what
18   a "VE unit" is, but he's a doctor; he knows what he's doing.
19   *(She gets out of bed. BRAD remains beside the bed, watching the*
20   *doctor deliver the baby.)* Four years ago the FDA issued a
21   warning about VE deliveries. Vacuum Extraction. They
22   literally vacuum the baby out of the birth canal. Don't look so
23   shocked. It's true. They hook up this suction cup on the baby's
24   head, create a vacuum to suck the head up in there in the cup
25   tight, and then ... they pull the baby out. *(Pause)* I couldn't
26   push. They had to do something, right?
27 CLOE: It's a girl, Angel! I'm so proud.
28 ANGELA: I knew it! *(She jumps back in bed.)* A girl. Thank God.
29   Thank God she's here. Oh look at her, Brad! Brad?
30 BRAD: A girl? God. God. *(He walks aside.)* I'm tired.
31 ANGELA: Look at her, Brad. She's perfect. Just perfect. Ten little
32   fingers, ten little toes —
33 CLOE: They need to clean her up, Angel, weigh her, ya know.
34 ANGELA: And they whisk her away, just like that! I don't even get
35   to see what color — Why's she shaking like that?

1   CLOE: They're black. All babies' eyes're black when they're born.
2   They gradually change color, but hers'll be brown. I already
3   know that. Like mine. And she won't be a "Junior." Gramma's
4   baby won't be a "Junior." That's the most important thing.
5   Babies deserve …
6   ANGELA: But it's *not* the most important thing. The baby's
7   shaking. Shaking violently. The doctor and the nurse grab her
8   from me and rush her out of the room and the doctor's yelling
9   things. I don't know what. It's like I can't hear … *(To BRAD)*
10   What's wrong? What's happening? Where are they taking
11   her? Brad?
12   BRAD: I'm so tired. *(He flops into the bedside chair and falls asleep.)*
13   ANGELA: A seizure. My baby's having a seizure? I don't
14   understand this.
15   CLOE: *(To audience)* Can you believe it? His mother gives 'em
16   this dog. "They're a family now," she says. "Daddy, Mommy,
17   baby — and a dog. Every family needs a dog. If she couldn't
18   give my son a boy, at least I can give him a dog." A real piece
19   of work, that woman!
20   ANGELA: She's in intensive care. I don't know what's wrong.
21   What's wrong with my baby?
22   CLOE: *(To ANGELA)* Doctor says the baby had a seizure. He don't
23   know why. He's looking at possible …
24   ANGELA: *(To the audience)* But he does know. That doctor does know
25   what could have caused this. He won't say it, and I haven't read
26   the warnings, so I'm having trouble putting all the pieces
27   together. Something doesn't add up. I mean, four years ago I was
28   graduating from high school. I wasn't reading FDA warnings.
29   And when I discovered I was pregnant, I went to Lamaze classes.
30   I did the exercises. I took my vitamins. I did everything the
31   midwives told me to do. I did not read FDA warnings.
32   CLOE: Midwives. My Angel gets midwives. Not even the same
33   midwife every month. That's Medicaid for you. They need to
34   save their pennies, so my precious Angel gets midwives, and
35   her precious baby ends up with seizures. I blame the midwife.

1   And that Brad? He sleeps. He's tired. And now he's got — a
2   dog? What a loser.
3 BRAD: I am so tired.
4 ANGELA: Brad, you can sleep here. *(She indicates the bed.)* I can't
5   sleep anyway. *(He climbs into bed while she speaks to the
6   audience.)* I can't! How can I sleep? The doctors keep coming in
7   and going out with one piece of good news for every two pieces
8   of bad news. That's what doctors do, I guess. That's what they
9   did with Mom — when she was dying. Give hope, take it away.
10 CLOE: Her mother died just nine months ago. *(Smiles.)* That's why
11   we have a baby here now. Angie was so upset. She was in
12   shock. She forgot to take 'er pills. But it'll all work out. The
13   baby's name is *not* Brad; that's what's important here. I've
14   had my fill of Brads. *(Pause)* Every Brad who walked into my
15   fifth-grade classroom was a problem. Most of 'em on Ritalin.
16   You ever seen a kid on Ritalin? It's a lot like a cat with its tail
17   on fire. God Almighty. ADD, my butt. They just need a good
18   spanking, that's all. My kids, her dad included, were raised
19   before Spock — when spankings were still good for kids.
20 ANGELA: Nanna? I don't understand what's happening. They say
21   she might have had a stroke. Why would she have a stroke?
22   They're asking me all kinds of questions about Mom's
23   diabetes. Do you think the baby has diabetes? Was it the
24   epidural? Did that cause this? Was it my fault?
25 CLOE: You did nothing wrong, Angela. She's going to be fine. We
26   have never had a baby born with any problem in this family,
27   and we're not going to start now. The important thing here is
28   to think of a good name.
29 ANGELA: Maria. I'm going to name her Maria after Mom. I like
30   it — Maria.
31 CLOE: Maria's a beautiful name. And if she's lucky, the kid will
32   grow up to be like Angela's mom, you know. *(Pause)* 'Course
33   she never took care of her diabetes right. Had three kids, total.
34   Two by my boy. She shouldn't a done that. She should have
35   been more careful. But she was a good woman. My boy really

1   loved her. I told Angel that at her funeral. Maria and him, they
2   just decided they wanted different things after awhile. Hurt
3   Angie the most, I suppose. He's a good man, my boy.
4   BRAD: *(Sits briefly.)* I need a nap.
5   ANGELA: I'm hearing words. Words I don't know. I'm afraid to
6   ask what they mean. I'm afraid it will be worse than what it
7   sounds like. MRI, PET Scan, CAT Scan, EKG, EEG …
8   They're not even words. They're letters. Letters. They're
9   performing letters on my baby.
10   CLOE: He loved Maria. Really did. *(Pause)* I think he still does.
11   ANGELA: Nanna? Do you know what the letters mean?
12   CLOE: Now you have to think positive. They're doing a lot of tests
13   trying to decide what, if anything, happened. It's their job to
14   paint the worst possible picture. That's what doctors do; they
15   make you worry. When I had your aunt, they had to pull her
16   out. Grabbed her with forceps and pulled her out. Pretty
17   much the same thing as this vacuum thing they did on you. I
18   didn't dilate, but I'd had one kid already, so they just pulled
19   her out. I was in labor for about as long as you, too. Probably
20   longer. I didn't get an epidural though.
21   ANGELA: Do you think it was the epidural? Did that cause this?
22   If only I'd —
23   CLOE: You cannot blame yourself for this, Angel. Besides, there's
24   nothing wrong with her. She's my beautiful great grand baby.
25   ANGELA: *(Addressing audience)* But there is. Maria's sedated.
26   They're keeping her drugged so she doesn't have any more
27   seizures. She doesn't even move — except for breathing. And
28   that looks like an effort. I'm not allowed to hold her —
29   CLOE: Good news! You can go home today. Guess they're going to
30   have to keep little Maria here for a few more days so they can
31   do some tests. Their specialist doesn't come in until Monday.
32   So they need to keep Maria at least until then.
33   ANGELA: I can't believe what I'm hearing. The specialist doesn't
34   "come in" until Monday? *(She yells Off-stage.)* Call her in.
35   Now. Make her come in now! Fix my baby! Now!

1　CLOE: They're taking Maria a few buildings down to do the PET
2　　　　Scan. They're gonna set up a room for you to use each day
3　　　　when you come to visit her. The nurses will show you. Doctor
4　　　　says he'll stop by before you leave, case you have questions.
5　　　　Not that there's a lot he can tell you at this time.
6　ANGELA: At this time? He hasn't told me a lot at any time. Aren't
7　　　　doctors supposed to know what's wrong?
8　CLOE: Doctor left this prescription for some pain medication. He
9　　　　said "script." Just like ER. He said it'd be best if you tried
10　　　　Tylenol first, since you're nursing. Anything that goes into you
11　　　　could end up in your milk and into Maria. Let's get you home
12　　　　so you can catch up on your sleep. Relax some, ya know?
13　BRAD: *(Lying in bed and mumbling)* I am so tired.
14　ANGELA: *Now* they're concerned about what goes into me? While
15　　　　I was in labor, they put all kinds of stuff into my IV. Didn't
16　　　　that go into the baby? Did that stuff cause all this? *(Pause)*
17　　　　What? Sleep? Relax?
18　CLOE: Your dad's been looking into this Vacuum Extraction
19　　　　delivery thing. Did some research on the 'Net. Seems they did
20　　　　a special report on *20/20* about this a few years back. He says
21　　　　this VE thing causes all kinds of problems. Birth defects.
22　　　　Deaths. He thinks we need to call a lawyer.
23　ANGELA: A lawyer? Dad? What are you saying? Birth defects?
24　　　　Nobody has said anything about birth defects! Dad? Daddy!
25　CLOE: Sweetheart, they're just looking at worst-case scenarios right
26　　　　now. Did the doctor ever mention a C-section? Did you sign an
27　　　　"informed consent?" Think, Angel. We need to be sure about
28　　　　what happened. If that doctor did something wrong, we need to
29　　　　think about protecting your rights. Maria's rights. If she's going
30　　　　to have special needs, well, you need to be compensated for that.
31　ANGELA: *(Addressing audience)* Special needs. That's another way
32　　　　of saying deformed or retarded. My child is not normal? My
33　　　　child is not perfect? Nanna? Daddy?
34　BRAD: *(Struggles out of bed.)* You know, you gotta stop talking
35　　　　about it all the time.

1   ANGELA: "Stop telling everyone?" What?
2   CLOE: Well, Sweetie. It's Brad. He wants you to stop telling
3   everyone everything. This is our business. Nobody else's. Just
4   ours. Everybody don't need to know this.
5   ANGELA: But … *I* need them to know it. Nanna!
6   CLOE: No you don't, Honey. You just keep it to yourself. In my
7   day, we handled things quietly. You can too.
8   BRAD: Can anybody see I am trying to sleep? I'm tired. *(He crawls*
9   *into bed.)*
10 ANGELA: He's tired? All he's done is sleep. *(Pause)* I come home
11   from the hospital with no baby. Empty arms. Empty cradle.
12   This is the first time without her since she was conceived. In
13   me, she was safe. Protected. I took her to the grocery store, to
14   the dentist, shopping. I ate the broccoli, carrots, even peas. I
15   slept with her. I read her the Dickens and the Dinesen. I
16   played Mozart for her. I bought a white crib with just the right
17   slat-width. For her head, you know? I dressed the crib with
18   Winnie-the-Pooh sheets. *(Pause)* She was loved. She was safe.
19   In me. *(Pause)* I think I ate the right foods. How do I know if
20   I ate the right foods?
21 CLOE: You young mothers! You're always worried about
22   everything. *(To the audience)* They're always worried about
23   doin' the right thing, eatin' the right foods. Good grief. In my
24   day, we just ate. That was the thing — just eat. Eat for two,
25   they'd say. All these books, all this La-maze stuff. Pure trash.
26   If they'd just have left her alone, my granddaughters — both
27   of 'em — would be fine. Vacuum extraction! Sounds like
28   something I'd do to my carpet. *(ANGELA paces.)*
29 BRAD: I'm so tired.
30 ANGELA: Look at her, Brad. *(BRAD doesn't respond.)* She just sleeps.
31   Why does she sleep all the time? *(Pause. She looks at BRAD.)*
32   They bring her to me to nurse, and all she does is sleep.
33 CLOE: They've got her all doped up, Sweetheart, to prevent more
34   seizures. What's with Bradley? All he does is sleep!
35 ANGELA: Now Nanna! Don't start on Brad! Please?

1 **CLOE:** *(To audience)* If I started on 'im, I'd never stop. What a
2   loser my Angel picked! *(Pause)* They're talking epilepsy now.
3   Cerebral Palsy. The tests don't show nothing. You gotta hand
4   it to Angel, though. She's a rock. Like her mother. Like me.
5   You can't tell her there's anything wrong with that baby.
6 **ANGELA:** Her hand moved! Look! See? Well, it did. I saw it. I
7   know it did. The doctors are saying that that hand just lays
8   there lifeless —
9 **CLOE:** "Just lies there lifeless." What do they know, stupid
10   doctors? Do they watch her all the time? Every moment of
11   every day? Angela does. Angela knows. If she says the baby's
12   hand moved, then the baby's hand moved. There's nothing
13   wrong with that baby. The father? Now that's another story.
14 **ANGELA:** My grandmother. She hates Brad. She doesn't even try
15   to hide it.
16 **CLOE:** Why should I try to hide anything? He's worthless like his
17   mother. Stupid woman brings him a dog. A dog! Can you
18   imagine? Bringin' a lousy mutt into Angie's house? At a time
19   like this? With a sick baby?
20 **ANGELA:** Dog! I can't think about a dog. Brad, put it out in the
21   yard. Please.
22 **BRAD:** I'm too tired.
23 **ANGELA:** It's not a housedog. It's not any kind of dog, yet. Put it
24   out in the yard!
25 **BRAD:** Can't you do it?
26 **ANGELA:** *(Addressing audience)* He needs to take a nap. Keeps
27   him busy, sleeping does. So he doesn't have to think. *(Pause)*
28   My father wants me to sue the doctors, the hospital, everyone
29   involved, the dog. He'd sue the dog if he could. *(Pause)* He
30   wants me to sue them for damaging my child.
31 **CLOE:** Then mister junior doctor says: *(Adopting her imitation of*
32   *the doctor's voice:)* "Your baby can go home today, Mrs.
33   Brodski. Test results show that Maria had a stroke sometime
34   after she was born and that caused the seizures. Bye-bye!"
35 **ANGELA:** A stroke? Wait! How? Why?

1 CLOE: *(Doctor's voice)* "We may never know all the answers to
2   those questions."
3 ANGELA: Do "we" know *any* answers to any questions? Some? One?
4   Doctor? Could it have been caused by the Vacuum Extraction?
5 CLOE: *(Doctor's voice)* "Absolutely not! VE's a safe method! This
6   could have been caused by any number of things."
7 ANGELA: Such as?
8 CLOE: *(Doctor's voice)* "Such as — any number of things. We just
9   don't know. The tests only show that she had a stroke — not
10   what caused it. The good news is that babies heal very quickly.
11   Especially their brains. Here, I've written down the number of
12   a local support group that you might want to contact."
13 ANGELA: Support group? There's a support group for this? This
14   is a big enough problem that there's a support group and yet
15   we don't know what causes it?
16 CLOE: *(Doctor's voice)* "The nurses will demonstrate the exercises
17   you'll need to do with — with — the baby to prevent muscle
18   atrophy. They'll give you an alarm blanket, to alert you if she
19   stops breathing. Be sure to lay her on her back. Be sure that
20   her head is aligned. Bye-bye!"
21 ANGELA: There's nothing wrong with this baby!
22 CLOE: *(Resuming her own voice)* Sweetheart, your daddy's only
23   looking out for your best interests. He's my boy, God love him,
24   but we both know how he gets. Keeps talking about them
25   Vacuum Extractors. Just talk to the lawyer, then he'll let you be.
26 ANGELA: There's nothing wrong with this baby! See? Her hand
27   moved.
28 BRAD: I'm tired. I think I'll take a nap. *(He curls up in a fetal
29   position on the bed.)*
30 ANGELA: There's nothing wrong with my baby. Suing would be
31   saying there's something wrong with my baby. *(Pause)* There's
32   nothing wrong with my baby. *(ANGELA curls up in the chair
33   and cradles her baby.)*
34   *The End*
35

Blackberry Picking
by Sam Smiley

Sam Smiley's book *Playwriting: The Structure of Action* is widely used in America and abroad. He headed dramatic writing programs at the universities of Indiana, Missouri, and Arizona. Twenty-two of his stage plays have been produced. He also writes screenplays and serves as a story consultant for major film projects. He has written freelance scripts for major TV series, served as head writer for the TBS series "The Catlins," and worked as a story consultant for producers at Warner Brothers, Twentieth Century Fox, and ABC Television.

Playwright's Production Suggestions

This play focuses on the characters and their inner responses revealed physically. So, as is true of Shakespeare's plays, the actors can and should create the setting; no scenery is necessary. The characters' dialog and reactions to their surroundings should establish the milieu.

Lighting, sound, props, and costumes are quite important, though they too can be simply handled. The lighting should suggest bright morning sunlight in the central acting area, and the surrounding edges should be shadowy to suggest the surrounding forest. The natural sounds of birds and humming insects could nicely provide a soft background to the action. Music in the style of George Winston might precede and follow the action. The specific props called for in the script serve an important function in the action and should be the actual, realistic items. The clothes of the three people in the play help characterize them, and the descriptions of those costumes in the script provide helpful hints for assembling them.

Address all inquiries concerning performances, readings, or reprinting of this work *or any portion thereof* to Dr. Sam Smiley, 5799 N. Via Amable, Tucson, AZ 85750-1312. For details, see "Part II: Securing Rights for Your Production," pages 241 to 250.

1   The play's action takes place early one summer morning in a
2   meadow near a forest.
3   *CHARACTERS:* MARTHA — a professor. CALVIN — her husband,
4   also a professor. BLUE — a young woman.
5   *SETTING:* No scenery is necessary — only lights, props, costumes,
6   sound, and of course actors.
7
8   *(From the shadows of a forest where birds chirp and insects buzz,*
9   *MARTHA walks into a sunny meadow. A slender, almost frail*
10   *woman, she wears khaki pants, a purple shirt, an orange scarf,*
11   *and a wide-brimmed straw hat. She carries two galvanized*
12   *buckets and stops to look around. CALVIN trudges into view*
13   *carrying a picnic basket, a blanket, and two folding camp chairs.*
14   *He wears well-worn L.L. Bean clothes, gold-rimmed glasses, and*
15   *a baseball cap. She is smiling; he is not.)*
16   **MARTHA: Oh, here we are. Our enchanted meadow — sunlight**
17   **and tall grass, blackberries and butterflies.**
18   **CALVIN: Yes, we made it. After getting up at the crack of dawn**
19   **and trudging over hill and dale through the forest into clouds**
20   **of mosquitoes ...**
21   **MARTHA: Calvin, listen! Just listen. Do you hear anything?** *(Beat)*
22   **You can't hear it?**
23   **CALVIN: Sure, I can. I'm not deaf.**
24   **MARTHA: Well, you act like it. Life is so wonderful when you stop**
25   **and listen to it.**
26   **CALVIN: Martha, life doesn't make any noise. A living being can**
27   **squeak or howl or talk, but life itself is absolutely silent.**
28   **MARTHA: Yes, dear ... now just listen for a moment.**
29   **CALVIN:** *(He listens.)* **Can you give me a clue?**
30   **MARTHA: I knew you couldn't hear it. You said you could, but**
31   **you can't.**
32   **CALVIN: I hear it.**
33   **MARTHA: What do you hear?**
34   **CALVIN:** *(Guessing)* **Insects.** *(More certain)* **Bugs.**
35   **MARTHA: No. That's what you've harped on all morning —**

1   gnats, mosquitoes, ticks …
2   CALVIN: … and chiggers. That's what I hear. I hear chiggers.
3   MARTHA: Calvin. You can't hear chiggers.
4   CALVIN: *I* can. Right this minute I hear herds of them creeping
5   toward me, and soon we'll be scratching like dogs scratch
6   fleas. *(He deposits his burden.)*
7   MARTHA: Oh, stop.
8   CALVIN: Well, you sprayed yourself all over with DEET.
9   MARTHA: Calvin, listen to nature's music — crickets, cicadas,
10   birds. The birds always sing so happily here in our
11   wonderland. I can hear cardinals, larks, and … titmice. Just
12   listen to them singing their lovely little arias. *(They listen to*
13   *bird calls until suddenly a crow caws.)*
14 CALVIN: Would you call that Verdi or Mozart? *(Calling out)* Hey,
15   Mr. Crow. Swoop down here and eat these chiggers.
16 MARTHA: This is my favorite spot on earth, our secret lair in the
17   woods. *(Romantically)* Do you remember how many Fourth of
18   Julys we've picnicked here? Especially that first one. You
19   were so romantic.
20 CALVIN: *(Gruffly)* I'm still romantic.
21 MARTHA: *(Taking his hand)* You don't sound like it this morning.
22   *(She beams at him until he slowly breaks into a smile, puts his arm*
23   *around her, and recites.)*
24 CALVIN: I arise from dreams of thee
25   In the first sweet sleep of night,
26   When the winds are breathing low,
27   And the stars are shining bright.
28   I arise from dreams of thee,
29   And a spirit in my feet
30   Hath led me — who knows how?
31   To thy chamber window, Sweet!
32 MARTHA: I love it when you recite Shelley. *(Kisses his cheek.)*
33 CALVIN: Hmmm, I thought we came out here to pick
34   blackberries.
35 MARTHA: Oh, you! Northern Wisconsin is always so beautiful

195

1   this time of year. *(She moves off, and CALVIN unfolds a camp*
2   *chair.)* **The grass is dotted with little yellow daisies, purple**
3   **asters, Queen Anne's Lace ...**
4   CALVIN: **... ragweed, golden rod. Pretty soon I'll be sneezing like**
5   **a zebra.** *(Beat)* **I'm hungry.** *(He begins exploring the picnic*
6   *basket.)*
7   MARTHA: **It's too early to eat. We still have to do some blackberry**
8   **picking.**
9   CALVIN: **Well, if you're going to flit from flower to flower, I'm**
10   **going to watch the show.** *(He sits.)*
11   MARTHA: **Fine. You rest a minute while I explore this wonderland**
12   **of butterflies.**
13   CALVIN: **Keep your eye peeled for the Mad Hatter.** *(He finds*
14   *something in wax paper and sniffs it. She wanders farther and*
15   *farther away, while he unwraps a deviled egg.)*
16   MARTHA: **I can see Whites, Monarchs, Skippers. And oh, Calvin,**
17   **over there's a pale yellow Swallowtail with black wing tips and**
18   **tiger stripes. This is a butterfly lover's dream.**
19   CALVIN: **Or an insect nightmare. This place is crawling with ants**
20   **trying to steal our food.**
21   MARTHA: **And look over by the woods — a pair of black and**
22   **orange Checkerspots.** *(Just as he starts to take a bite of egg, she*
23   *yells.)* **Calvin!** *(He jumps up, juggling the half-eaten egg.)*
24   CALVIN: **What?** *(Eases toward her.)* **What is it — a snake, a skunk?**
25   MARTHA: **Someone's been picking our berries.**
26   CALVIN: **No!**
27   MARTHA: **Yes.** *(Then whispering)* **And look over there. It's a tent.**
28   CALVIN: **A what? Where?**
29   MARTHA: *(Still whispering)* **Right over there.** *(They draw together.)*
30   CALVIN: **I don't see anything.**
31   MARTHA: **Over there in the shadows — see that dark shape?**
32   CALVIN: *(Beat)* **That isn't a tent ... it's a bear.**
33   MARTHA: **Calvin, wipe your glasses. That's a pup tent.**
34   CALVIN: **What are dogs doing in a tent?**
35   MARTHA: **No ... a two-man tent.**

1   CALVIN: Well, what do you know! I better go get my shotgun.

2   MARTHA: Your what? You don't even own a shotgun.

3   CALVIN: Well, if there are two men hiding out in our woods, I
4   better get one.

5   MARTHA: Calvin, we don't know who it is. Maybe it's Boy Scouts.

6   CALVIN: Well, I don't want a bunch of pimple-faced punks
7   plundering our timber. They'll scare off all our snakes and
8   skunks, not to mention trampling our milkweed and horse-
9   nettle.

10   MARTHA: Calvin, stop! Boy Scouts take an oath to preserve the
11   flora and fauna.

12   CALVIN: I don't believe a word of it. All Boy Scouts do is salute
13   and go skinny dipping.

14   MARTHA: Look. Someone's crawling out of the tent.

15   CALVIN: I better get a stick. If they come after us, you can spray
16   'em with DEET.

17   MARTHA: Shhh! It's a ... I think it's a woman. A young woman.

18   CALVIN: I definitely need a stick.

19   MARTHA: *(Waving)* Hello there. *(BLUE walks into view. She wears*
20   *worn-out sneakers, tattered low-slung jeans, and a tank top that*
21   *shows her midriff. She has silver rings in her ears and belly*
22   *button, and a set of earphones around her neck, the wire*
23   *disappearing into a pocket.)*

24   BLUE: Hey, wha-sup? Real groovy day, huh? *(They stare at her.)*
25   Isn't this a awesome meadow ... and the forest won't quit. So
26   whatcha doin'? *(Beat)* Hey, I bet you two came out here to pick
27   blackberries, right? I tell ya one thing — they're scrumptious.

28   MARTHA: Yes, I noticed someone has already picked quite a few.

29   BLUE: *(Grins.)* You nailed me. Look — purple hands. I'm the
30   guilty party, but since I'm camping out here, I just helped
31   myself. *(Offers to shake.)* My name's Blue Sky. *(CALVIN shakes*
32   *hands gingerly.)*

33   CALVIN: I'm Calvin Curtis, and this is my wife, Martha. How'd
34   you get such a strange name?

35   BLUE: My real name's Smith, but I like Sky better. And when I

1   was born my mom said my face was blue. So there you are.
2   I'm Blue Sky.
3 MARTHA: Well, Miss Sky, what exactly are you doing here on our
4   property ... besides camping out and eating blackberries?
5 BLUE: Oh, uh ... well, I'm camping out here doing a summer
6   research thing, uh, project.
7 CALVIN: What do you study — spiders, slugs, stink bugs?
8 BLUE: *(Laughs.)* Yeah right. I study insects at the University of
9   Wisconsin-Madison.
10 MARTHA: How nice. My husband's a professor there. *(BLUE*
11   *grows more cagey.)*
12 BLUE: Cool. *(To CALVIN, kidding)* What do you teach, animal
13   husbandry?
14 CALVIN: *(Chuckles.)* No, I teach dead poets. They're not my
15   students; they're my subjects. Tell me, since you study insects,
16   do you know anything about chiggers?
17 BLUE: A little. And I know lots about the moths and the beetles.
18 CALVIN: They're musicians, right?
19 BLUE: Dude, you got a Smashmouth sense of humor. I love poets
20   too, you know, like Nelly and L L Cool J. *(The names mystify*
21   *CALVIN.)* Tell me about your dead poets.
22 CALVIN: The ones I'm talking about write romantic poetry.
23 BLUE: Romantic, huh? Then you must be quite a lover, Calvin.
24   *(They grin at each other.)* Hey, ya know, I once read a book by
25   Shelley. *Frankenstein.*
26 MARTHA: Shelley's wife, Mary, wrote that.
27 BLUE: Oh, yeah? *(To CALVIN)* Well, could ya recite one of his
28   poems? *(He's delighted.)*
29 CALVIN: Sacred Goddess, Mother Earth,
30   Thou from whose immortal bosom
31   Gods and men and beasts have birth,
32   Leaf and blade, and bud and blossom,
33   Breathe thine influence most divine
34   On thine own child, Proserpine.
35 BLUE: Man, you're good. You sound like an antique Eminem.

1   CALVIN: *(Glowing)* Now, maybe you could tell me about chiggers.

2   BLUE: Sure. I got a poem about 'em.

3   There is a little chigger

4   That isn't any bigger

5   Than the point of a very small pin.

6   The lump that he raises

7   Just itches like the blazes

8   And that's where the rub comes in!

9   *(CALVIN laughs, but MARTHA does not.)*

10 MARTHA: Obviously, Miss Sky doesn't know much about

11   chiggers.

12 BLUE: Oh, yes I do. Chiggers are the larvae of the harvest mite.

13   An adult feeds on plant juice, but for a larva to become a

14   nymph, it needs a meal of mammal protoplasm. When you

15   walk through tall grass, the hairs on the legs of chiggers catch

16   on your clothing, and then they crawl upward. They climb

17   and climb until they find a patch of tender skin with hair on

18   it — like around your ankles, knees, or groin. And here's the

19   gross part. Right in that tender area, a chigger grabs one of

20   your hairs and pukes into the follicle pore.

21 MARTHA: Charming.

22 BLUE: Chigger puke has an enzyme that dissolves the walls of

23   your skin cells so they rupture and protoplasm runs out.

24 CALVIN: Then what happens?

25 BLUE: The chigger laps up the protoplasm, burps, releases his grip,

26   falls to the ground and begins its transformation into a nymph.

27   But you're left with a big red bump that itches like blazes.

28 MARTHA: That's informative, but you don't exactly talk like an

29   entomologist.

30 CALVIN: No, she's quite informative. I never realized that I'm

31   allergic to chigger puke.

32 MARTHA: Miss Sky, I'm acquainted with the faculty of the

33   University's Entomology Department. Who's your major

34   professor?

35 BLUE: Oh. Well, uh, Professor, uh, Sandler. Yeah, Professor Adam

1   Sandler.
2   MARTHA: I don't believe I know him.
3   BLUE: *(Quickly)* Well, don't sweat it. Hey, let me show you some
4   stuff I've done for my project. *(She rushes off to her tent.)*
5   MARTHA: There's something's fishy going on here.
6   CALVIN: Fishy? You think she's been in our pond as well as the
7   blackberry patch?
8   MARTHA: Calvin, I'm a member of the Entomology faculty and
9   teach in the Russell Labs building. Ken Raffa is our forest
10   insect specialist. There is no Professor Adam Sandler.
11   CALVIN: *(Thinks a moment.)* I've heard that name before ... maybe
12   a politician or something.
13   MARTHA: If she's lying about what she's doing here, then maybe
14   she's a criminal and we should call the sheriff.
15   CALVIN: She's not a criminal just because she has a pierced navel
16   and tattooed buttocks.
17   MARTHA: Tattooed what? How did you see that?
18   CALVIN: Those low-slung jeans.
19   MARTHA: Well, she is trespassing on posted land. Our land. We
20   could prosecute her. *(He starts to protest.)* I'll face her down,
21   and you order her off the property.
22   CALVIN: Me? I wouldn't even know she was here, if you hadn't
23   dragged me through the woods and into the bugs. *(BLUE*
24   *returns with sheets of construction paper.)*
25   BLUE: I couldn't find my notebook, but here's some sketches I've
26   been doing.
27   MARTHA: I don't mean to be unfriendly, Miss Sky, but you see, I
28   also teach at the University ... in the Entomology Department.
29   BLUE: Aw oh.
30   MARTHA: We have no Professor Sandler. *(BLUE looks guilty.)* My
31   dear, after years and years of teaching, I can read the face of
32   any student who lies to me.
33   BLUE: Listen, Miz Curtis, you got me all wrong. I really am a
34   student.
35   MARTHA: Perhaps. But surely not a university student. And I

1   seriously doubt that you're out here doing research.

2 BLUE: Sure I am.

3 CALVIN: Is there anyone with you in that two man, uh, two person

4   tent? *(BLUE nods no.)*

5 MARTHA: How old are you — sixteen — and you're out here all

6   alone?

7 BLUE: Yeah, but considering where I grew up, I can take care of

8   myself.

9 CALVIN: Where'd you park your car? *(She blinks at him.)* How'd

10   you get here?

11 BLUE: The only car I ever had was a pile of junk in an empty lot.

12   It wouldn't run, but I slept in it. I got out here by hitchin'

13   rides and walkin'.

14 MARTHA: Where are your parents? *(BLUE looks back and forth*

15   *between them and suddenly seems out of breath.)*

16 BLUE: I got no parents. None I'd claim anyway. *(She looks up at*

17   *them with tears in her eyes.)*

18 MARTHA: *(To Calvin)* She's probably lying again. *(BLUE throws*

19   *down her drawings defiantly.)*

20 BLUE: No, I'm not! I'm protecting myself. I graduated from high

21   school in South Chicago a month ago, and I been workin' ever

22   since at a Burger King and livin' with my mom. But two

23   weeks ago she got busted again for sellin' crack and I didn't

24   want to hit the streets so I just took off.

25 CALVIN: Where's your father?

26 BLUE: Never met him. *(To MARTHA)* You said you could look at

27   someone's face and tell if they're lying. *(Approaching her)* Look

28   me right in the eye and judge for yourself. *(As the women stare at*

29   *each other, CALVIN picks up the drawings and looks at them.)*

30 CALVIN: Martha. Look. Look at what she's done. *(MARTHA pays*

31   *no attention.)* You told *me* to listen. Now, you come look.

32   *(CALVIN holds up the drawings one at a time. They are large,*

33   *bright studies of butterflies.)*

34 MARTHA: You drew those?

35 BLUE: *(Shrugs.)* All I had was cheap paper and colored pencils

1   from Walgreens.

2   MARTHA: They're superb. The most detailed renderings I've ever

3   seen.

4   CALVIN: She's a lepidopterist. *(CALVIN goes on showing drawings*

5   *as they talk.)*

6   BLUE: A butterfly lover? You're kidding. Me too. I mean, I'm no

7   expert like you, but I'm crazy about 'em. I read that

8   butterflies love the edge of a forest. That's why I'm living out

9   here. *(Warming up to the subject)* Did you know that all these

10   wildflowers are dependent on butterflies for pollination? That

11   means no butterflies, no flowers. And butterfly caterpillars

12   are food for wild animals and birds, which means when the

13   butterfly population goes down, birds and animals suffer too.

14   Butterflies have been around for millions of years, much

15   longer than humans. But I'm sure you know lots more about

16   'em than me. *(As BLUE's enthusiasm grows, MARTHA responds*

17   *more and more sympathetically.)*

18   MARTHA: Well, for one thing, they show that non-aggressive

19   creatures can thrive in nature.

20   BLUE: Right, an' butterflies live everywhere on earth, from the

21   Sahara to the North Pole.

22   MARTHA: You really do know a lot. I'm amazed with you, Blue,

23   amazed at your interest, your knowledge, not to mention your

24   artistic talent. If you're making such wonderful drawings, you

25   have every right to be out here in our woods.

26   BLUE: Thanks, Miz Curtis.

27   MARTHA: *(Cordially)* I'm Martha. How would you like to pick

28   some more berries with us?

29   CALVIN: And join our picnic.

30   BLUE: Love to. Let's go. *(She hooks MARTHA'S arm, and the two get*

31   *the buckets and head for the blackberries, both chattering about*

32   *butterflies. CALVIN lags behind to put the drawings down safely.)*

33   MARTHA: *(Calling back)* Come on, Calvin. We've got work to do.

34   CALVIN: In a minute. *(To himself)* Got to spray myself with DEET.

35   *The End*

A Play about Color

by Norman A. Bert

**from materials submitted by Nadia Bodie, Heidi Dier,
Kevin Garnepudi, Brian Griffin, Hershell Norwood,
Seung-joo Park, Ricky Ramón, Michele Rodriquez,
Lei Ting, and Keith West**

Norman Bert has taught theatre on the college level since the mid-1970s. He teaches playwriting and script analysis at Texas Tech University. He has directed over 30 productions and served as an ACTF adjudicator. His published books include *Theatre Alive: An Introductory Anthology of World Drama* and *The Scenebook for Actors*.

The contributors are students in American colleges and universities. Some of them are American citizens, and others are not. They responded to an invitation to contribute their thoughts about being ethnically diverse in America. They contributed their lives.

Playwright's Production Suggestions

This play is imagistic, rhythmic, and idea-based rather than being story- and character-based. To perform it well, the actors must play the images in the speeches and concentrate on the rhythms of the piece.

If the play is too long for performance slot, the producers should feel free to cut speeches or segments.

The titles of the play's segments should be displayed by projection or on title cards. The set might be dressed with images that reflect the ethnic diversity that makes up the United States. One option would be to arrange large, abstract, colorful objects around the stage with the titles printed on their backs; as each title is announced, the actors could turn an object around to display the title.

Address all inquiries concerning performances, readings, or reprinting of this work *or any portion thereof* to Norman A. Bert, 5704 Nashville Avenue, Lubbock, TX 79413. For details, see "Part II: Securing Rights for Your Production," pages 241 to 250.

1   The action takes place now on a stage.

2 ***CHARACTERS:*** WOMAN 1, WOMAN 2, MAN 1, and MAN 2 —

3   four performers of any age or ethnicity.

4 ***SETTING:*** The scenery indicates no specific location. It might provide

5   levels, chairs or stools, and tables to provide variety in staging.

6

7 **WOMAN 1: This is a play about color.**

8 **MAN 1: A play about the color *[1] of pride.**

9 **WOMAN 2: A play about the pride * of color.**

10 **MAN 2: A play about the color * of anger.**

11 **WOMAN 1: The color of fear.**

12 **MAN 1: This is a play about the colors * of America.**

13 **WOMAN 2: Red, white, * and blue.**

14 **MAN 2: Black, brown, * and white.**

15 **WOMAN 1: Red and yellow, black and white, and red and white**

16   **and blue.**

17 **MAN 1: This is a play about us: Students * in America.**

18 **WOMAN 2: Students * who are different.**

19 **MAN 2: Students of color.**

20 **WOMAN 1: This is a play about us.**

21 **ALL: This is a play about color.**

22

23

24   **WHO I AM / WHO AM I?**

25

26   *(The title is projected.)*

27 **WOMAN 1: Who * I am —**

28 **MAN 1: Who * am I?**

29 **WOMAN 2: Who * I am —**

30 **MAN 2: Who am I?**

31

32   [1] The lines of the play should sometimes overlap, like different pigments being layered on

33   a picture. An asterisk (*) indicates the beginning of the next line. In this footnoted case,

34   WOMAN 2 begins her line "A play about the pride of color" immediately upon MAN

    1's word "color"

35

1 ◊ ◊ ◊
2
3 MAN 2: I am Brian. I'm African American. Six hundred dollars,
4 and I can't cash a check.
5 WOMAN 2: I'm Heidi. My father's American. My mother's from
6 Korea. I bleached my hair. It's something different, which is
7 what I was going for. I think I like it.
8 WOMAN 1: I'm Nadia. I'm from the Bahamas. I'm special — not
9 because of where I was born, but because I'm a unique
10 individual, wanting to be the best I can be.
11 MAN 1: I'm Keith. I'm part Native American. I've got fair skin
12 and freckles. My hair is sandy, and my eyes are blue. I'm
13 proud of my heritage — on both sides of the family. Proud of
14 the Chickasaw, even if I don't look it.
15 WOMAN 2: I am Lei, and I am Chinese — from Taiwan. Being a
16 part of minority, I cannot stand up for myself with my poor
17 English. It is really hard sometimes.
18 MAN 1: Hi. I'm Kevin. My parents came here from India. I'm
19 Indian — Desi. I would never want to be anything but Desi.
20 WOMAN 1: I'm Michele. My daughter Miranda is four. Her
21 father was from Trinidad.
22 MAN 2: I'm Ricky. I'm Chicano. Do people really know who I am?
23 WOMAN 2: I am Seung-Joo. I am from Korea. I wonder whether
24 people understand me or not.
25 MAN 2: I'm Hershell. I'm African American. Being black means
26 you are born with a double conscience. Two worlds, two
27 realities you live in all the time. This is a strange condition. No
28 one tells you this. You watch it. You feel it. And one day you
29 are aware it's in you.
30 WOMAN 1: Who are we?
31 MAN 1: We are * the voices.
32 WOMAN 2: We are * the colors.
33 MAN 2: We are the voices of our colors.
34 ALL: This is our play. This is a play about color.
35

1   **I FELL IN LOVE WITH A COUNTRY ONCE**

2

3   *(The title is projected.)*

4   MAN 2: I fell in love with a country once.

5   WOMAN 2: My mom wants to go back to Korea next year. I'd like

6   to go. I love Korea. It's a beautiful place, the sort of country

7   that gets into your blood. And you just ache to go back, and

8   you cry when you leave it.

9   WOMAN 1: I was asked to sing the national anthem at the

10   graduation ceremony at Ohio State. I was totally surprised by

11   the invitation. I informed the supervisor that I was not

12   American, and was she positive I was the one she wanted. She

13   told me that it didn't matter if I could sing as well as my

14   department said and proceeded to tell me that she had two

15   black friends. Well — *(Pause)*

16   I told her I'd be happy to sing the national anthem. Why

17   wouldn't I be? It was in this country that I came into

18   womanhood. It was in this country that I got my first car, my

19   driver's license, my first big crush. It was this country that

20   provided me with friends. I was baptized here. So hell yeah,

21   lady, I'll sing the national anthem! And I did. And from the

22   beginning of the song 'til the end, I cried and laughed inside.

23   MAN 2: I fell in love with a country once,

24   And I loved it as much as my own.

25   Then the towers fell and I was alone.

26

27

28   **RACISM AND FEAR**

29

30   *(The title is projected.)*

31   MAN 1: That's just terrific. The sniper's Muslim. Now every piece

32   of white trash will think that I carry a gun — and a bomb!

33   WOMAN 1: Racism.

34   MAN 1: Racism * and fear.

35   WOMAN 2: Racism * and fear.

206

1   MAN 2: Racism and fear.

2   MAN 1: Some people are racist and don't even realize it.

3

4   ◊ ◊ ◊

5

6   MAN 2: Being black means you learn to read well the words in

7   other black eyes. Most important you learn to know not only

8   when to move but what move to make. No matter if it's literal

9   or symbol, the wrong move in the white man's eyes gets us all

10   killed. We learn well how to read words in other black eyes.

11 MAN 1: I'm not racist, even though it might come off as so. When

12   my parents came to this country in the '70s, they wouldn't let

13   my father be a surgeon. The exact words were, "We don't let

14   foreigners be surgeons, only Americans." Although my father

15   is now a successful doctor, since that day he has had nothing

16   but hatred to many white people. When I was little, some lady

17   at a Blockbuster thought she could cut in front of us, told us

18   to go back to our country. And proceeded to go to the front of

19   the line. We left Kentucky soon after, 'cause my dad didn't

20   want me to go through the same racism that he went through.

21   That was when I was five. I've never been able to get that

22   image out of my head.

23 WOMAN 1: A black person has white folks and their world forced

24   upon her. But like my grandmother says, there are some good

25   ones and some bad ones, too. Yet because they all seem to be

26   related, what is really the place of a black person in all this? As

27   far as I can see, they kill each other over riches and possession

28   every day. So, I wonder, what do they want to do to me?

29 MAN 1: It's funny: when my dad wants to talk about white people

30   on the cell phone, he'll only talk in Telegue — my native

31   language. He thinks the world's out to get us.

32 WOMAN 1: If I tell them, will they attack me?

33 WOMAN 2: *(Spoken simultaneously with following line.)* Will they

34   attack me?

35 MAN 1: *(Spoken simultaneously with previous line.)* Racism and fear.

1   **WOMAN 1:** If I tell them, * will they attack me?

2   **WOMAN 2:** *(Spoken simultaneously with following line.)* **Will they**

3   **attack me?**

4   MAN 1: *(Spoken simultaneously with previous line.)* **Racism and fear.**

5

6   ◊ ◊ ◊

7

8   **MAN 2:** The wrong move in the eyes gets us all killed.

9

10

11   **I'M PROUD**

12

13   *(The title is projected.)*

14   **WOMAN 1:** I was asked to sing the national anthem. I wasn't an

15   American but I was a part of the community and very proud

16   * of it.

17   **WOMAN 2:** I'm * proud.

18   **MAN 1:** I'm * proud.

19   **WOMAN 1:** I'm * proud.

20   **MAN 2:** I'm proud.

21

22   ◊ ◊ ◊

23

24   **MAN 1:** Going to pow-wow or dances with other tribes always

25   brings pride to my heart. After all these years of families

26   hiding their blood, we have something to be proud about.

27   Grand parade into the circle, holding the American flag after

28   the lead dancer enters. It's now our flag too. My uncles were

29   fighting and dying for that flag in war, even when they were

30   being look down upon by whites.

31   **WOMAN 1:** I'm proud. Damn proud.

32   **MAN 1:** I don't act black, 'cause I'm not. I'm Indian, and damn

33   proud. I would never want to be anything but Desi.

34   **WOMAN 1:** I'm proud. * Damn proud.

35   **MAN 1:** I'm * proud.

1   WOMAN 2: I'm * proud.
2   MAN 2: I'm proud.
3
4
5   **I DON'T LIKE YOU, EITHER**
6
7   *(The title is projected.)*
8   WOMAN 2: And guess what, Whitey? We don't really like you
9   either!
10
11   ◊ ◊ ◊
12
13   WOMAN 1: Honky,
14   Hiemie,
15   Limey,
16   Mick.
17   MAN 1: Commie,
18   Nazi,
19   Yanqui,
20   Kraut.
21   WOMAN 2: White Eyes,
22   Red Neck,
23   Squarehead,
24   Yid.
25   MAN 2: Gringo,
26   Anglo,
27   Dago,
28   Dog.
29   WOMAN 1: Shylock,
30   Polack,
31   Paleface,
32   Frog.
33   MAN 1: Schiksa,
34   Cracker,
35   Goomba,

1   Wop.
2   ALL TOGETHER: Mr. Charlie,
3   Little Eva:
4   We don't really
5   Like you either!
6
7   ◊ ◊ ◊
8
9   WOMAN 2: No one worries about getting stuck with a stinky
10   roommate. They worry that their roommate will be too
11   different, too weird, too preppy, too dorky. Never stinky. No
12   one thinks about the stinky roommate.
13   MAN 2: So shut up, cracker.
14   MAN 1: Dumb white eyes!
15
16   ◊ ◊ ◊
17
18   MAN 1: Complaints in the news about Native American gambling
19   halls and bingo halls. Mainstream Indians don't understand
20   why they can't gamble as well. I see streams of busses and
21   vans filled with little old ladies pouring their money into the
22   halls. Most are white. I have to think, nice revenge!
23   WOMAN 1: She proceeded to tell me that she had two black
24   friends. "First of all," and I said this to myself, "if you have to
25   tell someone how many black friends you have, they won't
26   find it very impressive."
27   MAN 1: For the last time, I'm Indian — not Hispanic, not Black,
28   definitely not Pak, or anything else you ignorant people think.
29   MAN 2: So shut up, cracker.
30   WOMAN 1: Honky,
31   Hiemie,
32   Limey,
33   Mick.
34   MAN 2: Gringo,
35   Anglo,

1   Dago,
2   Dog.
3   ALL TOGETHER: Mr. Charlie,
4   Little Eva:
5   We don't really
6   Like you either!
7
8
9   DATING A COLOR
10
11   *(The title is projected.)*
12   WOMAN 2: I would like to marry a guy who is black and white
13   mix, so we can have an Asian, black, and white mix baby.
14   WOMAN 1: Date me, * date my color.
15   MAN 1: Date me, * date my color.
16   WOMAN 2: Date me, * date my color.
17   MAN 2: Date me, date my color.
18   MAN 1: Yeah I'm out with a white girl. Get over it, redneck.
19   WOMAN 1: I saw this really cute white guy in the food store. I said
20   hello, but he ignored me. To console myself, I said that he was
21   probably occupied with his shopping list. But in most cases,
22   they're just not interested. He saw a color and not a beautiful
23   woman. That's too bad, for him — and me. I did date a white
24   European once, but he was different. He was from
25   Czechoslovakia, and he wasn't concerned about my color. He
26   thought I was pretty and funny, and that was it. He told me
27   that his people worked and prayed hard. If they ever fell in
28   love, well that was good. A good woman was a good woman. I
29   remember he called me Nadiezdha.
30   MAN 1: Date me, * date my color.
31   MAN 2: Date me, date my color.
32   WOMAN 2: My American friends said that my eyes are pretty, but
33   while I were in Taiwan my eyes are so normal. People in
34   Taiwan like big eyes and my eyes are small. I guess it is one
35   good reason being a minority. I also have a white girl friend

211

1   who said she wants to be Asian, so she can get laid everyday. I
2   do not know where she got this idea from.
3   MAN 1: When I was dating a white girl a white cop pulled me over.
4   First he said that I was turning out of a non-turning lane.
5   Nope. Then I was running a red. Nope. After those two failed,
6   he said that I was speeding — forty-seven in a forty-five.
7   That's crap. Then he thinks that it's impossible for a colored
8   kid to have a BMW. So he pulls out my girlfriend, and asks if
9   she's OK, while I have my hands on the hood for going two
10   miles over the speed limit. He implies that I raped her —
11   probably gonna kill her. It's not possible for a rich, proper
12   white girl to love a foreigner. I have never seen worse racism
13   in my life.
14   WOMAN 2: "I want to marry a rock star," I said.
15   "Which one?" my sister said.
16   "Clark. Brett."
17   "Both of them?"
18   "Sure. Or one can be my pool boy."
19   Then she changed the subject.
20   MAN 1: She said: "Once you go black, you never go back, right?"
21   I said: "I'm not black."
22   WOMAN 1: Date me, * date my color.
23   WOMAN 2: Date me, date my color.
24
25
26   IDENTITY: I'M SPECIAL
27
28   *(The title is projected.)*
29   WOMAN 2: I'm special.
30   WOMAN 1: I'm special, * not because of where I was born but
31   because of who I am.
32   MAN 1: I'm * special.
33   WOMAN 2: I'm * special.
34   MAN 2: I'm special.
35   WOMAN 2: I wonder what people think about me.

1   ◊ ◊ ◊
2
3 MAN 1: Even though I was taught to be racist, I believe that
4   everybody is equal, although sometimes my thoughts drift. I
5   was just worried that you might get a wrong impression of me.
6 MAN 2: It's a strange phenomenon living black. It's something
7   your total body and being is aware of before your mind is able
8   to see it. That's why it happens at birth. *(Pause)*
9   When you wake up mornings to that scent of grandma's
10   kitchen. It's southern love that lets you know "I'm home
11   again." And when the big fish fry on Friday night stirs people
12   to come together, being black brings a warm smile to all the
13   faces. But don't let nobody start that laughter 'cause it won't
14   quit 'til the wee hours of the dawn. When you laugh black,
15   you really * laugh.
16 WOMAN 2: I don't like to blend in. I want to stand out of the
17   crowd. But not in that loud, obnoxious way. Quietly.
18 MAN 1: I never thought of myself as Hispanic American before.
19   Maybe Mexican. Or Chicano. Which? OK, Chicano.
20 WOMAN 2: Yes: Stand out. But * quietly.
21 ALL: *(Repeating, getting quieter and quieter until they fade out)* **Quietly,**
22   quietly, quietly, quietly, quietly, quietly, quietly, quietly ...
23
24
25   **COLOR ME SMART**
26
27   *(The title is projected.)*
28 WOMAN 1: What color * is the mind?
29 WOMAN 2: What color is ignorance?
30 WOMAN 1: Color * me smart.
31 MAN 1: Color * me smart.
32 WOMAN 2: Color * me smart.
33 MAN 2: Color * me smart.
34
35   ◊ ◊ ◊

213

1   WOMAN 2: I want you to go to other countries wherever you
2   cannot understand their languages, because I want you to
3   have a being stupid experience like me.
4   MAN 1: Got to remember to look up, look them straight in the eyes.
5   They don't understand. They won't understand.
6   WOMAN 1: What color * is the mind?
7   WOMAN 2: What color is ignorance?
8   MAN 1: It's funny how when people find out that I'm Desi, not
9   African American, they seem to treat me with more respect,
10   and respect my intelligence.
11   WOMAN 1: What color * is the mind?
12   WOMAN 2: What color is ignorance?
13   MAN 1: Remember being taken out of class in freshman year of
14   high school for "Minority Counseling." They were concerned
15   the little Indian kids weren't able to get good grades. I had a
16   4.0 at the time. When I got back to class, everyone kept staring
17   at me. Then the jokes and put-downs started. They didn't
18   know my family background, until then.
19   MAN 2: Diversity Training! Everyone at Notre Dame was expected
20   to attend this workshop. They taught us how to act around
21   and how to treat and work with people of color. They taught
22   us how to be sensitive. Are we that different that people need
23   to be taught how to treat us? I didn't know I was a minority
24   until I went to Notre Dame. Constantly I was reminded that I
25   was different by professors and my roommates and dorm
26   mates. One time one professor said she would provide me
27   extra assistance because she knew where I came from. *What?!*
28   Where did she think I was from? The Land of the Dumb
29   where only people of color live?!
30   WOMAN 1: The words of W.E.B. Du Bois:
31   WOMAN 2: The words of color:
32   MAN 2: "Either the United States will destroy ignorance, or
33   ignorance will destroy the United States."
34
35

1   **BELONGING**

2

3   *(The title is projected.)*

4 WOMAN 1: I feel lonely.

5 MAN 2: Lonely.

6 WOMAN 2: Lonely.

7 MAN 1: Lonely.

8 MAN 2: Why do people give me that look?

9 WOMAN 2: I feel isolation of other people.

10 MAN 1: When you meet another Desi, you're instantly friends and

11   have a connection.

12 WOMAN 2: I feel lonely often. I feel I am different and never can

13   fit into the majority's society. Being a part of minority, I

14   cannot stand up for myself with my poor English. It is really

15   hard sometimes. I am adjusting my feeling all the time. I need

16   to tell myself all the time that I am important; I have my value

17   to be here. I don't need to worry about people who cannot

18   appreciate me.

19 WOMAN 1: I feel * lonely.

20 MAN 1: Why do people * give me that look?

21 WOMAN 2: I feel isolation of other people.

22 MAN 1: Inter-Tribal Dances in Odessa. Master of Drum has to ask

23   audience members not to toss tobacco onto the drum itself. I

24   feel embarrassed that the audience would do this, in their

25   attempt to "honor the drum." Feel like I'm an outsider as

26   well. Just another tourist watching the pretty Indian

27   costumes. Looking white didn't work on the Indian side of the

28   family either. Growing up, we wouldn't play Cowboys and

29   Indians. We'd play Custer and Indians. I was passing,[3] so I'd

30   play Custer. Even got scalped by my younger cousin. She was

31   about four or five at the time. *(Pause)*

32   Never fit in with the Indian cousins — those that looked

33   like it. Their friends were Osage, and never really trusted me,

34

35   [3] "Passing" — appearing to be Anglo rather than Indian.

215

1   even though I was family to my cousins.
2   WOMAN 1: I feel * lonely.
3   MAN 1: Why do people * give me that look?
4   WOMAN 2: I feel isolation of other people.
5   MAN 2: I feel the wall between people.
6
7
8   COLOR IS THE FIRST THING PEOPLE NOTICE.
9
10   *(The title is projected.)*
11   WOMAN 1: No matter what they say, color is the first * thing
12   people notice.
13   MAN 1: Color is the first * thing people notice.
14   WOMAN 2: Color is the first * thing people notice.
15   MAN 2: Color is the first thing people notice.
16   MAN 2: Saw *White Man's Burden* this morning. An alternate
17   reality where blacks were the "superior" race and whites were
18   the "niggers." Hm.
19   WOMAN 1: We blocked the curtain call for *Damn Yankees* and
20   everything seemed to be going well until someone on the line
21   pointed out that I was placed right next to the only other black
22   girl in the cast. He made me begin to think about whether this
23   was a conscious or subconscious decision. I'll never know.
24   What I find interesting is that I never thought of black and
25   white to the degree that Americans do. I've never thought of
26   one color being lesser than the other, not even when we were
27   taught about slavery in class in my country. I never thought
28   about any of these things until I started schooling here.
29   MAN 2: Beware of the blackface jiggle and jive, the jingle and
30   song. The trickster's grin has many meanings. Even death
31   sometimes is his motivation.
32   WOMAN 1: Miranda came home from day-care today and said,
33   "Mommy, the kids at school say I'm black and white. Am I
34   black and white?" I told her, "You're a lovely shade of tan.
35   And you look like my daughter."

1   MAN 1: Wow, I'm the only person that's not white in this class,
2   and that class, * and that class, and that class, and that class,
3   and that class …
4   WOMAN 2: I bleached my hair. It's something different, which is
5   what I was going for. I think I like it.
6   MAN 1: I wonder if I would get those looks in the honors dorm if I
7   was white.
8
9   ◊ ◊ ◊
10
11   WOMAN 1: This is a play about color.
12   MAN 1: A play about the color of pride.
13   WOMAN 2: A play about the pride of color.
14   MAN 2: A play about the color of anger.
15   WOMAN 1: The color of fear.
16   MAN 1: This is a play about the colors of America.
17   ALL: This is a play about color.
18   *The End*
19
20
21
22
23
24
25
26
27
28
29
30
31
32
33
34
35

Demetra Tseckares (seated) and Barbara Pinto star in Help Me, I'm Becoming My Mother, *one of ten short features in WHYY's production, PHILADELPHIA PERFORMS. Photo by Steven Katz.*

Help Me, I'm Becoming My Mother!
by Deanna Riley

Deanna Riley, a native southerner, lives and writes in Delaware where she teaches playwriting at Baltimore's Goucher College. Her work with the Maryland Public Television comedy show "Crabs" won two regional Best Entertainment Special Emmys.

Help Me, I'm Becoming My Mother! originally appeared in a three-character version in "Spotlights" and "Philadelphia Performs" on the Philadelphia PBS station WHYY-TV 12 in February 1992. Ms. Riley adapted the play to its present single-character version for stage presentation.

Production Suggestions

Experiment until you find a "Mother's voice" that is distinctly different from your own. Observe the stage-direction suggestions for pauses and vocal variations; you will, of course, want to develop your own phrasing and vocal qualities for the character, but do consider the suggestions the playwright makes. An understated, steady and rational characterization will be more effective in this piece than a bizarre, overly neurotic one.

Address all inquiries concerning performances, readings, or reprinting of this work *or any portion thereof* to Deanna Riley, 8 Wayne Dr., Wilmington, DE 19809. For details, see "Part II: Securing Rights for Your Production," pages 241 to 250.

1   The action takes place in a classroom.

2   *CHARACTER:* LYNN — a woman in her late twenties.

3   *SETTING:* LYNN sits in a child-sized chair.

4

5   **LYNN: I didn't mean for it to happen. It came upon me slowly.**

6   **Thought I had everything under control. But one day, I**

7   **couldn't deny it anymore. I was in the bathroom getting ready**

8   **for work. I looked in the mirror. There she was. Brushing her**

9   **teeth. My mother. That's tough in the morning. We even swish**

10   **and spit the same way.**

11   *(Whispers.)* **Help me. I'm becoming my mother.**

12   *(Apologetic)* **Not that it's necessarily bad. I love my mother.**

13   **It's just not what I wanted; what I planned. I wanted to be**

14   **strong. Independent. Different. Very different. I swore I would**

15   **never be even remotely like my mother. Cross my heart, hope**

16   **to die, stick a needle in my eye. The whole bit. But then I**

17   **began to notice little things. Words. Not my words. Mom**

18   **words. My mother's words.**

19   *(In mother's voice)* **Don't come out of that room until you**

20   **know how to behave.**

21   *(Normal voice)* **Do you know what I mean?**

22   *(In mother's voice)* **This is the last time I'm going to tell you.**

23   **I want you to eat every smell of it. Don't you think you'd be**

24   **more attractive with less make-up? How can they listen to that**

25   **racket?**

26   *(Normal voice)* **Why am I saying these things?**

27   *(In mother's voice)* **Because I said so.**

28   *(Normal voice)* **I don't understand how they just pop out of**

29   **my mouth.**

30   *(In mother's voice)* **Just wait, you'll find out.**

31   *(Normal voice)* **Strange things.**

32   *(In mother's voice)* **When I'm six feet under …**

33   *(Normal voice)* **That's exactly —**

34   *(In mother's voice)* **what I'm talking about** *(LYNN freezes in*

35   *horrified recognition. Regains her composure and continues.)*

1   *(Normal voice)* **Then one day I said *the* word.**

2   *(In mother's voice)* **Flagrant disobedience.**

3   *(Normal voice)* **It's actually two words. But I always**

4   **thought it was one.**

5   *(In mother's voice)* **Flagrant disobedience.**

6   *(Normal voice)* **When that unappetizing mouthful escaped,**

7   **two things happened. I had to suppress the sudden impulse to**

8   **rip out my tongue, while at the same time I felt strangely**

9   **powerful. "Please" is not the magic word, it's —**

10   *(In mother's voice)* **Flagrant disobedience.**

11   *(Normal voice)* **Finally, I understood why my mother used**

12   **it. It works. When you're eight years old, you don't know**

13   **what it means except pay attention or die. It mesmerizes you.**

14   **You can't move. Now I was truly terrified. I understood her.**

15   **And I began developing these mother myths. Mystifying**

16   **maternal abilities. I grew eyes in the back of my head. Instead**

17   **of ears, I have radar. I can hear cookie pilfering in the next**

18   **county. I can discover untruths without a lie detector. In**

19   **skillful and knowledgeable hands, mom ESP is a wonderful**

20   **thing. I am blessed to have these. Could have used them**

21   **earlier. But it's the other mother things that stick in your**

22   **craw. And I'm not just talking about the gray hairs, crow's**

23   **feet and wearing ugly sweaters because you're always cold.**

24   **When I was little, my mother was so bizarre. She'd write lists**

25   **on old envelopes. She wouldn't use notepads or regular paper,**

26   **but old envelopes.**

27   *(Whispers.)* **I'm saving old envelopes.**

28   *(Raising voice to norm)* **My friends think it's conservation.**

29   **It's genetic. I am exactly like her. My husband says that I'm**

30   **even hardheaded like her. Can't tell either of us what to do. I**

31   **know she's like that. But not me. Well, maybe just once in a**

32   **while. There was a time when I was thrilled to be just like my**

33   **mother. When I was nine years old, I got to iron my dad's**

34   **handkerchiefs. This was a big deal. Iron and fold. Iron and**

35   **fold. Iron and fold. I was so proud. That was the first time I**

1   felt exactly like my mom. But I didn't want the whole package.
2   *(Shouting)* Hear me, Mom? I don't want the whole package.
3   I don't want to be crazy, responsible or cold!
4   *(Lowers her voice.)* I want to be young. Forever. *(After a*
5   *pause, she smiles.)*
6   The other day, I told my little girl,
7   *(In mother's voice)* "Don't slouch. Straighten up."
8   *(Normal voice)* That was my mother's line ... Not anymore.
9   *(Lights fade to black.)*
10   *The End*
11
12
13
14
15
16
17
18
19
20
21
22
23
24
25
26
27
28
29
30
31
32
33
34
35

Bookworm
by John O'Brien

John O'Brien is a literary fellow of the National Endowment for the Arts and the author of ten published plays. For thirty-five years, he has taught English and theatre at Malden High School, Malden, Massachusetts.

Bookworm was first performed in the author's cellar during a thunderstorm on Halloween.

Production Suggestions

This monolog will play best if you accept the speaker as a rational, well-balanced individual. If he is exceptional at all, it is in the very excessiveness of his rationality and sense of control. Resist the impulse to make him grotesque; the play will do that for you. The script includes a wealth of background information on the character; don't overlook a single item in your preparation. For instance: Have you ever read the "Love Song of J. Alfred Prufrock" or "Invictus"? Ever listen to Bob Dylan records? If not, be sure to do so as you work on creating this character.

Address all inquiries concerning performances, readings, or reprinting of this work *or any portion thereof* to John O'Brien, 41 Delle Ave., Boston, MA 02120. For details, see "Part II: Securing Rights for Your Production," pages 241 to 250.

Sean L. Guarino as the man in Bookworm.

1   The action takes place in a small room used for book storage. The
2   time: 8:45 a.m.? Perhaps.
3   **CHARACTER:** A MAN — middle-aged? Perhaps.
4   **SETTING:** The room is lined with books. It is small, giving the effect
5   of a bomb shelter. On the Upstage wall is a clock reading 8:45.
6   The clock is not working.
7
8   *(The MAN is reading from a sheaf of papers.)*
9   **MAN: I have decided to write down a report of the experience I am**
10   **undergoing. That is the scientific approach. Though I am an**
11   **English teacher, my mind has a scientific bent. My father was**
12   **a biology professor, and from my early childhood he taught**
13   **me the proper way of responding to a crisis: keep your head,**
14   **examine the facts, list the alternatives open to you and choose**
15   **the best course of action. Father's premise was, and mine is,**
16   **that everything can be explained rationally. Father was fond**
17   **of quoting Sherlock Holmes' axiom that when you have**
18   **eliminated the impossible, whatever remains, however**
19   **improbable, must be so. I'll try to remember, to get a hold. I'll**
20   **go back a day. Yesterday, on the train going home from school,**
21   **I sat next to one of my colleagues, a history teacher. We talked**
22   **about the upcoming primary election on April 25th. The**
23   **date — that's the starting point. Let me see. Yesterday was**
24   **March 27th. No March 28th. Today is Wednesday. Last**
25   **Wednesday was March 22nd. I remember because Mary and**
26   **I had tickets to a revival of "Guys and Dolls." It was great fun.**
27   **I've been humming the tunes ever since … "Sit down, sit**
28   **down, sit down, sit down, sit down, you're rocking the boat."**
29   **What a show. That was Wednesday. On Thursday night we**
30   **were at our book discussion group. That's right. That was**
31   **Thursday. We discussed a book about American Indians. It**
32   **was by Edmund Wilson —** *Apologies to the Iroquois*, **that was**
33   **it. Friday was a Stravinsky concert at the New England**
34   **Conservatory. That was Friday. Great concert. Free, too. We**
35   **took the kids and stopped for pizza on the way home.**

Saturday was errands. Mary did a wash while I raked last year's leaves from under the slush in the yard. I cleaned the cellar, too, came across a picture of my grandfather, my father's father, with his corncob pipe and derby hat. I remember him at a St. Patrick's Day party, singing an old Irish song, "The Bog." The song went on and on and on, and so did Grampy. Pampy, they called him. Pampy. That was Saturday. March 25th. I stayed in the cellar a long time, studying Pampy's picture. I had not noticed, as a child, how closely Pampy resembled my father. Saturday night we stayed home and watched "The Blue Angel" on television. Sunday was church and afterwards a walk with the children and the dog along the Commonwealth Avenue mall. Sunday night Mary and I heard a harpsichord concert at the Museum of Fine Arts. Monday was school and a night of preparing classes and correcting papers. Yesterday, school again and a quiet night at home with my family. We listened to Bob Dylan records and played Crazy Eights. And then today. School starts at 8 a.m., and though I have no class until ten minutes of nine, I was in my room, as always, at 7:45. I hung up my hat and coat and scarf and went to the school library. After I browsed through the morning paper, I did what I could of the crossword puzzle. Then, at about 8:30, I suddenly got restless. I had forgotten my pipe, which I usually smoke before class, and I felt momentarily at loose ends. I left the library and wandered through the school corridors, past the auditorium and the natatorium, stopping after a while at a book storage room. It's really nothing more than an oversized closet. The door was open. The clock on the book room wall read 8:45. I sat, as I sit yet, in a chair with my back to the clock, to await the bell for my class.

I thought about the election, about Stravinsky, about church and harpsichords, about "The Bog" and "Guys and Dolls." I hummed. *(He hums, "Sit down, you're rocking the boat.")* I whistled. *(He whistles the same tune.)* I heard

1   footsteps approaching in the corridor, but at the last instant
2   the sound receded. No one passed the open door. I recited
3   poetry — Eliot's "Love Song of J. Alfred Prufrock," Henley's
4   "Invictus." I sang softly old songs of my childhood —
5   "Beautiful Dreamer," "You Ought to Be in Pictures," "Did
6   You Ever See a Dream Walking?" When I became aware that
7   time had stopped, I decided not to panic. Nor will I. There
8   must be a rational explanation. I will not call out. Nor will I
9   turn to look at the clock. I do not myself wear a watch. It has
10   always seemed to me that time is what we make of it, ours to
11   command, not to obey. I am in no discomfort. I can hear the
12   murmur of classroom activity. The books on the shelves are
13   reassuring, like old friends. There is no reason to worry. I will
14   wait for the bell. Not to do so would be to admit the possibility
15   of irrational forces at work. There are no such forces. If
16   something is wrong, it is simply that my mind is tired. I will
17   await the bell. The bell will ring. I am a teacher. I will answer
18   the bell. Tonight, Mary and I will play chess. The bell will ring
19   the next time the clock ticks. Nothing is out of the ordinary.
20   *(He lowers the paper. Lights darken. Fadeout continues until last*
21   *word.)*
22   My feet have gone to sleep. I'll untie the laces to loosen the
23   pressure. That's odd. The laces have come untied. They're
24   untied and they're moving. Nonsense. They can't be moving.
25   They are not wriggling. My shoelaces are not wriggling. They
26   are not brown. They are black. My shoelaces are black, and
27   the linoleum is white. It is not green. There is nothing pushing
28   between the cracks in the floor. The books on the shelves are
29   not stones. The are books. I am a teacher. I am sitting in a
30   room at school, awaiting the bell. It is Wursday, Mapril 92nd.
31   My grandmother was Mampy. She sang "Beautiful
32   Screamer." My wife is an Iroquois. My father was Stravinsky.
33   My mother raked frozen leaves in the spring. My shoelaces
34   are not stirring. They are not stirring. They are shoelaces.
35   They are not ... They are ... They ... *(The door slams shut.)*

1   When you have eliminated the impossible, whatever
2   remains, however improbable, must be so. *(He tries to stand,*
3   *falls back into the chair.)*
4   *(Singing)* "Sit down, sit down, sit down, sit down, sit down,
5   you're rocking the boat." *(Blackout)*
6   *The End*
7
8
9
10
11
12
13
14
15
16
17
18
19
20
21
22
23
24
25
26
27
28
29
30
31
32
33
34
35

Marla, You're On

by Julianne Bernstein

Julianne Bernstein Theodoropulos received her M.F.A. in playwriting from Rutgers University and serves as guest artist and teacher for Thespian festivals throughout the country, at McCarter Theatre in Princeton, and at George Street Playhouse in New Jersey.

Ms. Bernstein wrote *Marla, You're On* while taking a playwriting class from Milan Stitt at the University of Michigan. Read about Mr. Stitt in the introduction to his play, *Labor Day*, also in this book.

Playwright's Production Suggestions

Marla goes from acting hostile and defensive to friendly and open in a very short time. The key to making these transitions work is based on two things: Establishing the reality of the "peeping Tom" and Marla's objective — to get the role! If you can make "getting the role" extremely important and the stakes very high, then you will discover how the "peeping Tom's" behavior and your reactions to him will carry you from one transition to the next until you reach the end where Marla is vulnerable — almost transparent.

Address all inquiries concerning performances, readings, or reprinting of this work *or any portion thereof* to Julianne Theodoropulos, 811 Corinthian Avenue, Philadelphia, PA 19130. For details, see "Part II: Securing Rights for Your Production," pages 241 to 250.

1   The action takes place in a New York apartment in the present.

2   ***CHARACTER:*** MARLA — 23. She wears a matching jacket and skirt

3   with a blouse that is buttoned up to her neck. The outfit is not very

4   flattering as it makes her look heavier than she actually is.

5   ***SETTING:*** MARLA's apartment is simple but respectable. On the

6   Stage Right wall, slightly Downstage, is a window. Center Stage

7   is a modest-looking sofa.

8

9   *(MARLA enters clutching a script. She closes the door behind her,*

10   *takes off her jacket. She crosses to the window, opens it a little, and*

11   *looks out. She doesn't see what she is looking for so she crosses to*

12   *the couch and settles herself down into it as if she is about to watch*

13   *her favorite old movie and does not want to be disturbed.)*

14 MARLA: *(Reading)* "The Center of My Soul: A Two-Character

15   Play in Three Acts." One more. One more reading. And it's

16   mine. *(She looks Stage Right toward the window. Crosses to it for*

17   *a better view.)*

18   *(Out the window)* Damn! Thought maybe the police pulled

19   you in by now. Well, get out of here you horny high-riser! You

20   don't impress me. Go down to the diner on Seventy-ninth

21   Street. Meet some of the customers I wait on. You'll see. Now,

22   move away from there. Thank you! *(Toward the window)* Go

23   park yourself in front of Sharon's apartment. She's probably

24   prepping for tomorrow as well. No. She won't. I won't. I will

25   not let Sharon Beedles get this part. I will not. I can

26   understand her landing that national commercial. OK, she's

27   the Madonna of Maidenform, there's no denying. But this

28   part. No. I will not let Sharon Beedles get this part. The only

29   other blond, five-foot, one-inch green-eyed* actress looking

30   for work. And she happens to be queen of the D-cups.

31   Probably has an agent handling each one. *(She takes off the*

32   *note attached to the script and reads it.)*

33   "Miss Thompson. Read over act three, scene two for final

34   reading tomorrow." Final reading. Final audition. Final

35   chance at any part ever again. *(Pause)* No, Marla, stop this.

.

1	*(Reading)* **Act three, scene two.**
2	*(Reading)* **"Elizabeth's bedroom. Elizabeth is seated on her**
3	**bed with Victor looking down at her. She reaches up to**
4	**Victor's face, pulling him down to her. They kiss."** Nice, I like
5	that. I can see it, too. *(As she reads the following line of dialog,*
6	*MARLA's talent as an actress should reveal itself clearly. She is a*
7	*very good one, who knows what she is doing.)*
8	*(Still reading)* **"Don't go away this time. This is for you."**
9	*(She repeats the line as she crosses to the refrigerator exploring*
10	*different ways of saying it. She looks toward the window shouting*
11	*out the line exuberantly and confidently.)*
12	No! Not for *you!* This is for — what?! Binoculars?! Some
13	help. *(She pulls down the shade.)*
14	*(Reading)* **"She reaches up to Victor's face pulling him**
15	**down to her. They kiss. They kiss again. She unbuttons her**
16	**blouse, exposing her breasts."** *(She stops. Rereads.)*
17	**" ... unbuttons ... exposing her ... "** Oh. OK, her breasts. My
18	... breasts. Yes. B-R-E-A-S-T *(Pause)* S. *(She rereads the note.)*
19	**"Act three, scene two."** Right. **"Final reading ... tomorrow."**
20	I'll give Sharon a call and congratulate her. *(Pause)* Wait a
21	minute. It's only part of the scene. Just ... part of the scene. A
22	natural part ... of a scene. *(A man whistling from outside the*
23	*window is heard. She runs over and lifts up the shade.)*
24	Hey! What are you whistling for? Maybe if you were
25	serious, I'd — hey, you've been out there almost two weeks,
26	now. The same thing every day for two weeks. Every single day.
27	*(Softly)* Except for last Friday. What happened? *(Pause)*
28	Nothing! Nothing! I didn't say ... a thing. *(She pulls down the*
29	*shade and goes back to the script and rereads it. She starts to*
30	*unbutton her blouse saying the line "Don't go away this time. This*
31	*is for you." She then tries to lift it over her head but stops midway.)*
32	Hey, uh ... I was going to call the police, but I — I'll give
33	you a chance to explain first. *(Pause)* Well? *(Pause)* I see you
34	scrapped the binoculars. You don't need them. I mean, there's
35	only — *(Looking down)* — two taxi lanes between us. *(Pause)*

1	And why don't you come out from around the side there? I
2	mean, it looks like you're hiding ... or you're uncomfortable
3	or something. Are you? Well ... uh ... see, I'm an actress, see,
4	and I've almost got it. This part in this play. A real play in a
5	theatre, you know? Finally. The thing is ... is that I have to
6	take off my blouse. See, I need you to — You know, acting is
7	really funny. Because most of the time when you're acting, it
8	seems so real that it's not acting. it's more like ... trying
9	different ways to work out the same ... real ... things. Oh, I
10	don't know. You're disgusting. My boyfriend would never
11	behave that way. Well, Bob's not exactly my boyfriend. He's
12	this guy I've been seeing. For about three weeks now. Twice.
13	I've been seeing him ... twice. Hey. Hey! *(She goes and picks up*
14	*the phone.)*
15	· Hi, Bob? It's me, Marla. You know. The casting call. The
16	industrial for G.E. I read for the stupid housewife. Yeah. Yeah.
17	*(Pause)* Right. I enjoyed it. I mean I thought they'd never call
18	our numbers but I didn't mind waiting. Talking. Anyway,
19	thanks for the coffee. Howard Johnson's across the street.
20	Remember? *(Pause)* I can't believe I spent all my change on
21	subway tokens. Anyway, I need someone to help me take off
22	my blouse. No! I mean — what I mean is — there's this part.
23	This scene. I mean — *(Pause)* Yeah. Me, too. I gotta go, too.
24	Listen. Uh ... maybe we'll see each other or something.
25	Maybe we'll do lunch again. *(Pause)* Oh. No problem. I love
26	that place. It was my pleasure. Yeah. *(She hangs up and looks*
27	*out the window. Pause)* Uh ... wait a minute. Don't go away.
28	*(She crosses away into her living room.)*
29	No. I can't. He stares. A starer. Two weeks. All he's done is
30	watch me. Look at me. And now he's ... doing the same thing.
31	Watching ... looking ... *(She goes back over to the window.)*
32	Hey, you changed your shirt. Nice shirt. I like the color.
33	They call it rhubarb, I think. I love food colors. You know —
34	watermelon, tangerine, champagne ... Anyway, I told Bob
35	how I felt. That I thought that there was something really

1   good between us and we should give it a shot. From the way
2   his artichoke salad reappeared on his plate, I don't think he
3   agreed. *(Pause)* See, it's a two-character play. Two people
4   together ... on stage ... together. And in the third act, they're
5   nude. Making love, I suppose. But not right there on stage,
6   though. We allude to the fact. Suggest it, you know? See,
7   acting isn't really acting. I mean, in the script the two
8   characters ... don't ever really do it. They actually don't ever
9   come close. Because the lights go black and they play is over.
10   So if they don't ever do it, what the hell is the point? *(Pause)*
11   Where are you going? Are you coming back? *(She remains at*
12   *the window and waits for him to return.)*
13   I don't need him, anyway. *(She crosses to a record player.)*
14   Where's that old Sinatra record? *(She searches through a*
15   *pile of records and pulls one out. She puts it on. It is old and*
16   *scratched and it starts to skip. She takes the needle off, carelessly*
17   *scratching the needle along the grooves.)*
18   Maybe the lights. *(She goes over to the lights and turns them*
19   *off.)*
20   No. Dim. Dim. Don't go completely off. *(She turns them back*
21   *on.)*
22   I can't even set a mood. *(She goes back toward the window.)*
23   Hey, there you are. I *am* going to get this job, tomorrow.
24   Because I'm sick of staying home every Saturday night
25   practically making love to a script. Yeah. I do. I mean, when I
26   pick up a script, you know, I'm real gentle-like. You don't
27   want to push anything. If it's not good ... right ... you don't
28   want it. It feels wrong. Because it is wrong. Wrong. See, if
29   you're good enough at what you're doing, you know, the
30   acting — making the acting, real, and the real, actual. It's
31   fantastic. Because you get to be so much like the role you're
32   playing that in a lot of ways you're not really there. And you
33   don't have to worry about anything. Even the morning after.
34   You know, the sequel? When you turn over. The damp Sears
35   pillow against your cheek. And you open your eyes and don't

1	know where the hell you are, and that's when the camera's
2	coming in for a close-up. The script. Right next to you.
3	Between the sheets. Lying face up. Open to the last page of the
4	scene you were working on the night before. Sometimes,
5	though, it's closed. Back to the beginning. Page one. Staring
6	you in the face. *(Pause)* Sorry. Show's over. You can go now.
7	Sorry. *(She walks away from the window. She stops, picks up the*
8	*script, turns back to the window, looks out and smiles a half smile*
9	*of recognition and relief. She takes a deep breath and the lights*
10	*fade to black as she starts to unbutton her blouse, repeating the*
11	*line, "Don't go away this time. This is for you.")*
12	*The End*
13	
14	
15	
16	
17	
18	
19	
20	
21	
22	
23	
24	
25	
26	
27	
28	
29	
30	
31	
32	
33	
34	* *These lines can be edited according to the physical characteristics of the actress reading them.*
35	

Homer

by Robert L. Lippman

Bob Lippman, a psychologist in private practice in Elizabethtown, Kentucky, is a member of the Dramatists Guild.

Homer was first performed at Illinois Wesleyan University's 11th Annual Writer's Conference in 1987.

Production Suggestions

Avoid faking the cigarette. If smoking is a problem in your setting, have Homer see a "No Smoking" sign and return the cigarette to its pack; if you make this choice, eliminate the ashtray called for in the description of the setting. If you use a real pot but do not have a live partner to hand it to, place it on a table where the therapist could reach it.

Address all inquiries concerning performances, readings, or reprinting of this work *or any portion thereof* to Dr. Robert L. Lippman, PO Box 206, Elizabethtown, KY 42702. For details, see "Part II: Securing Rights for Your Production," pages 241 to 250.

1   The action takes place at 4:00 p.m. in a psychologist's office.

2   *CHARACTER:* HOMER — about 38. A husky six-footer, he wears a

3   shirt open at the neck, regular slacks, and work boots.

4   *SETTING:* Homer sits in a black leather chair facing the audience. To

5   his right is a small square table with an ashtray. On the floor,

6   beside his left foot, is a brown cardboard box folded closed, five

7   inches high.

8

9   **HOMER: Is it all right to smoke?** *(He lights a cigarette.)* **I've never**

10   **been in this place before ... I've always been able to handle**

11   **my own problems. But, this, my wife leaving me ... It's over a**

12   **year now and her going with a guy who is loser. He has no**

13   **ambition, been at the same job for fifteen years. He works**

14   **with her in the sportswear plant ... She operates a sewing**

15   **machine. He has a beat-up car. There is nothing to him. And,**

16   **now, if you can't get her to come in, she will go through with**

17   **the divorce.** *(He leans forward.)*

18   **It's true, I've not been there for her. I've concentrated on**

19   **the business. Rock quarrying isn't the easiest thing to do. And**

20   **with no education, I've done fine. And I can even handle the**

21   **bankruptcy which I know will be a hassle. They're going to**

22   **claim I sold a truck I shouldn't have. But I can handle that.**

23   **I've never been shy. I can always speak up for myself.**

24   *(Bending down, he picks up the box.)*

25   **Here, let me show you something.** *(Gently he removes a gray*

26   *pot, 3¹/₂ inches high, 4¹/₂ inches wide.)*

27   **This is made from mussel shell. It's about twelve or**

28   **thirteen hundred years old. I found it in Caneyville ... made**

29   **by the Indians who lived there. There are lots around. But you**

30   **have to know where to look. I got into this through my work.**

31   **We would find different things at the sites. I got carried away**

32   **you could say. I would go to conventions in different states**

33   **and pay hundreds of dollars a piece. You gotta be careful**

34   **though ... there are counterfeits; you gotta know the artifacts.**

35   **But this I found myself. Here!** *(He hands it to the therapist.)*

1   You know how to do this? How to find them? *(He gets up,*
2   *spreads his feet apart, and with an imaginary prod, makes a*
3   *"hole" in the earth, very gently.)*
4   You take a piece of metal, stainless steel, like a radio antenna
5   but it's not an antenna. You use it as a prod and when you hear
6   that special sound, a *ping*, you know you've hit something …
7   And this is what I found … Look at it. It even has handles …
8   you have to look close … handles for string or something, to
9   hold it up. And the feel. Here it is smooth. *(Taking it from the*
10   *therapist, he touches the bottom and the lower half.)*
11   But here, *(Top half)* the feel, they make it this way on
12   purpose, the bumps … But she wants to take the children.
13   *(Still holding the pot, he looks at therapist.)*
14   I want her back. Can you get her back? If I can't have her,
15   at least Chris, the older boy … I was fourteen when my father
16   died. Chris is eleven. Everything fell apart. We fished
17   together. I dropped out of school. He was my best friend. I was
18   always big for my age … But I know I can change. I'm
19   changing already. *(With his hand, he wipes tears away … looks*
20   *around; then back at the therapist.)*
21   When we first got married I drove a truck cross-country to
22   Texas, to Mexico. And for four or five years we never had sex.
23   We were married and never had sex. Not before, not after the
24   marriage. Then after four or five years, we have sex. I never
25   understood that. *(Pain here)* The sex started after Ellen got
26   scared of this other woman who worked for a supplier. We just
27   spoke. There was nothing else … On one trip … it was in
28   Texas, just outside of Oklahoma, I picked up this girl
29   hitchhiking. She was dirty. Her hair was dirty. You could tell
30   she came from a good family. I bought her a meal and we
31   talked. We stayed in the same hotel room. She wanted to have
32   sex with me. I wouldn't. I wanted her to call her parents. She
33   wouldn't. Her mother had remarried. *(Noticing the pot in his*
34   *hand, he puts it down and lights a cigarette.)*
35   There was some difficulty. I don't know what. But she

1   wouldn't call home. She was seventeen. I wanted to take her
2   home. But people would get the wrong idea and I couldn't get
3   my wife to understand, could I? So, I had to let her go. *(Tears*
4   *come. With a wrinkled handkerchief, he wipes his brows and eyes.)*
5   Doc! You think you'll be able to get us back together
6   again? ... If you can, this is yours. *(He picks up the pot.)* ... You
7   gotta be careful. There are lots of counterfeits. *(He "pings" it*
8   *with his wedding ring finger, listens to the sound and places it*
9   *back in the box.)*
10   *The End*
11
12
13
14
15
16
17
18
19
20
21
22
23
24
25
26
27
28
29
30
31
32
33
34
35

Part 2
Securing Rights for Your Production

Securing Rights for Your Production

Why Secure Rights?

A play producer's first responsibility is to secure performance rights for the "property," the script. If you do not have a designated producer, *you* should take care of this legal detail. Three reasons make it important for performers to be scrupulous about securing performing rights to the plays they do:

Artistic Reasons: New plays are the lifeblood of the theatre, and playwrights are your fellow artists. Knowing you are performing their plays and (when appropriate) receiving money for your use of their property encourages playwrights to turn out more and better scripts. You owe it to your art and your fellow artists to secure rights.

Ethical Reasons: Using a script without permission is theft. It does not suddenly become theft when you join a semi-professional acting company. As a person of integrity you owe it to yourself to secure rights.

Legal Reasons: It's the law. Neglecting to secure performance rights lays you open to fines, lawsuits, and other sanctions.

How to Secure Rights for Scripts in This Anthology

In order to make it easier for you to secure performance rights, the playwrights of scripts in this book have agreed to special arrangements. These arrangements apply to scripts in this anthology only.

To secure rights for your production:

1. Using the following descriptions, decide which kinds of production you are doing.

2. Fill out the Performance Agreement Form or Performance Report that corresponds to your type of production. You may either tear out the form included in this book or photocopy it.

3. In the case of Competition or Full-Scale Amateur Productions, send the P.A.F. and royalty payment to the address at the end of the introduction to

your script. Do this *at least* two weeks prior to your performance.

4. In the case of Class Projects and Departmental Juries, you may complete and send the Performance Report after the production.

Types of Productions

Class Projects and Departmental Juries. These performances are open only to students and instructors of your institution. There is no advertising outside your institution and no admission is charged. For **Class Projects and Departmental Juries**, no royalties are charged; however, since many playwrights like to know when their property is being used by students, you are encouraged to fill out the Optional Performance Report and send it to the author as a courtesy.

Competition Performances. This category covers performances done for contests sponsored by recognized state, regional, or national organizations; these performances have no production budget, and no admission is charged the spectators. **Competition Performances** must pay a nominal $5.00 royalty and secure permission by filing the appropriate Performance Agreement Form.

Full-Scale, Amateur Productions. These productions have no restrictions in terms of production budget, size of audience, admission charges, or publicity, but the performers are not members of Actors Equity. **Full Productions** must pay royalties ($20.00) for the first performance and ($15.00) for each subsequent performance, and they must secure rights by filing the appropriate Performance Agreement Form.

Other Productions. All other productions, including performances by Equity companies and productions to be broadcast or produced as movies, must negotiate rights and royalties with the playwrights or their agents.

Optional Performance Report for a
Class Project/Departmental Jury Production

of the play _____

by _____, playwright,

as the script is printed in *More One-Act Plays for Acting Students.*

This is to inform you that we of the _____

department of _____ *(institution),*

at _____

_____ *(address),*

performed the above-named script as a Class Project or Departmental Jury on

_____ *(dates).*

This performance had no audience other than students and instructors of our institution. We did not advertise the performance outside our institution, nor did we charge admission to the performance.

We included the playwright's name in all printed announcements or programs.

If we perform this production of this script under circumstances other than those listed above, we will first negotiate performance rights for those performances in a separate document.

We think the playwright would be interested to know the following details about our production and/or responses to the script:

_____

_____

_____

_____

_____

_____

_____

_____

_____

_____

_____

_____

Signed: _____

Title or Position: _____

Date: _____

At your option, send this completed form, or a photocopy thereof, to the playwright or playwright's agent as indicated in the script's introduction. No royalty payments are required for Class Project or Departmental Jury performances of the scripts in this anthology.

Performance Agreement Form for a
Competition Performance

of the play _____

by _____, playwright,

as the script is printed in ***More One-Act Plays for Acting Students.***

We hereby request permission to perform the above-named script in

competition under the auspices of _____

_____ *(sponsoring organization)*, a

recognized LOCAL, STATE, REGIONAL, NATIONAL *(circle one)*

organization, on _____ *(dates)*

at _____
(name and address of performance place).

We hereby certify that this performance has no production budget and that no admission will be charged to attend the performances.

If we perform this production of this script under circumstances other than those listed above, we will first negotiate performance rights for those performances in a separate document.

In consideration of the right to perform the script under the above-specified circumstances only, we enclose herewith the sum of $5.00.

We further agree to include the playwright's name in all printed announcements of the performances and to include in all programs the playwright's name and the following statement: "*(Title of play)* is performed by special arrangement with the playwright."

Signed: _____

Title or Position: _____

Date: _____

Producing
Organization: _____

Address: _____

Telephone Number: (   ) _____

At least two weeks prior to the performance dates indicated above, send this completed form, or a photocopy thereof, along with a check for $5.00, to the playwright or playwright's agent as indicated in the script's introduction.

Receipt of this form and royalty payment by the playwright or agent automatically secures performance rights to this play under the competition circumstances and limitations specified above.

Performance Agreement Form for a
Full-Scale, Amateur Production

of the play   _____

by   _____, playwright,

as the script is printed in *More One-Act Plays for Acting Students.*

We hereby request permission to present   _____ *(number)*

performances of a Full-Scale Amateur Production of the above-named script

on _____ *(dates)*

at _____
(name of performance space)

at _____
(address).

We hereby certify that this is a non-Equity production.

If we perform this script under circumstances other than those listed above, we will first negotiate performance rights for those performances in a separate document.

In consideration of the right to perform the script under the above-specified circumstances only, we enclose herewith $20.00 for the first performance and $15.00 for each subsequent performance, being a total of $ _____

We further agree to include the playwright's name in all printed announcements of the performances and to include in all programs the playwright's name and the following statement: "*(Title of play)* is presented by special arrangement with the playwright."

Signed: _____

Title or Position: _____

Producing
Organization: _____

Address: _____

Telephone Number: (   ) _____

At least two weeks prior to the performance dates indicated above, send this completed form, or a photocopy thereof, along with a check for the royalties to the playwright or playwright's agent as indicated in the script's introduction.

Receipt of this form and royalty payment by the playwright or agent automatically secures performance rights to this play under the Amateur Production circumstances and limitations as specified above.

Part 3
Rehearsing the Play

The third part of this book provides assistance for actors who are preparing a play without a director. Depending on your experience, you may want to use this section in different ways. Relatively inexperienced actors may want to read and use most of the materials as they work at developing their own rehearsal methods. Actors with considerable experience and training may find much of the material unnecessary; even these actors, however, are likely to encounter rehearsal problems for which they have no immediate solutions, and in cases like these, they may find some of the suggestions helpful as trouble-shooting tools.

Scheduling the Rehearsals

Sample Rehearsal Schedules

Here are samples of three approaches to preparing a play. If none of them suit your needs exactly, borrow some ideas from them and construct your own schedule. The "Rehearsal Calendar" which follows the third sample schedule provides a convenient place for you to record your plans.

Sample Schedule A: This loosely organized schedule demands considerable self-discipline and inventiveness from actors.

Learning about the characters and the play through read-throughs, discussion, improvisations, and research. Approximate number of rehearsals: _____.

Session with a coach to check progress and get suggestions.

Dealing with technical details such as blocking and memorization. Approximate number of rehearsals: _____.

Session with a coach to get feedback and suggestions.

Polishing the play for performance. Approximate number of rehearsals: _____.

Performing.

Sample Schedule B: This schedule forms the basis for the rehearsal session guides *(pages 261 to 275).*

Analyzing the script.
Reading the script together.
Improvising.
Playing the given circumstances.
Investigating character identity.
Playing the intentions.
Rehearsing with a coach to get feedback and suggestions.
Incorporating technical elements.
Repeating earlier concentration points (optional, as needed).

Getting off book.
Bringing it all together.
Rehearsing with a coach to get feedback and suggestions.
Repeat of synthesizing rehearsal (optional, as needed).
Final dress rehearsal.
Performing.

Sample Schedule C: This schedule will work best if you have a coach who will give a lot of time and guidance to your project.

Individual script analysis.
Read-through: group script analysis.
Improvisations.
First blocking rehearsal.
Second blocking rehearsal.
Monitored blocking rehearsal.
Revising your blocking.
Characterization: given circumstances.
Characterization: character analysis.
Characterization: objectives.
Memorization: putting down the book.
Memorization: confirming your memory.
Monitored characterization rehearsal.
Characterization: bringing it all together.
First technical rehearsal.
Second technical rehearsal.
Pacing rehearsal (with a coach's assistance).
Final dress rehearsal.
Performance.

Rehearsal Calendar

Play title: _____

Actor's name: _____ Telephone: _____

Actor's name: _____ Telephone: _____

Actor's name: _____ Telephone: _____

First rehearsal. Date: _____ Place: _____ Time: _____

    Concentration point: _____

    Warm-up leader: _____

Second rehearsal. Date: _____ Place: _____ Time: _____

    Concentration point: _____

    Warm-up leader: _____

Third rehearsal. Date: _____ Place: _____ Time: _____

    Concentration point: _____

    Warm-up leader: _____

Fourth rehearsal. Date: _____ Place: _____ Time: _____

    Concentration point: _____

    Warm-up leader: _____

Fifth rehearsal. Date: _____ Place: _____ Time: _____

    Concentration point: _____

    Warm-up leader: _____

Sixth rehearsal. Date: _____ Place: _____ Time: _____

    Concentration point: _____

    Warm-up leader: _____

Seventh rehearsal. Date: _____ Place: _____ Time: _____

    Concentration point: _____

    Warm-up leader: _____

Eighth rehearsal. Date: _____ Place: _____ Time: _____

    Concentration point: _____

    Warm-up leader: _____

Ninth rehearsal. Date: _____ Place: _____ Time: _____

    Concentration point: _____

    Warm-up leader: _____

Tenth rehearsal. Date: _____ Place: _____ Time: _____

    Concentration point: _____

    Warm-up leader: _____

Eleventh rehearsal. Date: _____ Place:_____ Time: _____

    Concentration point: _____

    Warm-up leader: _____

Twelfth rehearsal. Date: _____ Place: _____ Time: _____

    Concentration point: _____

    Warm-up leader: _____

Thirteenth rehearsal. Date: _____ Place: _____ Time: _____

    Concentration point: _____

    Warm-up leader: _____

Fourteenth rehearsal. Date: _____ Place: _____ Time: _____

    Concentration point: _____

    Warm-up leader: _____

Fifteenth rehearsal. Date: _____ Place: _____ Time: _____

    Concentration point: _____

    Warm-up leader: _____

Sixteenth rehearsal. Date: _____ Place: _____ Time: _____

    Concentration point: _____

    Warm-up leader: _____

Seventeenth rehearsal. Date: _____ Place: _____ Time: _____

    Concentration point: _____

    Warm-up leader: _____

Eighteenth rehearsal. Date: _____ Place: _____ Time: _____

    Concentration point: _____

    Warm-up leader: _____

Performance. Date: _____ Place: _____ Time: _____

    Warm-up leader: _____

Approaching Rehearsals

Productive Rehearsal Attitudes

Forming good mental attitudes toward time, performance level work, and characterization will help make your rehearsals efficient and productive.

First, determine to use **time** well. Remember that, in contrast to space arts like painting, theatre is a time art. The clock, therefore, is one of your most important tools. Never call off a scheduled rehearsal. Even if you don't feel like rehearsing, do it anyway. Nothing can hurt your performance more than skipping rehearsals. Then, once you start to rehearse, rehearse; don't let yourselves wander off on some conversational by-way. And give it a full shot. If you decide on a 1½-hour rehearsal, rehearse for 90 minutes, not 75; if you can't maintain concentration for 90 minutes, try two 50-minute sessions instead.

Second, commit yourselves to concentrating on performance-level work. As Stanislavski said, every rehearsal should be a performance and every performance just another rehearsal. Never permit yourself to "just walk through the scene" — **act** it. Every time. You will progress farther and faster. And never comment when you make a mistake. Breaking character during rehearsals builds bad habits that may haunt you in performance. Furthermore, once you crack, it takes extra time and energy to get back into character.

Finally, work on **characterization** in every rehearsal. Even if you don't think a particular rehearsal has much to do with characterization (for instance, blocking or tech rehearsals), use the time to create your character. Aim to learn something new about your character in each session, and write down these discoveries to help solidify your gains. If you start getting bored, experiment with giving your character a different voice, posture, or personality. And *never* tell yourself or your partner that you need to wait for costumes (or props, or the "real stage," or the Second Coming) before you can really get into character. This game, called Waiting for Santa Claus, is a device poor actors use to deceive themselves. If a costume or prop item is that important, bring it to rehearsal yourself.

Rehearsal Session Procedures

Begin your rehearsal with about five minutes of vocal and physical warm-ups. Warming up will make your rehearsal more successful. Not only will warm-ups help you prepare your body and voice for the different demands you are about to make on them, but they also will prepare you psychologically. If you notice, for instance, that the second or third run through your play is better than the first, there's a good chance you're using your first run-through as a warm-up; this is a bad habit for actors to form. And equally important, warm-ups provide a clear transition from everyday life to the time you will spend in rehearsal; if you don't do warm-ups, you will find it more difficult to stop visiting and start concentrating on rehearsal. Divide the responsibility for warm-ups between you and your partner so that neither one of you have to find and lead them all the time. If you don't know any warm-up exercises, several books in the bibliography will give you ideas. A good warm-up session includes activities to do four things: warm up the body, warm up the voice, loosen up the actors' sense of play, and get the actors into character.

Once you start through a scene, work straight through it without stopping for anything. The scripts in this book are short enough to go straight through the entire play without a break. Your rehearsal will be far more productive if you don't stop to discuss each problem that occurs. Many of these problems ("Should I hold the broom in my right hand or my left?") solve themselves in successive repetitions simply through the magic of doing; stopping to talk about them wastes your time and breaks your concentration on character.

After you finish a run-through, briefly discuss the major things you want to change. Briefly. Spend your time rehearsing, not talking about rehearsing. If you are spending more than one-third of your rehearsal time talking, you're talking too much. And don't try to solve all the problems in any one of these discussion periods; focus on two or three major changes. The other problems will wait, or, more likely, solve themselves.

Conclude your rehearsal by summarizing your progress. Talk briefly and specifically about what you have accomplished and what you need to do next time you rehearse. And before leaving, be sure you've agreed on the next rehearsal time and that you've cleaned up the space.

Rehearsing for Specific Objectives

Analyzing the Script Individually

Objective:

To discover as much about your play as you can on first acquaintance.

Techniques:

Begin by reading straight through the script. Aim during this first reading to discover the life of the script. You may find that reading the play aloud helps you feel its rhythms and get immediately in touch with its characters. Reading a script demands a different approach from reading an essay, short story, or poem. If, like most people, you have not read a lot of scripts, you might want to look over "How to Read a Playscript" *(page 277)* before approaching the play itself.

Immediately after your first reading, without taking a break, jot down your first impressions of the play. Aim at description, not evaluation. If you must evaluate, focus more on the positive than the negative; the point is to accept and understand the play on its own terms. Some sample descriptive statements might be: "The play moves fast/slowly." "It is funny/sad/like a soap opera." "It is realistic/a moodpiece/weird."

Next analyze the play in detail. The "Study Questions for Individual Script Analysis" on pages 278 to 280 can help you avoid overlooking important aspects of the play. In order to keep your analysis specific and precise, write down your observations.

When you think you've learned everything about the play that you can in one session, give yourself a short break, and then read straight through the script again; aim to see the play as a whole.

Progress assessment:

Take a few moments to register what you have accomplished: What did you know about the script before your first reading, or even immediately *after* the first reading? How much do you know about it now? Congratulate yourself on the difference.

Two further suggestions:

First, don't start memorizing yet; you've got plenty of time, and memorizing too soon may make it harder for you to experiment freely with the script and your role. Second, you may want to highlight your lines, but you're better off not underlining them; underlining fills spaces you may later want for writing notes, and it makes lines harder to read.

Read-Through: Analyzing the Script Together

Objective:

To agree with your fellow actor(s) about the nature of your script.

Techniques:

Begin by reading through the script together. Don't interrupt your reading in order to correct mistakes or try different interpretations; work for flow and worry about improvements later. During this rehearsal, concentrate on your character but don't push; characterization needs to develop naturally throughout the rehearsal schedule. For instance, if you settle on a particular "voice" for your character at this early rehearsal, you may not feel free to experiment with other, potentially better voices later.

After the read-through, briefly tell each other how you understand the play. one way to do this is to share your responses to the "Study Questions for Individual Script Analysis" *(pages 278 to 280)*. You may want to discuss your different ideas briefly, but don't let this discussion become heated or lengthy; if you simply register your opinions and then move ahead, you'll save time and your disagreements will begin to solve themselves.

Next, read straight through the script again.

Now, using the "Discussion Guide for Group Script Analysis" *(page 280)*, talk about the play. If you agree, you might write down your responses to the questions. If you don't readily agree, discuss your opinions *briefly*, and then read through the script again. After re-reading the play, see if you can reach agreement. If so, write it down; if not, write down your different responses and let it go at that.

Improvising

Objective:

To trigger your imagination for creative play interpretation.

Techniques:

Prepare for this rehearsal by dividing your script into three segments which are roughly equal in length. If, as suggested on page 220, you already divided your play into episodes, you can base these segments on that work; you may need to group some of the smaller episodes together to provide three larger segments for rehearsal purposes. In order to save rehearsal time, do this work before coming to rehearsal; it may be more efficient to assign this task to one partner rather than spending unnecessary time negotiating segment breaks.

Starting with a lively set of warm-ups will help this rehearsal immensely. You need to approach improvisation with a sense of adventure and playfulness, with the intention of taking risks and making mistakes. Warm-ups will help you tune in to your play impulses. You might conclude your warm-up session by playing Leap-Frog all around the rehearsal area. This game will thoroughly activate your body and will help you get past the fear of looking silly — a fear that can destroy improvisations.

After warm-ups, read through the first segment of your play. Now put down the scripts, and without speaking, pantomime your way through the section. Talk about what happens in this segment: Who is doing what to whom? What is different at the end than at the beginning? Try to decide this without looking at the script. Now pantomime your way through the section again. Still without looking at the script, decide what physical activity is similar to the human event in this part of the play: Boxing? Seduction? Hide and seek? Rape? Ping-Pong? A cat with a mouse? Forget the play for a moment and pantomime that activity, complete with appropriate non-verbal noises such as grunts, screams, or laughter. Now re-read the segment you're working with, and then put down the scripts and pantomime it again, this time incorporating some of the behavior of the physical activity you experimented with. Conclude your work on this segment by reading through the scene while doing the pantomime. Don't worry if it doesn't look "realistic"; right now you're after the primitive, underlying lives and conflicts of the characters, not a realistic performance of the scene.

Before going on to the next part of the script, you may want to do a transitional improv to provide variety and help you move from one section to the next. Some suggestions:

Fight-Dance-Fight. Start a slow-motion, no-contact fight with your partner. Do this in character, and be sure to involve your whole body. Gradually let the fight shift into a slow-motion dance, and then change it back into a fight again. For an interesting and productive variation, try switching characters for Fight-Dance-Fight.

263

Jungle/Barnyard. Pick an animal that your character reminds you of. Imitate the animal, complete with sound, walk (crawl?), and gesture. Once you've "got it," encounter your partner in his/her "animal state." What happens?

Wake-up. Lie on the floor, and completely relax. Imagine yourself to be your character asleep in the early morning of the day on which the events in your play take place. What is your character dreaming about? Morning comes, and your character wakes up, gets out of bed, yawns and stretches hugely. Suddenly an idea or image or memory pops into your character's mind and you freeze in mid-stretch. Tell your partner what stopped your stretching.

After the transitional improvisation, approach the second segment of the script using the sequence for the first one. Continue to alternate between script-based improvs and transitional improvs until you are through the play.

Progress assessment:

Tell each other one thing you learned about your own character, one thing you learned about each other's character, and one thing you learned about the play.

Problems? If the improvs seem to fall flat and you're learning nothing about your roles, you probably are not committing yourselves fully enough or going far enough with the exercises. In such a case, you might want to ask someone else to help you by directing your improvisations. The assistant's job would be to tell you what to do next, suggest new moves, and push you to experiment further.

Playing the Given Circumstances

Objective:

To **real**-ize your character's situation in terms of time and place.

Techniques:

Prepare your mind for this rehearsal by scouring your script for every scrap of evidence it can give about the location and time of your play. *Where* the play occurs includes not only the country, city, and immediate surroundings (represented by the set), but also what the location and every part of it *means* to your character. *When* the play occurs includes not only the calendar and clock time, but also the psychological moment in your character's life. Writing down all the information you discover about the place and time will help you be specific and is a good device to help you internalize what you have learned. Prepare physically for the rehearsal by collecting any hand props you will need. From now on, use your props in every rehearsal.

Begin by arranging the rehearsal furniture you think you will need, and then do your warm-ups.

After warm-ups, get in "places" to begin your play, and pause. In your mind, go over all the details you discovered about the time and place of your play. Visualize your set as that place; let yourself, as your character, enter into that time. When you sense that both you and your partner are ready, begin the play. Don't worry if you misjudge each other's readiness to start; you can iron out the details later. Go straight through the play, and concentrate *at every moment* on your character living in the time and place of the play.

After your run-through, talk about the beginning of the play. Which one of you gets the scene underway? How will this initiator know when the passive partner is ready? Once you've settled this detail, share your individual lists of time-and-place data. Don't waste time debating your differences — just listen to each other.

Run through the play again. If your perceptions of time and place had significant differences, you might follow this run-through with a brief discussion of any major contrasts in your ideas.

Once you are in places for the next run-through, pause a little longer before starting the action, and imagine where your character has been and what s/he has been doing immediately prior to the play's beginning. If you can visualize this "moment-before" in considerable detail, and if you make a habit of going through it like a mental play-before-the-play prior to each entrance, you'll never suffer the embarrassment of coming on stage out of character. Perform the play, and then briefly discuss anything you'd like to change about your scene. If you have time, it would probably be a good idea to go through the play a fourth time before quitting; remember to concentrate on making real the time and place of the action.

Progress assessment:

Conclude your rehearsal by each telling the other one thing you learned about your character or play during the session.

A note on set arrangement and blocking: You will be wise to postpone blocking until you are more familiar with your characters and the play. Many directors pre-block plays before characterization work, but before blocking, they have invested *days* of study in understanding the script; in contrast, as actors without a director, you will be developing your basic understanding of the script through the rehearsal process itself. At this point, then, simply arrange the furniture you need, and let your characters move around the set as the action and their relationships demand. Gradually, you will discover natural, meaningful blocking patterns.

If, however, you do decide to block before this rehearsal, begin by arranging your set. The "Blocking Checklist" on pages 285 to 286 has some suggestions for set arrangement. Once the set is arranged, act your way straight through the script, and then discuss one or two changes you need to make in your blocking; again, the "Blocking Checklist" may be of help. Avoid getting picky, at this early stage, about specific gestures or body positions; such fine-tuning this soon will waste your time and may inhibit development of your character. Repeat the sequence of acting and discussing until you are satisfied with the blocking. You'll save a lot of time erasing if you wait until the end of the rehearsal before making blocking notes in the script's margins.

Investigating Character Identity

Objective:

To deepen your acquaintance with your character.

Techniques:

Prepare mentally for this rehearsal by combing your script for every scrap of evidence about *who* your character is. Using the "Character Analysis Questions" on page 281 or the "Character Profiles" on pages 282 to 283 may help you avoid overlooking important pieces of data. Making written notes will help your memory and attention to details. Prepare for the rehearsal physically by assembling a costume. Resist the temptation to postpone using your costume — especially if the costume is different from what you usually wear in public (for instance, a bathrobe) or less than you usually wear (for instance, a swimsuit). In particular, you should rehearse in the shoes your character will wear during the performance, and if your character will be costumed in a skirt, you should wear one during rehearsals — especially if you don't normally dress that way. These costume items should become a regular part of your rehearsal because they fundamentally affect the way people move and behave.

Begin your rehearsal by arranging your set and doing your warm-ups. Then, aiming for concentration and performance quality, act your way straight through the play.

After the first run-through, take about ten minutes to introduce your characters to each other. Each pretend that your character is an old acquaintance of yours but that your character and partner have never met. Tell your partner the things that are really important for understanding who your character is. You may want to ask each other some questions about each other's character, using the same premise of never having met the person before. Have fun with this; the more you can enter into the game, the more you are likely to learn from it.

Now, act your way through the play again. Follow this run-through with a gossip session about your characters. Pretend your characters are mutual acquaintances of you and your partner. Give each other the *real* scoop about your characters. Let the gossip get a little catty; after all, it's for your characters' own good.

Follow the gossip session with another run-through. During the moments of concentration before the beginning of your play, visualize yourself as your character.

After this run-through, you might tell each other how you and your character are similar and different. What can you draw on from your life to apply to this character? How do you have to change yourself to become this character? If you have time, follow this talk session with a fourth run-through.

Progress assessment:

Conclude your session by telling each other how you feel about your progress. This might be a good time to check your schedule to be sure you are rehearsing frequently enough to be ready by the performance date.

Other techniques:

If the introduction or gossip exercises don't work for you, or if they work so well that you want more of the same, invent your own games. For instance, you might compose obituary notices for your characters (imagine they died immediately after the end of the play). Or you might play the role of an FBI agent doing a security check on your partner's character who has applied for a position with the Bureau; grill your partner for details about the applicant.

Playing the Intentions

Objective:

To focus on the chain of intentions which make up your role.

267

Orientation:

If Character A tries to force her will on Character B, and Character B not only resists but also tries to force his will on Character A, the result is conflict and drama. Most plays consist of a lively chain of shifting conflict. The moment one character has no intention at all, drama ceases to exist, the play gets boring, and the actors begin to fall out of character. The following suggestions will help you investigate the intentions of your characters.

Techniques:

The best preparation for this rehearsal is writing out your character's "through line of action." You may want to refer to the "Guidelines for Constructing a Through Line of Action" on page 284. Although writing out a through line of action takes time and hard work, it pays huge dividends.

Start your rehearsal by arranging your set and doing warm-ups. Then act the play, focusing with complete concentration at every moment on what your character is trying to accomplish during that moment, and on the transitions from intention to intention.

After the first run-through, compare your character's super-objective with that of your partner's: What is the overall objective of each of your characters? How do their different objectives bring them into conflict? When and how is the major conflict resolved?

Next, play through the script again. Concentrate on living out your character's through line of action.

After this run-through, you might see if you can help each other with one or two moments when one or the other is not sure about his/her character's intentions. For instance, your partner might say, "I don't really know why I make that first exit." Or you might say, "I get lost during your speech on page fifteen. I don't know what I'm supposed to be doing, and my mind starts to wander. What do *you* think my character is trying to do during your speech?" Remember while you talk, that it is each actor's own business to determine his/her character's intentions; the point of this discussion is not to take away that responsibility and privilege but only to get assistance in problem solving.

Don't let this discussion drag on and on; rehearsing is doing, not talking about doing. If you find you are talking more than rehearsing, you may even want to use the clock to limit your discussion times. Continue your rehearsal by repeating the sequence of acting and discussing, focusing at every moment on your character's intentions.

Progress assessment::

You might conclude this rehearsal by telling each other what moments in the play you each feel especially good about. Celebrate these bright spots and determine to let them spread through the rest of the play.

Incorporating Technical Elements

Objective:

To check the play's set, props, and blocking.

Techniques:

Prepare for this rehearsal by collecting any props and costume items which you haven't already been using. If you've postponed attending to these technical elements, procrastinate no longer. Handling actual props will help you invent characteristic business with them; wearing the actual costume will help you develop characteristic mannerisms.

Begin the rehearsal by arranging your set and props and getting into costume. Using the questions about set arrangement in the "Blocking Checklist" on pages 285 to 286, look at your set from the audience's perspective, and make any necessary adjustments.

When you're satisfied with the set, do your warm-ups, and then perform the play. If the presence of new props and costume items or a different set arrangement causes some awkward moments, avoid breaking character; dealing with the problems *after* the run-through will be far more efficient.

After the run-through, critique your blocking using the "Blocking Checklist" *(pages 285 to 286)*. If you begin to find quite a few problems, limit yourself to talking about one or two, and then correct them while acting the play. After the second run, deal with a couple more improvements and put them into effect. Continue by repeating the acting/critiquing sequence.

Progress assessment:

At the end of the session, if you discovered your play is still missing props, decide which one of you will bring them. Take stock of what remains to be done on your play. Do you need another session on blocking and tech? Or do you need to return to the concentration point of an earlier rehearsal? If you are still dependent on the book and you're having a real problem keeping your place in the script while handling the props, maybe you should devote a rehearsal to getting off book. In the midst of considering what you still have to do, remember to notice and celebrate all the progress you've made so far.

Getting Off Book

Objective:

To free your mind and hands from dependence on the script.

Orientation:

If you've rehearsed frequently and with concentration, and if you've made a practice of going over your lines by yourself outside of rehearsal, you may already be very nearly lines-perfect. If so, you might well eliminate this rehearsal or combine it with another one. If you do a memorization rehearsal, be sure to concentrate on acting and characterization along with the memorization. So-called "lines rehearsals" in which actors sit and read lines back and forth without movement and characterization are wrong in theory and inefficient in practice. Such practices reinforce the erroneous idea that the bare words have an importance of their own separate from the characters' lives. Furthermore, by eliminating character and movement, "running lines" cuts the actors off from major aids to remembering the lines.

Techniques:

After warm-ups, begin by putting the scripts down and acting your way straight through the play. Don't stop if you or your partner forget lines. Don't check the script. Don't break character, apologize, or curse yourself, your memory, or the play. If you go up on a line, focus on what your character is trying to accomplish at that moment and ad-lib your way through the spot. If your partner gets lost, don't feed him/her the line; instead either jump ahead to your next speech or ad-lib to call your partner back to his/her character's intention. If both you and your partner get lost, don't stop; muddle through to the conclusion, and stay in character. The goal, of course, is a word-perfect performance exactly as the lines are written. But stopping now in the middle may just train your mind to block up at the same place each time. An ad-lib is better than breaking character.

After the run-through, pick up your scripts and each choose one spot where you lost a line. Go over these two places together several times. Then act through the play without the script again. Continue to alternate between runs-through and work on specific lines until your time is gone or until you've done a performance without memory lapse.

Once you are confident of your lines, check to see that the lines you are speaking correspond to those in the script — that comfortable but inaccurate ad-libs have not crept in. You can do this either by running the play once, script in hand, or else by asking your partner if s/he is aware of any inaccuracies in your lines.

Progress assessment:

If you are word-perfect, congratulate each other and celebrate. If one or both of you still have memory problems, pinpoint them and determine to have those spots learned before the next rehearsal.

Rx:

Persistent memory problems are indicative of concentration problems. Probably the forgetful actors are not concentrating, or else they are concentrating on the wrong things (for instance, their memory problems instead of their characters). If you repeatedly stumble over a particular spot, check your through line of action; chances are you are not clear about your character's intention at the trouble point.

Bringing It All Together

Objective:

To pull the elements of the play together into a satisfying performance.

Techniques:

After arranging the set, do your warm-ups; commit yourself to them so your first run-through will be the best you are capable of.

With full concentration, act the play. Focus on making it performance quality — the best you can do. Remember that when you perform it for your audience, you probably won't have a chance to go through it once "dry" in order to get in the mood.

After the run-through, evaluate your play. Since you are within your own performance, you may find it difficult to view your show objectively; you may realize later (probably after the rehearsal is over, or even after the final performance) that you've given a few aspects of your performance more

271

attention than they deserved while ignoring other important elements. One way to minimize this danger is to have a director watch you and give feedback, but even directors can have blind spots. Another solution is to use some kind of a check list; you might construct your own check list by including the concentration points from your previous rehearsals, or you could use the "Final Performance Feedback Sheet" on page 289.

Remember that rehearsing is doing. Don't talk it to death. Limit yourselves to dealing with one or two points, and then do another run-through.

Progress assessment:

If, by the end of your rehearsal, you still have work to do, return to this concentration point in the next session.

Dress Rehearsal

Objective:

To try out your play under performance conditions.

Techniques:

Prepare for dress rehearsal by scheduling the performance space for your use; if possible, schedule your dress rehearsal at the same time of day as final performance. The reason for this timing is to prepare for events that happen at the same time each day (such as a freight train which thunders past your building daily at an hour which coincides with your performance). In order to provide a "test audience," you might want to invite several friends to watch, and if the performance program will consist of several plays done in succession, you may want to arrange for a couple of other shows to join you.

Meet long enough before the announced time of your rehearsal to do warm-ups and get into costume. If, at performance, you will have to arrange your set and props in full view of the audience or under some kind of time constraints, simulate those set-up and strike circumstances during dress rehearsal.

Prior to your show, stay backstage or sit in the audience as you will at final performance. Refrain from burning off useful energy by fussing around stage or bantering with your audience.

At the announced time, set your stage, announce your play, and perform it. When you're done, take your bows, strike your set, and exit.

When you see your friends afterward, remember that if you ask them how they liked your play you are trapping them into flattering you. Just thank them for their presence and for being a good audience. If they want to tell you how they felt about the show, they will do it without your prompting.

Progress assessment:

When the audience is gone, evaluate yourselves. How efficient was your set-up and strike? Do you need to run through those procedures once or twice to correct problems? Did you get together soon enough to get your warm-ups and costuming done? Or did you get together too soon and end up with too much waiting time? How did the presence of the audience affect you? Did you crack? Rush? Make inappropriate eye contact with the audience members? Did you fail to hold for laughs or other audience reactions? What might you do to improve the experience for yourselves or your audience?

Assisted Rehearsals

Objective:

To get feedback and advice from a knowledgeable theatre person.

Orientation and preparation:

Since you can't step off stage to watch yourselves perform, you may profit from the criticisms of an experienced observer. If your instructor doesn't include monitored rehearsals as a regular part of the course, look for a helper who has had some experience acting or directing. Decide when you want your "coach" to attend rehearsals; probably two visits will be sufficient. Depending on you and your coach, you may want to specify what you want feedback on. You could use the "Feedback Sheets" on pages 287 to 289 or make up your own. Even if you just want general, non-directed feedback, there may be one or two specific details you want comments on; if so, you'll be wise to tell the critic before performance rather than expecting him/her to pick out small details from a plethora of impressions after the fact.

Get together soon enough to do warm-ups, get into costume, and set the stage before the scheduled arrival of your observer. if you are ready before s/he arrives, don't just sit around and get nervous. Some suggestions of what to do until your coach arrives:

- Do a full run-through of your play, and follow it with a normal self-criticism session; you may discover a few last-minute improvements you can make.

- Do some of the transition improvs from the rehearsal session titled "Improvising" *(pages 262 to 264)*, or play around with some of the characterization exercises from the session on "Investigating Character Identity" *(pages 266 to 267)*. These activities will give you a fresh look at your characters which will enliven your performance.

As soon as the observer arrives and gives you the go-ahead, perform the play. Resist any impulses to visit with the coach before performing. Excuses, questions, explanations, and introductions at this point are a waste of everyone's time. They are probably a device you use unconsciously to postpone performance.

After the performance, learn all you can from the observer. Realize that learning to deal profitably with criticism is a valuable part of your training as an actor. Some suggestions:

- Write down notes of the coach's observations to help your memory.

- Do not argue or offer excuses or explanations; you can evaluate the criticisms later.

- Do not respond to criticisms with, "Oh, yes, I know"; if you knew, you should have corrected the problem.

- Make sure that you understand the suggestions; if you're not sure what a particular comment really means, ask.

Progress assessment:

After the coach leaves, discuss the criticism with your partner. Be sure you both agree on what the observer said. You may want to decide which comments are useful and which you don't agree with, but don't waste time or energy indulging in self-pity, self-recrimination, or arguments with the absent critic. Instead, decide what you need to do to incorporate the useful observations, and either get to work right away or set up your next rehearsal time. Be sure to end on a positive note; *especially* if the criticism was brutal, tell each other at least one aspect of your performance each of you was happy about.

Performing

Objective:

To share your finished art work for the mutual enjoyment of yourselves and your audience.

Techniques:

Prepare for performance by taking care of yourself. Save partying until afterward, and get to bed on time the night before. Watch what you eat prior to performance; do eat, but refrain from heavy, hard-to-digest foods. Avoid alcohol, uppers, and downers; no matter how these drugs make you feel, their effect is to diminish your rational control. Don't buy a little phony self-confidence at the cost of your ability to concentrate.

Before performance, take care of warm-ups, costuming, and props, and then do what you can to maintain concentration. This doesn't mean going into a trance, but it does mean refraining from loud or physical interaction with others which will burn off energy you should pour into your performance.

When your time comes, perform with all the concentration, energy, awareness, and commitment you can muster.

If your instructor gives oral feedback after your scene, take notes just as you did during monitored rehearsals. The note-writing will help reinforce the learning process, and the activity will help you deal with any negative, post-performance emotions you may experience.

Finally, thank your partner for his/her work, return all borrowed props and costume items, and begin looking for the next show to try out for.

Rehearsal Tools

How to Read a Playscript

A script is a technical document intended for the use of performers and technicians in staging a play. Because of this, playscripts should be read differently than essays, short stories, or poems. The following suggestions will help you be more efficient in reading a script.

1. In your first encounter with a script, read it *straight through*. The novelist expects the reader to read the novel in several sittings with sizable time gaps between; the playwright expects the audience — including you, the reader — to absorb the play in a single, sustained encounter.

2. Read at a rate slightly faster than the spoken word. Don't underline; it slows you down.

3. As you read, imagine the events happening on a stage, not "in real life."

4. Do not focus on word play or symbols. Although these may be present and can add to the enjoyment, they are not what the play is about.

5. Do not focus on philosophical meanings. The ideas in a play add to its power, but they usually are not why the play was written or what the play is about.

6. Focus on character identities and relationships between characters. Changes within and between characters are particularly important, because human change is *action*, and action is what plays are all about.

7. Focus on situations and events. "Situations" are periods of static human relationships; they may contain tension and conflict, but they are unchanging. "Events" are changes in human relationships; they are transitions from situation to situation. Most plays consist of an alternating sequence of situation — event — situation — event — situation.

8. Watch for physical actions and behaviors ("business") which are implied in the dialog. Not all actions are spelled out in the stage directions. For instance, in *A Streetcar Named Desire*, Blanche says to Stella, "Are you deliberately shaking that broom in my face?" To motivate that line, the

277

actress playing Stella must, immediately before the line, have the broom somewhere in the direction of Blanche's face, even though the stage directions say nothing about the gesture.

9. If you want to take notes on the play (a wise activity), do so after reading the script, not during the reading.

   Note: These suggestions will work not only for the short scripts in this book, but also for full-length scripts, scripts by Aeschylus and Shakespeare — any scripts.

For more help in how to read a playscript, see the Book List section on "Script Analysis," page 293.

Study Questions for Individual Script Analysis

As you study your script, seek what is *unique* about your play. Almost all plays show *selfish* characters in *conflict* with each other, and almost all plays keep the audience in *suspense* about what will happen; how is your play different from all other plays? Play analysis is an on-going task. Be prepared, therefore, to learn new things about your play and to change your ideas throughout the rehearsal process.

A. The action of the play

1. In thirty words or less, summarize the story of your play.
2. How are things different at the end of your play than at the beginning? In other words, what changes in the course of the play? (Answer this question in one sentence.)
3. How does the play arouse interest? Sustain interest? Satisfy interest? (Use one sentence for each answer.)
4. What is the primary focus of the play? In other words, what is most important in the script: Telling a story? Depicting a character? Communicating ideas to the audience? Dazzling with spectacle?

B. The characters in the play

1. In twenty-five words or less, describe each character.

2. What is the basic relationship between the characters? For instance, are they lovers? Parent and child? Business associates? Total strangers? Master and servant?

3. What is the central goal, motive, or desire of each character? (One sentence per character.)

4. What obstacles keep each character from accomplishing his/her goal immediately? (One sentence per character.)

5. What is the central conflict? How does it develop? And what is the result? (One sentence per question.)

C. The style of the play

1. What is the dominant mood of the play? Be as specific as possible. Some samples: hilarious, hateful, frightening, silly, mystifying, cerebral, anxiety-producing.

2. Where does the action occur?

3. When does the action occur?

4. How is the world of the play like the real world?

5. How is the world of the play different from the real world?

D. The plot of the play

1. Divide the play into episodes and summarize each episode in one sentence. A typical romantic play, for instance, might have the following episodes: (1) Alvin asks Jane to marry him. (2) Jane rejects Alvin on account of his name. (3) Alvin wins Jane by changing his name to Elmer.

2. What is the relationship between episodes; how does the plot progress from episode to episode? You will probably need to write a short paragraph to cover this. Some sample plot progressions: (i) Chronological and causal: Episode A *causes* episode B. Episode B in turn *causes* episode C. Episode C concludes the play. (ii) Chronological but not causal: Episodes A, B, and C happen first, second, and third in the time of the story, but the earlier episodes don't really *cause* the later ones. (iii) Non-chronological. Episode B is a "flashback"; in the time of the story, the episodes occurred in the order B, A, C. (iv) Other: some modern plays have no relation to "real" time and arrange their incidents rhythmically, similar to movements in a symphony.

E. The ideas of the play

1. What philosophical ideas or questions does the play suggest? (Use one sentence for each idea or question.)
2. What is the theme of the play? (Limit yourself to one or two sentences.) A theme may be an idea that is repeated until it dominates a play (technology threatens our humanity); or it may be a topic established by varied but related ideas and questions (how people respond to technology).
3. How important are ideas to the play? (Limit yourself to one sentence.) Answers might range from "This play exists for the sole purpose of establishing its theme" to "Any ideas found in this play are purely incidental to the main focus on telling the story."

Further Study:

While the above questions will help you understand your script, they barely scratch the surface of play analysis. To develop your dramatic analysis capabilities, continually read and view plays, and read books such as those listed in the Book List section titled "Script Analysis," page 293.

Discussion Guide for Group Script Analysis

The following questions are intended to help actors talk productively about their script. It's a good idea to write down a summary of the responses to each question.

1. What happens in this play? Try to summarize the action in one sentence, and then, if necessary, expand on it.
2. Where and when does it happen? Deal first with map-and-clock reality: "It happens on June 6, 1942, in a hospital room in southern California." Then deal with socio-psychological time and place: "It happens immediately after their divorce and before the birth of their child, and it occurs on *his* turf."
3. How are the characters involved in what happens? Who makes it happen? Who profits/loses/changes the most as a result? Who is in control at each moment in the play?
4. How does the plot progress? How many episodes or scenes are there and what is the relation of each scene to the ones that precede and follow it? Can you graph the emotional intensity of each scene?
5. What is the play's style?

Character Analysis Questions

1. What do other characters say about your character? Make a *complete* list. For each statement indicate whether you think the speaker is correct, is mistaken, or is lying.

2. What does your character say about himself/herself? Be complete. Again, indicate whether your character is truthful and accurate about each statement, ignorant about himself/herself, or intentionally exaggerating, minimizing, or falsifying.

3. What does your character do, and what do these actions reveal about his/her person?

4. What do the stage directions say about your character?

5. What is your character's super-objective? The super-objective is the one thing your character most wants to accomplish in the play. Compose the super-objective carefully.

   a. Start it with a purpose statement: "I want to ... " or "I must ... " or "I have to ... "

   b. Follow with an **active** verb: "I want **to kill** ... " or "I want **to seduce** ... " or "I want **to cure** ... " or "I want **to tame** ... " (Avoid static verbs and verbs such as "to show" as in "I want to show I am honest.")

   c. Follow the second active verb with an object that relates you to others in the play: I want to kill **the king**, I want to seduce **my servant**, I want to cure **my patient**, I want to tame **my lover**.

   d. Be sure the super-objective is specific to the play and at the same time deals with the entire role in the script. In *Oedipus Rex*, for instance, a good statement would be: "Oedipus wants to heal Thebes by punishing the murderer of Laius." An overly broad statement would be: "Oedipus wants to win everyone's admiration." This seems to be a life-long goal of Oedipus but is too general for this single event in his life. A sample of a super-objective that is too small might be, "Oedipus wants to learn his own identity." Actually he doesn't settle on this purpose until well into the play, and after he discovers who he is and blinds himself, the play still goes on for some time.

Sample Character Profiles

To play your character well, you need to know a great many more details about him/her than you will ever share with the audience on stage. Here are three character profile outlines you may use to fill in your character's background. When you add details from your imagination, be sure they fit with the character as portrayed in the script.

Profile 1: Six Traits of Character

This six-trait scheme comes from Sam Smiley's book, *Playwriting: The Structure of Action*, pages 83 to 91.

1. Biological traits: Is the character human or non-human? Male or female?

2. Physical traits: Include here all details about the character's body, voice, costume, manner of walking, and tempo — in other words, everything the audience can *see* and *hear* about the character.

3. Attitudinal traits: What is your character's basic outlook on life? Include such details as characteristic moods and habits.

4. Motivational traits: What are your character's goals, motives, drives, and desires? Also include your character's fears and hatreds.

5. Deliberational traits: What does your character think about? How does your character think? To what extent is your character ruled by mind rather than heart (emotions) or belly (desires)?

6. Decisional traits: What, if any, decisions does your character make? How does s/he go about making decisions?

Profile 2: The Bone-Structure of a Character

This three-part outline comes from Lajos Egri's book, *How to Write a Play*, pages 36 to 38.

Physiology

1. Sex
2. Age
3. Height and weight
4. Color of hair, eyes, skin

5. Posture
6. Appearance
7. Defects
8. Heredity

Sociology

1. Class
2. Occupation
3. Education
4. Home life
5. I.Q.

6. Religion
7. Race, nationality
8. Place in community
9. Political affiliations
10. Amusements, hobbies

Psychology

1. Sex life, moral standards
2. Personal premise, ambition
3. Frustrations, chief disappointments
4. Temperament
5. Attitude towards life
6. Complexes, obsessions, inhibitions, superstitions, manias, phobias
7. Extrovert, introvert, ambivert
8. Abilities, talents
9. Qualities

Profile 3: Identification of a Character

Jim Cash, film writer and teacher at Michigan State University, developed the following profile for his own use and for his students:

1. Name the character. Male or female.
2. Birthdate and birthplace.
3. Education
4. Occupation.
5. Height, weight, eyes, and hair.
6. Marital status.
7. Children.
8. A significant event that happened at the age of ten.
9. At the age of twenty.
10. At a later age.
11. Ten statements of information about this character — what s/he thinks, feels, cares about, hopes for, believes in, the conflicts and harmonies in his/her life, any kind of information that gives the character dimension.

Constructing a Through Line of Action

1. Go through your script and make a mark at every place where your character changes from one intention to another. The time between each mark is a "beat" or "unit of action."

2. In a notebook, write down two things for each beat. First, write down the intention. Use the same format as for the super-objective *(page 281)*. Second, write down what happens to the intention and how it changes to the next one. Typically, intentions are either fulfilled, defeated, postponed, or modified.

3. Don't forget to treat your character's *entrance* as a beat, complete with intention and transition to the next beat.

4. Avoid the following constructions for intentions: "to show ... ", "to express ... " *Especially* if what follows is an emotion.

5. Be sure your statement of intentions includes the *why* behind the physical act. **Wrong:** "He wants to sit down." **Right:** "He wants to infuriate the Emperor by sitting down."

6. As much as possible, make your intentions concrete and specific. Avoid vague intentions.

7. Intentions should all differ from each other. This is especially the case when they follow each other in adjacent sequence; it is also usually the case when two similar beats are separated by several other beats. At the very least, they should build in intensity.

8. Each beat should relate to the character's super-objective. The relationship need not be *stated*, but it should be relatively obvious.

For more details on this technique, see page 294 of the Book List.

Analyzing Your Lines

Every line — every *word* — in your role means something specific to your character. Furthermore, your character wants to accomplish something as a result of every line s/he speaks. These six steps will help insure none of your lines are meaningless or purposeless (in other words, *dead*) when you say them.

1. Look up all words whose definition or pronunciation you are uncertain of.

2. What is the **sub-text** of the line? That is, what does the line mean *to the*

character who says it? One way to discover sub-text is to paraphrase the line. Sample: Line: What time is it? Various sub-texts might be: (a) How long until my execution? (b) You are *really* late! (c) I think I missed my wedding.

3. Decide on the **verbal action** of the line. That is, what is your character *trying to accomplish* by saying the line? Sample: For the sub-texts in item #2 above, the respective verbal actions might be: (a) To discover if I still have time to escape from death row. (b) To insult my "friend." (c) To find out if I've avoided a marriage I really didn't want.

4. Notice all **images** in the line. An image is a verbal expression of a sensory experience or object which the speaker is remembering or imagining. Be sure you are able to visualize, in your mind's eye, the images your character talks about; focus on these images every time you rehearse or perform the role.

5. Don't skip a line. The point of this exercise is to help you deal with lines you've been ignoring (running them over your lips but bypassing your character's head). The line you are tempted to skip as "obvious" is likely the one that most needs work.

Blocking Checklist

A. Arranging the set.

1. Where is the audience in relation to your set?

2. How many entrances/exits do you need, and where are they? Are they located so that they maximize the effect of important entrances or exits? Upstage-center doors, for instance, make it difficult for actors to exit without turning their backs on the audience.

3. Where is the furniture? Where are important props such as telephones? Is your set cluttered with unnecessary furniture? Is the furniture arranged so that it shares the play with the audience? The following arrangement, for instance, will make it difficult for the audience to see the face of an actor in Chair "B" and may hide an actor in Chair "A" behind the downstage actor.

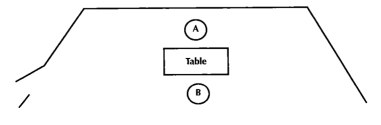

Rearrange the set like this:

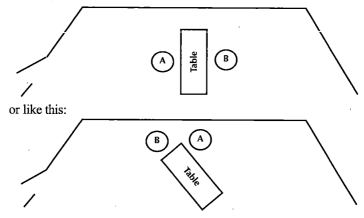

or like this:

B. Checking the blocking.

1. Does the blocking share the play with the audience? Usually minimize blocking which places the actor's back to the audience or which conceals upstage actors behind downstage actors.

2. Does the blocking focus attention on the dominant actor at each moment? In the course of a single scene, the action may belong to one character for a while, then shift to another; at times, two or three characters may share the scene. The blocking should enhance the focus.

3. Is there an appropriate amount of movement in the scene? Begin with the amount of movement the action would seem to demand in real life, and then heighten this by adding crosses and making them larger (don't forget to motivate each cross). Modify your blocking by considering the characters' relative tempos. In *A Streetcar Named Desire*, for instance, Blanche is likely to move often, quickly, and frenetically while Stella probably moves slowly, less often, more cow-like.

4. Does the blocking symbolize relationship by position and movement? For instance, in a scene where two lovers are "growing apart" the actors might gradually move further from each other. In a scene where one actor "talks down" to another, the persecutor might be standing upstage of the victim who might be seated or even lying on the floor. In a scene where two apparently equal characters are "sparring," their movement pattern might approximate that of two circling boxers.

For more details on blocking, check the Book List on page 294.

Feedback Sheet: Characterization

Play Title:_____

Character: _____ Actor: _____

1. Did the actor concentrate consistently?

2. Was the character believable?

3. Are there moments when the character's intentions need to be clarified?

4. Are there other useful comments?

Observer:_____

Date: _____

Feedback Sheet: Tech and Pacing

Play Title:_____

Character: _____ Actor: _____

1. Should any technical elements be changed?

2. Has the actor made progress in believability?

3. Are there sequences that should be faster, slower, louder, softer, etc.?

4. Were there lapses in line memorization?

5. Are there other helpful comments?

Observer:_____

Date: _____

Final Performance Feedback Sheet

Play Title:_____

Character: _____ Actor: _____

Technical considerations

Were there memorization lapses?

Were crosses, pictures, and business effective?

Was projection adequate?

Character portrayal

Were given circumstances consistent throughout?

Were intentions clearly and consistently played?

Did the actor clearly play the character's changes?

Was the characterization inventive?

Was there meaningful variety in the performance?

Was the energy level satisfactory?

Did the actor avoid over-acting?

Professionalism

Did the actor cooperate with fellow actors throughout the rehearsal period?

Did the actor take responsibility for rehearsal and production processes?

Did the actor maintain seriousness of purpose?

What did the actor do to help build cast morale?

Did the actor display willingness and ability to take direction?

Additional comments:

Evaluator: _____

Date: _____

289

Part 4
Book List

Rehearsal Helps

Rehearsing without a Director

Cohen, Robert. *Acting One*. 4th ed. Mountain View, CA: McGraw-Hill, 2001. "Rehearsing."

Felner, Mira. *Free to Act: An Integrated Approach to Acting*. New York: Holt, Rinehart, & Winston, 1990. "The Rehearsal Process," pp. 232–49.

Warm-ups

Barton, Robert. *Acting: Onstage and Off*. 3rd ed., New York: Harcourt, Brace, Jovanovich, 2002. "Relaxed Readiness," pp. 29–67.

Linklater, Kristin. *Freeing the Natural Voice*. Brooklyn: Drama Publishers, 1976. "Warm-up."

Machlin, Evangeline. *Speech for the Stage*. 2nd ed., New York: Routledge, 1992. "The Actor's Practice Routine" and "The Actor's Warm-up Exercises," pp. 239–43.

Script Analysis

Felner, Mira. *Free to Act: An Integrated Approach to Acting*. New York: Holt, Rinehart, & Winston, 1990. "The Elements of Dramatic Analysis," pp. 157–71.

Thomas, James. *Script Analysis for Actors, Directors, and Designers*. 2nd ed. Burlington, MA: Focal Press, 1998.

Waxberg, Charles. *The Actor's Script: Script Analysis for Performers*. Portsmouth, NH: Heinemann, 1998.

Improvisations

Gronbeck-Tedesco, John L. *Acting through Exercises: A Synthesis of Classical and Contemporary Approaches*. Mountain View, CA: McGraw-Hill, 1991. "Working Across the Given Circumstances," pp. 156–68.

Johnstone, Keith. *Impro: Improvisation and the Theatre*. New York: Theatre Arts Books, 1989.

Spolin, Viola. *Improvisation for the Theatre: A Handbook of Teaching and*

Directing Techniques. 3rd ed. Evanston, IL: Northwestern University Press, 1999.

Blocking

Cohen, Robert. *Acting One.* 4th ed. Mountain View, CA: McGraw-Hill, 2001. "Staging the Scene."

Dean, Alexander and Lawrence Carra. *Fundamentals of Play Directing.* 5th ed. New York: International Thomson Publishing. "Basic Technique for the Actor," and "The Five Fundamentals of Play Directing."

Character Analysis

Abbott, Leslie. *Active Acting: Exercises and Improvisations Leading to Performance.* Belmont, CA: Star Publishing Company, 1993. "Developing Your Characterization," pp. 115–24.

McGaw, Charles and Larry D. Clark. *Acting Is Believing: A Basic Method.* 7th ed. Belmont: Wadsworth Publishing Company, 1995. "Getting into the Part."

Constructing a Through Line of Action

Felner, Mira. *Free to Act: An Integrated Approach to Acting.* New York: Holt, Rinehart, & Winston, 1990. "Defining Beats," and "Building Beats into a Scene," pp. 232–49.

McGaw, Charles and Larry D. Clark. *Acting Is Believing: A Basic Method.* 7th ed. Belmont: Wadsworth Publishing Company, 1995. "Seeing a Part as Units of Action."

Memorization

Barton, Robert. *Acting: Onstage and Off.* 3rd ed., New York: Harcourt, Brace, Jovanovich, 2002. "Memorizing," pp. 238–39.

Cohen, Robert. *Acting One.* 4th ed. Mountain View, CA: McGraw-Hill, 2001. "Memorization Methods."

Dealing with Stage Fright

Barton, Robert. *Acting: Onstage and Off.* 3rd ed., New York: Harcourt, Brace, Jovanovich, 2002. "Stage Fright Substitutes," p. 33.

Cohen, Robert. *Acting One.* 4th ed. Mountain View, CA: McGraw-Hill, 2001. "Stage Fright."

Other Scripts by Writers in This Anthology

Patrick Baliani

All scripts are available from the playwright, 1750 Camino Cielo, Tucson, AZ 85718.

Eggs and Red Wine. A full-length play about Italian immigrant brothers who share a Thanksgiving in New Jersey.

A Namib Spring. A full-length play about one woman's struggle to overcome loss amid the cataclysm of Namibia's independence.

Oz. A full-length Enlgish translation of Marco Baliani's Italian political play.

Two From Tanagra. A one-act about the strained intimacy of two women, set against the idyllic coast of Crete.

Yerba Non Facta. A one-act in which overzealous "freedom fighters" discover they have stormed the wrong country.

Jan Baross

All scripts are available from the playwright, 6426 SW Barnes Rd., Portland, OR 97221.

Breaching. A two-act, three-character play about a man who becomes a whale to save the world.

Little Favors. A one-act, four-person comedy about a woman who is terminally self-sufficient.

Mata Hari. A tragi-comic monolog.

The Woman Who Walked With a List. A one-act, three-person comedy about family tragedies.

Daughters of Eden. A two-act, nine-person drama about a preacher who steals a town of women.

Norman A. Bert

All scripts available from the playwright, 5704 Nashville Avenue, Lubbock, TX 79413-4601.

Dr. Dixie Duzzett's Delight. A ribald, comic, one-act satire on modern sexual mores and addiction therapy.

The Dove, the Hawk, and the Phoenix. A one-act peace play.

Mixed Doubles. A one-act comedy about a marriage made in Montana.

Post Office. A one-act comedy about a couple bottled up in an open marriage.

Riders of the Golden Sphinx. A full-length spoof of Western melodramas, incorporating the Oedipus story and laced with classical cowboy songs.

Conrad Bishop and Elizabeth Fuller

Full Hookup. A modern tragedy in a trailer park. Available from Dramatists Play Service, 1987.

Get Happy: Acting Edition. A one-act play about teen alcohol abuse. Lancaster, PA: WoodWorkers Press, 1990.

Okiboji. A two-act comedy. In *Prima Facie 1991 Anthology.* Denver: Denver Center Theatre, 1990.

Mine Alone. Two-act drama. In *Prima Facie 1991 Anthology.* Denver: Denver Center Theatre, 1990.

Rash Acts: Eighteen Snapshots for the Stage. An anthology of short plays from two years of ensemble touring. Available from WordWorkers Press, 1989.

William Borden

All scripts available from the playwright, 7996 S FM 548, Royse City, TX 75189.

Garage Sale. A play about Warren, who is selling everything — pajamas, wedding pictures, his past.

I Want to Be an Indian. A play about a liberal who wants to be a Native American and gets his chance one night in a bar on a reservation.

Meet Again. A full-length romantic comedy with six characters who fall in love with unexpected people in unexpected lives.

Quarks. A ten-minute comedy about nuclear physics at a singles bar.

Turtle Island Blues. A full-length satire on American history with Columbus, Sitting Bull, and Leonard Peltier.

Linda Lee Bower

All scripts available from the playwright, 5025 Amesbury Drive #136, Dallas, TX 75206.

The Incredible Pregnancy Man. A wacky comedy.

Debra Bruch

All scripts available from the playwright, 209 Walker, Michigan Technological University, Houghton, MI 49931.

Damon's Cage. A strange and frightening one-act set in the after-life.

The Dividing Line. A one-act, full-length play about teens discovering how to live in this world by creating another.

The Exiled. A religiously oriented radio show about the coming-of-age of a young man.

The Union. A religiously oriented, fun one-act play for youth.

Wounded Healers. A religiously oriented readers theatre piece including mime and skits.

J. Omar Hansen

All scripts available from the playwright, 4497 S. Cameron Lane, Rexburg, ID 83440.

The Affairs of David Redding. A full-length history play about an Englishman executed in Colonial Vermont.

East of the Sun and West of the Moon. A full-length musical dramatization of the classic fairy tale.

The Home. A tragi-comic look at the problem of aging.

The Marriage. A dark comedy about the institution of marriage.

This Castle Needs a Good Scouring. A comic retelling of the Cinderella story; this play won the Great Platte River Playwrights Festival.

Bryan Harnetiaux

All scripts available from Dramatic Publishing Co., PO Box 129, Woodstock, IL 60098.

Dumb Luck. A full-length comedy.

The Killers. An adaptation of an Ernest Hemingway short story.

The Lemonade Stand. A 25-minute version of the script included in this anthology.

Long Walk to Forever. An adaptation of a Kurt Vonnegut short story.

Thin Air. A drama about the reunion of an old-time radio show cast.

Robert L. Lippman

All scripts available from the playwright, PO Box 206, Elizabethtown, KY 42702.

Ann and Aaron Read Freud. A two-act play in which a Rabbi tries to convince his art historian wife that Freud secretly strove to become the new Moses.

Freud in Rome. A two-act play in which the mysterious Miss Portero takes Sigmund Freud through his own troubled soul.

There Shall Come a Star Out of Jacob. A research-based one-act play in which Freud's ghost tells four psychoanalysts at a seance about his confrontation with the biblical Moses.

Wendy MacLaughlin

Crown of Thorn. Full-length play based on the life and philosophy of priest-scientist Pierre Teilhard de Chardin.

Love Taps. A collection of 10-minute plays connected by a shared focus on different forms of love.

Mirror/Mirror. Full-length play based on the life of Elizabeth Layton who cured manic-depression through art therapy.

The Secret Key. A children's play using puppets or live actors.

Watermelon Boats. Two girls age from 11 to 21 in 10 minutes. In *25 Ten-Minute Plays From Actors Theater of Louisville.* New York: Samuel French. Also in *One-Act Plays for Acting Students.* Colorado Springs, CO: Meriwether, 1987.

Madeleine Martin

All scripts available from the playwright, PO Box 53521, Lubbock, TX 79453.

Elizabeth the Fourth. A ten-minute, one-act about a mother and daughter in conflict over the daughter's impending abortion.

Family Values. A one-act in which a woman hangs out her bitter memories along with her laundry.

For Better or Worse. A monolog in which a woman makes detailed plans for a wedding she swears she doesn't want.

The Patrician Potty. A ten-minute play about a divorcing couple haggling over who gets custody of an antique toilet.

John O'Brien

All scripts available from Dramatic Publishing Co., PO Box 129, Woodstock, IL 60098.

Break a Leg.

Limbo.

The Man Who Died and Went to Heaven.

Mirrors.

Softy.

Sarah Provost

Both scripts are available from the playwright (10990 Massachusetts Ave., #4, Los Angeles, CA 90024) or through Rick Leeds, Agency for the Performing Arts, 888 Seventh Ave., New York, NY 10016.

The Home Team. A two-act romantic comedy for four men and three women, set in the bleachers of a little league game.

Six of One. A two-act comic drama for three men and four women about a man with six separate personalities, all of which are played by the lead actor.

William Reynolds

Both scripts are available from the playwright, 12342 Hunters Chase Drive #2425, Austin, TX 78729.

Something for Nothing. A one-act romantic comedy.

Welcome to the World. A one-act play about a cynical tour guide and his young client.

Deanna Riley

All scripts are available from the playwright, 8 Wayne Dr., Wilmington, DE 19809.

Bowling Balls and Babies. A comic monolog about pregnancy.

Christmas on the Moon. A children's holiday musical comedy about the first family on the moon, with songs by Cathi Norton.

How to Build a Better Baby. A one-act satire of upward mobility at Little Red Caboose University.

Memorandum Primer. A short satire on the actual meaning of office correspondence.

Procedures. A two-act farce set in an abortion clinic.

James I. Schempp

All scripts are available from the playwright, 723 Milligan Lane, West Islip, NY 11795.

Bathers. A one-act play for three women about substance abuse.

Outfoxed. A satire based on *Volpone,* set in a contemporary university.

Singing Vivaldi. A one-act farce.

The Song of Eddie King. A modern telling of the classic play *Oedipus Rex.*

Sisters in Partnership: Lora Lee Cliff, Cynthia Judge, and Janet Wilson

Umbilical Discord. A full-length, mad-cap comedy about three desperate sisters who will stop at nothing to prevent their mother from remarrying a Hawaiian. Scripts available from the playwrights, c/o Janet Wilson, 300 Harper Court, Normal, IL 61761.

Sam Smiley

Unless otherwise noted, all scripts are available from the playwright at 5799 Via Amable North, Tucson, AZ 85750-1312.

And Sometimes Light. A one-act comedy about an American tourist having a hard time in Barcelona.

Date. A gently comic one-act play about an old woman trying to make a connection with her granddaughter. Available in a published version from Samuel French, Inc.

Hemingway. A full-length play, for three men and two women, composed of numerous short cuttings from the works of Ernest Hemingway. Only available to amateur groups.

Property of the Dallas Cowboys. A rollickingly comic short play about a young woman, her opinionated mother, and a fast-talking cowboy in a Texas laundromat. In *One-Act Plays for Acting Students*, Colorado Springs: Meriwether, 1987.

Summer Lights. A play in the mode of Our Town that takes place on a farm in Indiana and traces the story of a boy's maturation paralleling his grandparents' aging and demise.

Milan Stitt

Back in the Race. New York: Dramatists Play Service, 1980.

The Runner Stumbles. New York: Dramatists Play Service, 1976.

Julianne Bernstein Theodoropulos

Unless otherwise noted, all scripts available from the playwright, 811 Corinthian Avenue, Philadelphia, PA 19130.

Autumn Leaves. In *Off-off Broadway Festival Plays: Sixteenth Series*. New York: Samuel French, 1991.

Pizza: A Love Story. A one-act comedy/farce for two women and three men in which merry mix-ups ensue when Janet would rather pop a pizza in the oven than have Jeffrey pop the question.

The Sampling Heart. A Norman Rockwellian one-act for three older actors which explores small-town prejudice and ignorance.

Scrabble. A one-act comedy about playing for points in which a man is caught cheating on two women.

Send Me a Picture, Love Peg. A full-length play, based on the writings of Willa Cather, about two women struggling to hold on to friendship.

Jon Tuttle

All scripts are available from the playwright, Department of English, Francis Marion College, PO Box 100547, Florence, SC 29501-0547.

A Fish Story. A full-length black comedy about a family not dealing very well with the death of a son; winner of the 1992 New Voices Award.

One Another. A mini-play about the ongoing chess match between the brain and the loins.

Remembering Us. A full-length psycho-drama about young, tortured love.

Synergy and Anarchy in the South. A companion mini-play to *I Wanna Be a Cowboy.*

Terminal Cafe. A full-length play about love and death in a Western mining town; winner of the 1991 New Voices Award.

Sharon Whitney

Anna's Latitude. A content Alaskan fisherwoman is invaded by her yuppie son from the Lower 48. Script available from the playwright, 2712 SW Patton Rd., Portland, OR 97201.

Girl Town. Boston: Baker's Plays, 1992.

A Cowboy's Sweetheart. A depression-era cowgirl fights her dad for a chance to rodeo. Script available from the playwright.

A Talk From Brother Bob. Portland, OR: Portland Review, 1989.

Totty — Young Eleanor Roosevelt. New Orleans: Anchorage Press, 1992.

Janet Wilson (of "Sisters in Partnership," q.v.)

Both scripts available from the playwright, 300 Harper Court, Normal, IL 61761.

Fired!?!? A short comedy about an employee getting the ax.

Richmond Mothers' Playground. A short comedy about a mom-and-tot clique.

About the Editors

Norman A. Bert and Deb Bert collaborate writing plays and theatre books. Norman earned his Ph.D. at Indiana University, specializing in dramatic theory and criticism. He has taught acting, playwriting, and other theatre courses since 1975. He currently teaches playwriting and dramatic analysis at Texas Tech University. He has been actively involved in the Playwriting Awards Committee of the Kennedy Center American College Theatre Festival and the Playwrights Program of the Association for Theatre in Higher Education. Norman has written over twenty-five play scripts, most of which have been published and/or produced, and has authored several books including *One-Act Plays for Acting Students, Play It Again: More One-Act Plays for Acting Students, The Scenebook for Actors*, and *Theatre Alive!,* an anthology of world drama with historical introductions.

Deb earned a B.A. in theatre arts from Montana State University — Billings where she graduated with high honors. A native of Montana, Deb writes under the pen name of Madeleine Martin. Her scripts have been produced in Montana, Texas, and off-off-Broadway in New York. She is currently writing a children's book as well as continuing to write plays.

When they're not absorbed in theatre-related activities, Norman and Deb enjoy traveling and spending quality time with their good friend and companion Geppetto, a Maltese.

Order Form

Meriwether Publishing Ltd.
PO Box 7710
Colorado Springs CO 80933-7710
Phone: 800-937-5297 Fax: 719-594-9916
Website: www.meriwether.com

Please send me the following books:

_____ **More One-Act Plays for Acting Students** $19.95
#BK-B130
edited by Norman Bert and Deb Bert
An anthology of one-act plays for one to three actors

_____ **New One-Act Plays for Acting Students** $19.95
#BK-B261
edited by Norman Bert and Deb Bert
An anthology of one-act plays for one to three actors

_____ **One-Act Plays for Acting Students #BK-B159** $19.95
edited by Norman Bert
An anthology of complete one-act plays

_____ **Theatre Alive #BK-B178** $49.95
by Dr. Norman A. Bert
An introductory anthology of world drama

_____ **The Scenebook for Actors #BK-B177** $16.95
edited by Norman A. Bert
Collection of great monologs and dialogs for auditions

_____ **Truth in Comedy #BK-B164** $17.95
by Charna Halpern, Del Close and Kim "Howard" Johnson
The manual of improvisation

_____ **112 Acting Games #BK-B277** $17.95
edited by Gavin Levy
A comprehensive workbook of theatre games

These and other fine Meriwether Publishing books are available at
your local bookstore or direct from the publisher. Prices subject to
change without notice. Check our website or call for current prices.

Name: _____ e-mail: _____

Organization name: _____

Address: _____

City: _____ State: _____

Zip: _____ Phone: _____

  ❑ **Check enclosed**
  ❑ **Visa / MasterCard / Discover #** _____
                                        Expiration
Signature: _____   *date:* _____
        (required for credit card orders)

Colorado residents: Please add 3% sales tax.
Shipping: Include $3.95 for the first book and 75¢ for each additional book ordered.

  ❑ *Please send me a copy of your complete catalog of books and plays.*

Order Form

Meriwether Publishing Ltd.
PO Box 7710
Colorado Springs CO 80933-7710
Phone: 800-937-5297   Fax: 719-594-9916
Website: www.meriwether.com

Please send me the following books:

_____ **More One-Act Plays for Acting Students** $19.95
#BK-B130
edited by Norman Bert and Deb Bert
An anthology of one-act plays for one to three actors

_____ **New One-Act Plays for Acting Students** $19.95
#BK-B261
edited by Norman Bert and Deb Bert
An anthology of one-act plays for one to three actors

_____ **One-Act Plays for Acting Students #BK-B159** $19.95
edited by Norman Bert
An anthology of complete one-act plays

_____ **Theatre Alive   #BK-B178** $49.95
by Dr. Norman A. Bert
An introductory anthology of world drama

_____ **The Scenebook for Actors   #BK-B177** $16.95
edited by Norman A. Bert
Collection of great monologs and dialogs for auditions

_____ **Truth in Comedy   #BK-B164** $17.95
by Charna Halpern, Del Close and Kim "Howard" Johnson
The manual of improvisation

_____ **112 Acting Games   #BK-B277** $17.95
edited by Gavin Levy
A comprehensive workbook of theatre games

These and other fine Meriwether Publishing books are available at
your local bookstore or direct from the publisher. Prices subject to
change without notice. Check our website or call for current prices.

Name: _____ e-mail: _____

Organization name: _____

Address: _____

City: _____ State: _____

Zip: _____ Phone: _____

❑ **Check enclosed**

❑ **Visa / MasterCard / Discover #** _____

Signature: _____ Expiration date: _____
(required for credit card orders)

Colorado residents: Please add 3% sales tax.
Shipping: Include $3.95 for the first book and 75¢ for each additional book ordered.

❑ *Please send me a copy of your complete catalog of books and plays.*